Enterprise Transaction Processing Systems

Putting the CORBA OTS, Encina++ and OrbixOTM to work

Ian Gorton *CSIRO and UNSW, Australia*

An imprint of **Pearson Education**

Harlow, England · London · New York · Reading, Massachusetts · San Francisco
Toronto · Don Mills, Ontario · Sydney · Tokyo · Singapore · Hong Kong · Seoul
Taipei · Cape Town · Madrid · Mexico City · Amsterdam · Munich · Paris · Milan

PEARSON EDUCATION LIMITED

Head Office
Edinburgh Gate
Harlow CM20 2JE
Tel: +44 (0) 1279 623623
Fax: +44 (0) 1279 431059

London Office:
128 Long Acre
London WC2E 9AN
Tel: +44 (0)207 447 2000
Fax: +44 (0)207 240 5771

Website: *www.awl.com/cseng*

First published in Great Britain in 2000

© Pearson Education Limited 2000

The right of Ian Gorton to be identified as author
of this work has been asserted by him in accordance
with the Copyright, Designs and Patents Act 1988.

ISBN 0-201-39859-1

British Library Cataloging in Publication Data
A catalogue record for this book is available from the British Library.

Library of Congress Cataloguing in Publication Data
Applied for.

All rights reserved; no part of this publication may be reproduced, stored in a retrieval system, or transmitted in any form or by any means, electronic, mechanical, photocopying, recording, or otherwise without either the prior written permission of the Publishers or a licence permitting restricted copying in the United Kingdom issued by the Copyright Licensing Agency Ltd, 90 Tottenham Court Road, London W1P 0LP.

The programs in this book have been included for their instructional value. The publisher does not offer any warranties or representations in respect of their fitness for a particular purpose, nor does the publisher accept any liability for any loss or damage (other than for personal injury or death) arising from their use.

Many of the designations used by manufacturers and sellers to distinguish their products are claimed as trademarks. Pearson Education Limited has made every attempt to supply trademark information about manufacturers and their products mentioned in this book. A list of trademark designations and their owners appears on page xvi.

CORBA is a trademark or registered trademark of Object Management Group, Inc. in the US and other countries.

10 9 8 7 6 5 4 3 2 1

Typeset by Pantek Arts, Maidstone, Kent
Printed and bound in the United States of America

The Publishers' policy is to use paper manufactured from sustainable forests.

*Enterprise Transaction
Processing Systems*

The Addison-Wesley Object Technology Series

Grady Booch, Ivar Jacobson, and James Rumbaugh, Series Editors

For more information check out the series web site [http://www.awl.com/cseng/otseries/] as well as the pages on each book [http://www.awl.com/cseng/I-S-B-N/] (I-S-B-N represents the actual ISBN, including dashes).

David Bellin and Susan Suchman Simone, *The CRC Card Book*, ISBN 0-201-89535-8

Robert V. Binder, *Testing Object-Oriented Systems: Models, Patterns, and Tools*, ISBN 0-201-80938-9

Bob Blakely, *CORBASecurity: An Introduction to Safe Computing with Objects*, ISBN 0-201-32565-9

Grady Booch, *Object Solutions: Managing the Object-Oriented Project*, ISBN 0-8053-0594-7

Grady Booch, *Object-Oriented Analysis and Design with Applications, Second Edition*, ISBN 0-8053-5340-2

Grady Booch, James Rumbaugh, and Ivar Jacobson, *The Unified Modeling Language User Guide*, ISBN 0-201-57168-4

Don Box, *Essential COM*, ISBN 0-201-63446-5

Don Box, Keith Brown, Tim Ewald, and Chris Sells, *Effective COM: 50 Ways to Improve Your COM and MTS-based Applications*, ISBN 0-201-37968-6

Alistair Cockburn, *Surviving Object-Oriented Projects: A Manager's Guide*, ISBN 0-201-49834-0

Dave Collins, *Designing Object-Oriented User Interfaces*, ISBN 0-8053-5350-X

Jim Conallen, *Building Web Applications with UML*, ISBN 0-201-61577-0

Bruce Powel Douglass, *Doing Hard Time: Designing and Implementing Embedded Systems with UML*, ISBN 0-201-49837-5

Bruce Powel Douglass, *Real-Time UML, Second Edition: Developing Efficient Objects for Embedded Systems*, ISBN 0-201-65784-8

Desmond F. D'Souza and Alan Cameron Wills, *Objects, Components, and Frameworks with UML: The Catalysis Approach*, ISBN 0-201-31012-0

Martin Fowler, *Analysis Patterns: Reusable Object Models*, ISBN 0-201-89542-0

Martin Fowler, *Refactoring: Improving the Design of Existing Code*, ISBN 0-201-48567-2

Martin Fowler with Kendall Scott, *UML Distilled, Second Edition: Applying the Standard Object Modeling Language*, ISBN 0-201-65783-X

Ian Gorton, *Enterprise Transaction Processing Systems: Putting the CORBA OTS, Encina++ and OrbixOTM to Work*, ISBN 0-201-39859-1

Peter Heinckiens, *Building Scalable Database Applications: Object-Oriented Design, Architectures, and Implementations*, ISBN 0-201-31013-9

Christine Hofmeister, Robert Nord, and Soni Dilip, *Applied Software Architecture*, ISBN 0-201-32571-3

Ivar Jacobson, Grady Booch, and James Rumbaugh, *The Unified Software Development Process*, ISBN 0-201-57169-2

Ivar Jacobson, Magnus Christerson, Patrik Jonsson, and Gunnar Overgaard, *Object-Oriented Software Engineering: A Use Case Driven Approach*, ISBN 0-201-54435-0

Ivar Jacobson, Maria Ericsson, and Agneta Jacobson, *The Object Advantage: Business Process Reengineering with Object Technology*, ISBN 0-201-42289-1

Ivar Jacobson, Martin Griss, and Patrik Jonsson, *Software Reuse: Architecture, Process and Organization for Business Success*, ISBN 0-201-92476-5

David Jordan, *C++ Object Databases: Programming with the ODMG Standard*, ISBN 0-201-63488-0

Philippe Kruchten, *The Rational Unified Process: An Introduction*, ISBN 0-201-60459-0

Wilf LaLonde, *Discovering Smalltalk*, ISBN 0-8053-2720-7

Dean Leffingwell and Don Widrig, *Managing Software Requirements: A Unified Approach*, ISBN 0-201-61593-2

Chris Marshall, *Enterprise Modeling with UML: Designing Successful Software through Business Analysis*, ISBN 0-201-43313-3

Lockheed Martin Advanced Concepts Center and Rational Software Corporation, *Succeeding with the Booch and OMT Methods: A Practical Approach*, ISBN 0-8053-2279-5

Thomas Mowbray and William Ruh, *Inside CORBA: Distributed Object Standards and Applications*, ISBN 0-201-89540-4

Bernd Oestereich, *Developing Software with UML: Object-Oriented Analysis and Design in Practice*, ISBN 0-201-39826-5

Meilir Page-Jones, *Fundamentals of Object-Oriented Design in UML*, ISBN 0-201-69946-X

Ira Pohl, *Object-Oriented Programming Using C++, Second Edition*, ISBN 0-201-89550-1

Rob Pooley and Perdita Stevens, *Using UML: Software Engineering with Objects and Components*, ISBN 0-201-36067-5

Terry Quatrani, *Visual Modeling with Rational Rose 2000 and UML*, ISBN 0-201-69961-3

Brent E. Rector and Chris Sells, *ATLInternals*, ISBN 0-201-69589-8

Paul R. Reed, Jr., *Developing Applications with Visual Basic and UML*, ISBN 0-201-61579-7

Doug Rosenberg with Kendall Scott, *Use Case Driven Object Modeling with UML: A Practical Approach*, ISBN 0-201-43289-7

Walker Royce, *Software Project Management: A Unified Framework*, ISBN 0-201-30958-0

William Ruh, Thomas Herron, and Paul Klinker, *IIOPComplete: Middleware Interoperability and Distributed Object Standards*, ISBN 0-201-37925-2

James Rumbaugh, Ivar Jacobson, and Grady Booch, *The Unified Modeling Language Reference Manual*, ISBN 0-201-30998-X

Geri Schneider and Jason P. Winters, *Applying Use Cases: A Practical Guide*, ISBN 0-201-30981-5

Yen-Ping Shan and Ralph H. Earle, *Enterprise Computing with Objects: From Client/Server Environments to the Internet*, ISBN 0-201-32566-7

David N. Smith, *IBM Smalltalk: The Language*, ISBN 0-8053-0908-X

Daniel Tkach, Walter Fang, and Andrew So, *Visual Modeling Technique: Object Technology Using Visual Programming*, ISBN 0-8053-2574-3

Daniel Tkach and Richard Puttick, *Object Technology in Application Development, Second Edition*, ISBN 0-201-49833-2

Jos Warmer and Anneke Kleppe, *The Object Constraint Language: Precise Modeling with UML*, ISBN 0-201-37940-6

To my parents, for making all this possible:
I'm eternally grateful.
To Jan, for everything.

Contents

	Foreword	*xi*
	Preface	*xiii*
	Acknowledgements	*xv*
	List of trademarks	*xvi*
1	**Introduction to enterprise transaction processing systems**	**1**
	Transaction processing: from mainframes to distributed systems	*1*
	The anatomy of enterprise applications	*3*
	Some examples of TP applications	*6*
	What is a distributed transaction processing monitor?	*8*
	Why are distributed TP systems attractive?	*9*
	The state of the market	*14*
	Summary	*16*
	Further reading	*16*
2	**Distributed transaction processing fundamentals**	**17**
	Introduction	*18*
	What is a transaction?	*18*
	Two-phase commit	*21*
	Transaction demarcation	*24*
	Resource manager access using XA	*26*
	Transactional remote procedure calls	*29*
	Heuristic outcomes	*30*
	Nested transactions	*32*
	Transactional queuing technology	*35*
	Locking	*37*
	Recovery	*39*
	System administration and monitoring requirements	*40*
	Summary	*41*
	Further reading	*41*

3	**Distributed transaction processing system architectures**	**43**
	Introduction	44
	The need for software system architecture	44
	A general transaction processing system architecture	46
	Application server architectures	49
	Summary	65
	Further reading	66

4	**The object transaction service**	**67**
	Introduction	68
	Background: CORBA	68
	OTS architecture and features	71
	Programming the CORBA object transaction service	76
	Recoverable resources	80
	Summary	81
	Further reading	82

5	**Transaction processing monitors: Encina and the OrbixOTM**	**83**
	Introduction	84
	Encina overview	84
	OrbixOTM overview	97
	Summary	104
	Further reading:	105

6	**Case study**	**107**
	Introduction	108
	The Stock-OnLine system	108
	Database design	115
	Summary	117
	Further reading	117

7	**Building the case study with OrbixOTM**	**119**
	Overview	120
	The Stock-OnLine CORBA interfaces	120
	The Subscriber client	123
	The StockFeed Client	141
	The StockDBMSAccess server	142
	Implementing the server object	150
	Communicating with MS SQL Server	157
	Summary	162

8	**Building the case study with Encina++**	**163**
	Overview	*164*
	The Stock-OnLine Encina interfaces	*164*
	Initializing the Encina++ client	*169*
	Performing transactions	*172*
	The Encina++ StockDBMSAccess server	*176*
	Security in Encina++	*191*
	Deploying and managing the server	*193*
	Summary	*196*
9	**Performance issues**	**197**
	Introduction	*198*
	Understanding application performance	*198*
	Test environment and results	*200*
	Base timings	*200*
	Performance under load	*203*
	Improving performance	*206*
	General performance tips	*208*
	Summary	*212*
	Further reading	*213*
	Index	*215*

Foreword

Whether you use the term *object*, *component* or *entity*, distributed object systems have many appealing characteristics. We all know of the advantages of object systems in projects. It is even more important that these techniques are used *in the large* in enterprise computing systems. Computer Science currently knows of no better way of defining interfaces, of separating concerns, and of inter-working across the boundaries that exist in our heterogeneous systems. How satisfying it is to make a normal invocation on an object that is implemented in a different programming language and object/component system, runs on a different operating system, across the network, and is owned by another company who's implementation details just aren't of concern to you.

But to use object technology in enterprise systems, it must provide enterprise characteristics such as security, management and transactions. The specifications for these are defined by CORBA, and by the EJB/J2EE specifications that bring CORBA more strongly into the Java world.

You want to be able to make a simple invocation on an object, but have the system level perform the security checking, provide the management data, and propagate any transaction context that is required for transactional semantics. If you invoke on two objects in different servers, and each object updates its own database then you want to make two simple object invocations. You want the system level to work out what needs to be done to propagate the transactional contexts, interface to the local transaction support at each site (e.g., via XA), and co-ordinate the two-phase commit. You want to worry about higher level business and architecture issues, not system issues.

Ian has concentrated on the transactional aspect of enterprise computing and written a terrific book that explains the standard, gives an overview of some of the products, and shows how they can be used to implement a common example. In just a couple of hundred pages he takes you from a basic knowledge of distributed computing to a clear understanding of the details of the standards and the products that implement them.

In case you think that transaction processing is passé, consider all of the e-commerce applications that you know of. Each one has a set of backend applications that need to be interfaced to the Web. Providing the Web interface is the easy bit – it's the backend integration, including the transaction semantics, that require the big effort.

The year 1999 has been an important one in distributed object computing, with the release of new core products – new ORBs, Naming Services and security – that take advantage of the last eight years of experience in their implementation and use. These scale, and they are fast! 2000 will see the release of the next generation of enterprise systems, adding transactions, management, and so on, to this new generation of ORBs. I hope that Ian can find the time to continue his work and provide insights and feedback on the new generation.

Seán Baker
Chief Scientific Officer, IONA Technologies

Preface

The recent merging of distributed object technology and transaction processing monitors has created a new class of technology known as Object Transaction Monitors (OTMs). OTMs typically contain a comprehensive set of features that make it possible to build enterprise-scale, high performance transaction processing systems.

As more systems based on OTMs are built, there's a need for software professionals new to the area to acquire an understanding of the concepts and features of the available OTM technologies. They also need to appreciate the important issues that drive a project's architecture, detailed design and programming. This book attempts to fill this niche, to educate people in the complexities of OTM technologies. The approach taken is necessarily a practical one. It attempts to distill several years of the author's consulting experience gained working with OTM technologies, and present the information in a way that is broadly useful and easily digestible for people who build OTM-based applications.

The aims of this book are to:

1. Explain the key underlying concepts and techniques of enterprise transaction processing technology (Chapters 1 and 2).
2. Discuss alternative architectural approaches for building object-oriented transaction processing systems (Chapter 3).
3. Describe the major features of the CORBA Object Transaction Service (OTS) and two products, OrbixOTM and Encina++, that support this service (Chapters 4 and 5).
4. Illustrate how to implement an example transaction processing system in C++ using OrbixOTM and Encina++ (Chapters 6, 7 and 8).
5. Discuss the performance characteristics of the examples, and introduce some techniques for improving performance.

Just as importantly, this book is not:

1. An introduction to CORBA/DCE and how to program these technologies. There are already many good books on these topics, several of which are referenced in the appropriate chapters.
2. A detailed description and evaluation of the techniques and algorithms employed in the internals of distributed transaction processing systems. Read Jim Gray's or Phil Bernstein's books for excellent coverage of these areas.

The intended audience for this book includes:

1. Project managers and system architects who need to understand the concepts of distributed transaction processing systems and the features supported by state-of-the-art products.
2. Professional software engineers who need to understand, evaluate and write programs using object-oriented transaction processing software.
3. Graduate-level and advanced undergraduate level students who study transaction processing systems and software.

The material in the book is roughly 50 per cent generic and 50 per cent reasonably specific to OrbixOTM and Encina++. This approach is deliberate, attempting to provide a balance between explaining general concepts and approaches and illustrating these in a concrete fashion with real products and code. For this reason, even if your projects don't specifically use the Iona or Transarc products (yes – there are many good alternatives!), there is still considerable value in at least the first six chapters, as well as Chapter 9.

What do you need to know to get the most out of this book? Certainly an understanding of the basic components in a distributed object system that uses CORBA or some similar technology should be considered a prerequisite. The code examples are written in C++, so a working knowledge of C++ will be useful. Also, when reading through the examples in Chapters 7 and 8, some understanding of basic RPC and/or CORBA technology is assumed. The examples do provide some explanation of the salient features that arise in the application code, but those new to this area should have a relevant reference book at hand.

The example code in Chapters 7 and 8 can be downloaded from the WWW site (**www.awl.com/cseng**). The code is based upon OrbixOTM 1.0c, and the Encina++ version in TxSeries 4.2. These products are therefore needed to build and run the applications, along with SQL Server 6.5. The code is built using Microsoft's Visual Studio version 5.0.

Of course, all faults and errors are indisputably my own.

Acknowledgements

I'd like to acknowledge the contributions of a number of people to the writing of this book. First to the many reviewers, including Paddy Nixon, David Hodge, Innes Ritchie and those who Sally never identified to me! Your feedback was greatly appreciated and has helped me to improve the quality of this book in a number of areas. I would also like to thank the many talented and dedicated professionals I have worked with over the past few years for the many long, involved discussions on applications and technologies. An incomplete list of these includes John Casey, Tony Parente, Mike Brady, Patrick Bryne, Daniel Tarudji, David Hodge, Paul Greenfield, John Colton, JP, 'Rendang' Rashid, Joe Piezuch, and many many more. In addition, many thanks to Elizabeth Law at IONA for helping with software distribution, and introductions to IONA technical staff.

Finally I'd like to express my gratitude to the people at Pearson Education who have made the publication of this book possible, including Sally Mortimore and Alison Birtwell. Your efforts are greatly appreciated.

CORBA is a trademark or registered trademark of Object Management Group, Inc. in the US and other countries. UML is a trademark of Object Management Group, Inc. in the US and other countries. Distributed Transaction Controller (DTC), SQL Server, Visual C++, Visual Studio and Windows are trademarks of Microsoft. Encina and Encina++ are trademarks of Transarc Corporation. Forte is a trademark of Digital Equipment Corporation. Oracle is a trademark of Oracle Corporation UK Ltd. OrbixOTM is a trademark of Iona Technologies. Sybase is a trademark of Sybase Incorporated. Top End is a trademark of NCR. Tuxedo is a trademark of USL, Inc. UNIX is licenced through X/Open Company Ltd. Visibroker ITS is a trademark of Inprise. WebLogic Enterprise is a trademark of BEA. All other trademarks are owned by their respective companies.

Chapter 1

Introduction to enterprise transaction processing systems

Transaction processing: from mainframes to distributed systems	2
The anatomy of enterprise applications	3
Some examples of TP applications	6
What is a distributed transaction processing monitor?	8
Why are distributed TP systems attractive?	9
The state of the market	14
Summary	16
Further reading	16

▶ TRANSACTION PROCESSING: FROM MAINFRAMES TO DISTRIBUTED SYSTEMS

To most software professionals, the mention of a transaction processing (TP) system conjures up images of huge mainframes, COBOL programs and 3270 terminals. These mainframe-based COBOL applications are the driving forces behind the operations of banks, airlines and all manner of financial institutions, to name just a few of the relevant vertical markets. What typifies all of these systems is their requirement for high levels of data integrity, scalable performance and the need to continue operating in the face of adversity. These are mission-critical, enterprise-scale systems which business and rather interestingly, society in general, rely upon.

It is undoubtedly true that the vast majority of today's on-line transactions are processed on mainframe-based systems, mostly by COBOL programs. In fact it has been estimated that there are 30 billion lines of operational CICS COBOL in existence today. However, distributed TP technologies for Unix and NT client–server systems are rapidly increasing their market share. A variety of distributed TP products are able to coordinate updates to one or more databases, maintain data integrity when machines and network connections fail, and provide high transaction rates and scalable performance for a range of applications.

The attractions of such technology are numerous. Systems can be constructed using cheap, commodity hardware and software technology. Compared to mainframe technology, the price/performance advantages are significant. In addition, it's possible to start small, and add processing capability as transaction rates grow. Technological obsolescence becomes less of a problem, as hardware and software can be upgraded in stages, spreading costs over time. This flexibility extends to being able to mix and match various development tools and system components such as databases from different vendors. Add to this the continuing ability to access all those old mainframe systems and data and you have a compelling story that most organisations can no longer ignore.

Until recently, distributed TP technology was largely procedural in nature. TP systems were typically written in C, and the products offered mainly C-based programming interfaces for constructing applications. Their procedural nature betrayed their heritage as products developed in the late 1980s and early 1990s when C was the predominant systems programming language. Examples include Tuxedo, Encina and Top End.

However, reflecting trends in software technology during the 1990s, object-oriented distributed TP technology is now emerging. Over a number of years, the Object Management Group (OMG) has been working to define the Object Transaction Service (OTS) as part of the Common Object Request Broker Architecture (CORBA) standard. This work has now reached fruition and a number of complete implementations of the OTS are now available from TP product vendors. These systems can coordinate transactions that involve multiple objects residing in various processes in a distributed system. These products combine the architectural advantages of distributed systems with the programming benefits of object-oriented design and implementation. This is a powerful partnership of technologies, one that will inevitably have a profound effect on next-generation TP applications. Products that fit into this category are known as Object Transaction Monitors (OTMs).

In this introductory chapter, some of the background and rationales for distributed TP technology will be explored. We'll also explain the fundamentals of transaction processing, and describe some real example applications that exploit this technology. This is not a technically complex chapter. It aims to provide the necessary background for much of the material that follows. Some of the historical perspective very much reflects the author's experiences over the last decade, and there are sure to be some readers who don't see things quite the same way. Still, in this rapidly moving industry our many different personal experiences lead to many differing perspectives, all of which are equally valid.

▶ THE ANATOMY OF ENTERPRISE APPLICATIONS

Enterprise applications are computing systems that are critical to the day-to-day operations of a business or organization. If an enterprise application fails or is unavailable, the business of the enterprise stops or is severely restricted in its operations. For example, as happened in mid-1999 to Qantas Airlines in Sydney, an airline without its reservation system cannot operate properly. It does not know who has tickets on which flight, or who has checked in, cancelled, or even selected a different flight. As a result, flights get delayed, cancelled or diverted, and customers get angry. These failures can cost enterprises millions of dollars a minute. Hence the viability of the organization itself depends on the performance and availability of these enterprise applications.

Enterprise applications require at least the following attributes:

- **High availability:** This includes $24 \times 7 \times 365$ operations, reliable hardware and software and rapid recovery from any failures that do occur.

It's interesting to note that a system with 99.9% availability is actually unavailable for over eight hours in a given year. With 99.999% availability, downtime is just over five minutes each year. For many enterprise applications, 99.9% availability simply isn't sufficient.

- **Integrity**: The application has to ensure high levels of data integrity and consistency. The data in the system's persistent storage must stay consistent despite transaction and system failure.
- **Scalability**: The application must be able to process the volume of transactions generated by large organizations and handle potentially tens of thousands of concurrent users. Scalability is becoming of paramount importance with the drive to e-business over the Internet. Suddenly a WWW-based system must support a vast number of users at peak times.
- **Security**: Enterprise applications must maintain security. This requires that access to the system is secure, controlled and audited.

Figure 1.1 shows an outline of the basic anatomy of an enterprise application that uses distributed object technology.

Let's briefly describe some of the key components of Figure 1.1:

- **Middleware**: There seem to be many debates about the precise meaning of middleware. In this book the term is really used as a synonym for '*software plumbing and associated services*' for constructing distributed software systems. By plumbing, we mean the basic pipes that enable data to be transferred between distributed processes. Middleware provides an abstract model that hides the low-level complexity of the programming interfaces for transport layer mechanisms such as TCP/IP sockets. If you're still confused, just think of middleware as a software infrastructure that makes it easier to write distributed systems! CORBA products are examples of middleware technologies.
- **Object transaction service (OTS)**: The OTS is a service that is typically built on top of a middleware infrastructure to provide distributed transaction processing capabilities. Application designers can then use transactions to ensure data integrity in their applications. Transactional access to resources basically guarantees that the changes made complete successfully and in their entirety, or fail completely.
- **Security service**: The security service typically stores information about the users and services in a distributed application. Users identify themselves to the security service, which uses passwords or

secure certificates to confirm that a user or service is who they claim to be. Security services also provide facilities such as access control and data encryption.

- **Directory service:** The directory service provides a location where services and applications in an enterprise system can advertise their location. Clients use the directory service to retrieve object or component references to services. These references can then be used to access the services that the component or object offers. As enterprise applications tend to be dynamic in nature, with various services starting, stopping and moving, directories are key components as they introduce a high degree of location-transparency into a system's architecture.

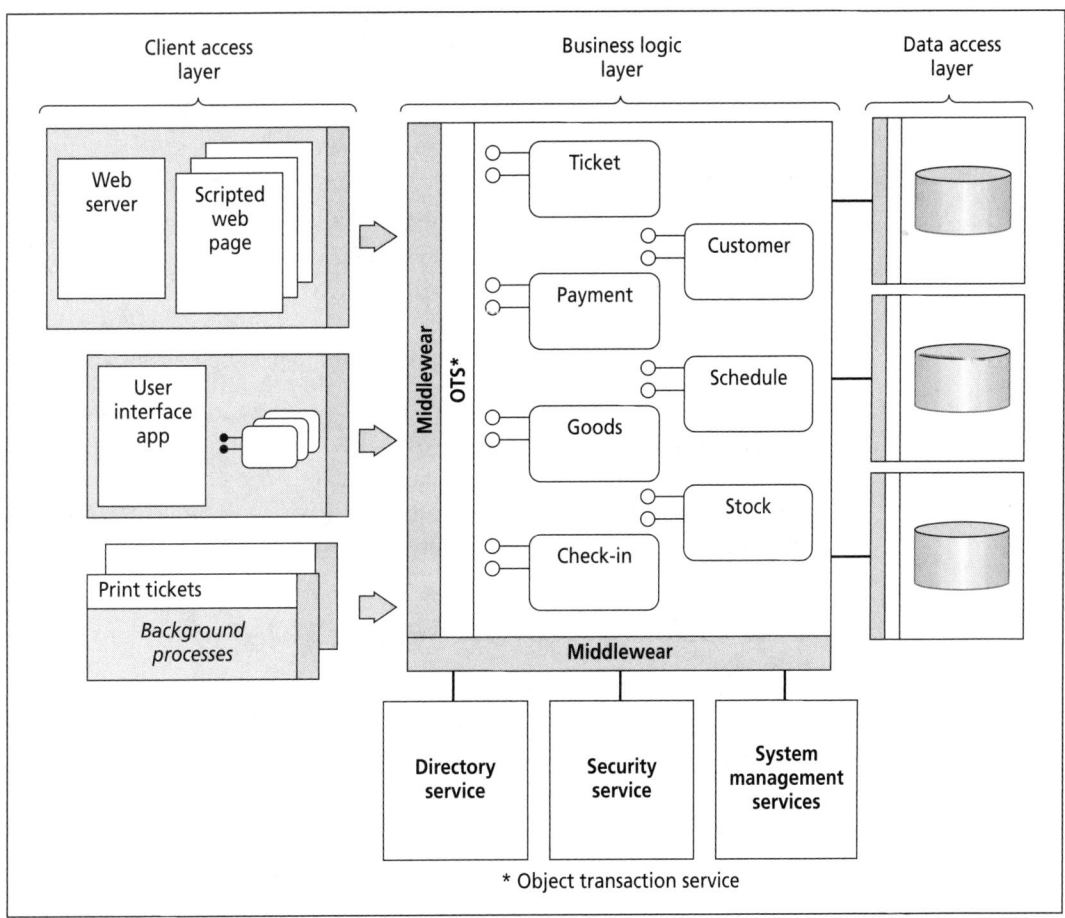

The basic anatomy of an enterprise application Figure 1.1

- **Management service**: Complex enterprise applications need monitoring, managing and maintaining. Without adequate support for auditing, event logging, alert and emergency handling and system configuration, distributed applications typically fail to meet their goals. Some brave souls feel that management infrastructure is something that can be mostly ignored, and then retrofitted to an application when it works. In my experience, I have found this to be untrue. Middleware products should provide adequate management tools and, ideally, hooks that allow management events to propagate through to some other, dedicated management tools such as Tivoli.

- **Client access layer**: The client access layer encapsulates client presentation and access services. It uses the services of the middleware and business logic layer to implement application-specific behavior. Clients may gain access to the application services via various mechanisms, including WWW-based HTTP protocols.

- **Business logic layer**: This layer comprises a set of server processes and components that accept client requests and implement the application business logic. Components and objects in this layer typically collaborate, access and update the persistent storage in the data access layer.

- **Data access layer**: This layer encapsulates the technologies and products needed to store and retrieve enterprise data. It comprises databases such as Oracle or SQL Server, gateways to legacy databases and interfaces to persistent queuing technologies such as MQ Series.

While all these components are important in enterprise applications, the OTS has a particularly pivotal role. The OTS services let application programmers focus on their application logic by giving them a simple programming environment where concurrent activities do not interfere with each other and persistent data remains consistent in the face of failures.

▶ SOME EXAMPLES OF TP APPLICATIONS

Enterprise transaction processing systems are deployed in many types of business applications. Here are some brief descriptions of three representative examples I've come across:

Customer billing

A large energy-provider with 16 million customers implemented a system to handle phone enquiries and payments by customers. Several hundred system operators received calls from customers. The operators used the system to display the customer details from a database, handle customer enquiries and submit bill payments. Payments and some customer requests caused the database to be updated, and requests for receipts and work orders (e.g. disconnect the customer supply) to be generated. The generated requests were transactionally fed into an accompanying workflow system for off-line handling. Interestingly, the main customer database was held on a mainframe. These records were downloaded to a large Unix-hosted Oracle DBMS, which was updated during the day due to customer requests. Each night, updated information was uploaded from Oracle to the mainframe so that the necessary batch processing could be run.

Airport management system

A major new airport required a way for all the 'off-the-shelf' airport subsystems to exchange information about significant events that occur. The airport comprises at least 40 information subsystems to handle functionality such as check-in, baggage handling and claim, arrival and departure information, gate allocation, and so on. A supplier who specializes in such systems typically provides each subsystem and the subsystems must be made to interoperate in the construction of the airport. In this example, a message broker application was built. The message broker provided a simple interface for airport subsystems to transactionally submit messages about events (i.e. plane XX has landed), and other subsystems to subscribe to a given set of event types. When a particular event type was submitted by a subsystem, the message broker ensured all subscribers to that event were informed that the event had occurred. The message broker ensured that messages could not be lost, and were delivered with a guaranteed quality-of-service. If messages could not be delivered, exception reports were raised. This loosely coupled solution proved to be extremely flexible, reliable and scalable.

Loan processing system

A bank wished to improve the automation of its on-line customer loan-processing centre. Customers wishing to take out a loan could phone the bank, and apply for a loan, and get approval or otherwise during the call. Difficulties included the fact that the data that needed to be provided and checked for each loan application was spread across a number of databases hosted by Unix and mainframe systems. Also, the performance of the system needed to scale to handle peak loads, as well as provide a high degree of security. The new loan processing system used a

TP monitor to transactionally coordinate requests and updates to and from the various databases involved in a single customer loan application. The TP monitor also provided the security levels needed, and the ability to scale to a high volume of simultaneous requests.

▶ WHAT IS A DISTRIBUTED TRANSACTION PROCESSING MONITOR?

A transaction is a set of operations that is treated as an indivisible unit of work, transforming data sets from one consistent state to another. Transactions must exhibit the so-called **ACID** properties of:

- Atomicity: Either all operations that are part of the transaction happen, or all fail.
- Consistency: A transaction moves data between application-defined consistent states.
- Isolation: Intermediate results of an incomplete transaction remain invisible to other concurrent transactions until the transaction completes (succeeds or fails). Essentially transactions acquire locks on the data they change, and appear to run serially.
- Durability: The results of successful transactions persist, even in the face of subsequent failures.

Transactions may complete in one of two ways. A successful transaction will commit. An unsuccessful transaction will abort, rolling back any changes to data made by the aborted transaction. The rollback process involves undoing changes to data and hence returning it to its previous, consistent state.

In distributed systems, a transaction may be spread across several machines, each running separate processes in the application. Consequently each process must coordinate its activities for the same transaction to ensure the transaction exhibits ACID properties. Of course, this is much more difficult in distributed systems, as network, process or hardware failures can cause a transaction to fail. In such circumstances, the failure must be communicated to all participating processes in the transaction, causing each to roll back any changes they have made on behalf of the transaction.

In order to deal with failure scenarios in distributed TP systems, two mechanisms are employed, namely *recoverable processes* and a *two-phase commit protocol*. These will be explained in detail in Chapter 2.

Products that support the development of transactional systems are known as TP monitors. A TP monitor will typically provide a number of services, as follows:

- **Application development environment**: TP monitors provide APIs to allow transactions to be defined and resolved, perform communications and transaction coordination, define security requirements, and handle aborts and exceptions in a distributed environment.
- **Runtime environment**: TP monitors provide an execution environment that manages transaction load across application servers, ensures server availability and data and transaction integrity in the case of failures, and provides fast response time and high transaction throughput.
- **Administration services**: TP monitors provide support for configuring, monitoring and managing servers, transactions and security.
- **Resource manager communication services**: TP monitors support the standard XA interface for coordinating distributed transactions with widely used database management systems such as Oracle and Sybase.

▶ WHY ARE DISTRIBUTED TP SYSTEMS ATTRACTIVE?

The early decades of commercial computing were dominated by large mainframe and minicomputer systems. Dumb, '*green-screen*' terminals gave simultaneous users the ability to time-share and access applications running on the host machine. Monolithic systems ran on the host, and merged presentation, business logic and database accesses in programs written in languages like COBOL, PL/1 and many, many others.

The 1980s, especially the end of the decade, saw some technologies become mainstream which radically changed the frontier of commercial computing. In no particular order, these were:

- Powerful, low-cost workstations and servers running Unix.
- Graphical user interfaces (GUIs), firstly on Macintoshes, and belatedly on PCs using Microsoft Windows and OS/2.
- Low-cost networking hardware technology and software protocols (e.g. TCP/IP) enabling communication between machines on heterogeneous networks.
- Database server technology from companies like Oracle and Sybase which ran on Unix-based servers.

The confluence of these technologies made it possible to consider building relatively high-performance, low-cost distributed systems. Not every multi-user system now needed to run on the mainframe. Typically these *client–server* systems (*see* Figure 1.2) would have a database server supporting tens of connected clients running on personal computers with GUI front-ends. Such systems were departmental in size, not enterprise-wide. Enterprise systems still ran on big machines. However, all this was sufficiently influential in the software industry to start the movement of 'downsizing' (or 'rightsizing' as it eventually became known by marketing departments).

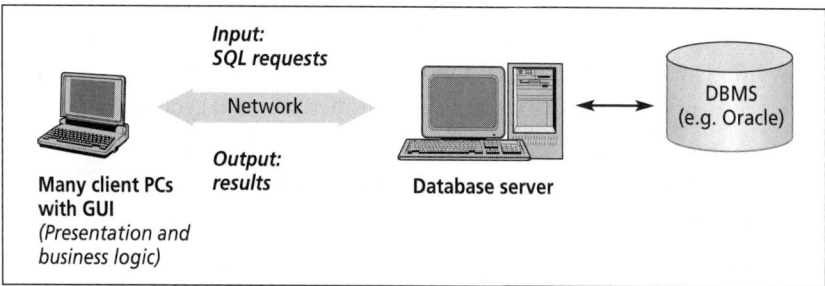

Figure 1.2   A two-tier client–server system

Key drivers in all this were cost and presentation technology. PCs were becoming cheap and relatively powerful, and PC software was starting to have an attractive look and feel. If you could get your application data in to your GUI, you could then (sometimes!) transfer it easily to your spreadsheet or word processor. And if your database server ran out of grunt, you could just upgrade the server machine every year or two, as Moore's Law proved to be correct. Upgrading a server gave the client PCs a much-extended life.

It didn't take long, though, for the industry to come up against the limits of these two-tier client–server systems. Despite ever-increasing processing power and multi-processor servers, two-tier systems didn't scale to thousands of users and geographically distributed enterprise-wide solutions. Connection management for thousands of users degraded the database server performance, and databases and networks became bottlenecks. Approaches such as stored database procedures helped, but these were proprietary solutions with all the attendant problems of vendor lock-in and so on. In addition, security needs became difficult to manage across multiple databases and single points of failure (e.g. the database server) made fault-tolerant approaches difficult.

Scalability and performance weren't the only problems. Large organizations quickly found themselves with many departmental systems, each with its own data and applications. In the rush to downsize, interoperability between departmental systems wasn't often top of the priority list of requirements. When a wider organizational view was taken, the major difficulties of integrating disparate systems using different technology, often with duplicate data, became apparent. Getting data from the Payroll system into the Human Resources (HR) system just wasn't easy. A general, consistent solution that could be utilized across the organization to integrate systems was obviously needed.

Finally, software engineering concerns also entered the fray. Clients in two-tier systems often tightly coupled presentation and business logic. As presentation and business functions are essentially independent architectural components, this was not a good idea. If a business requirement changed, as they do, finding and updating the code among the presentation logic was difficult. If presentation technology changed, as it tends to, incorporating code to use new visual components became a tedious and error-prone exercise. Clearly, a logical division between presentation and business logic was needed to aid software maintenance.

These pressures of enterprise-wide scalability, integration and improved software design requirements were key issues behind the introduction of an additional physical layer in distributed systems. As depicted in Figure 1.3, three-tier distributed systems cleanly separate presentation, business and data access logic across different machines. The

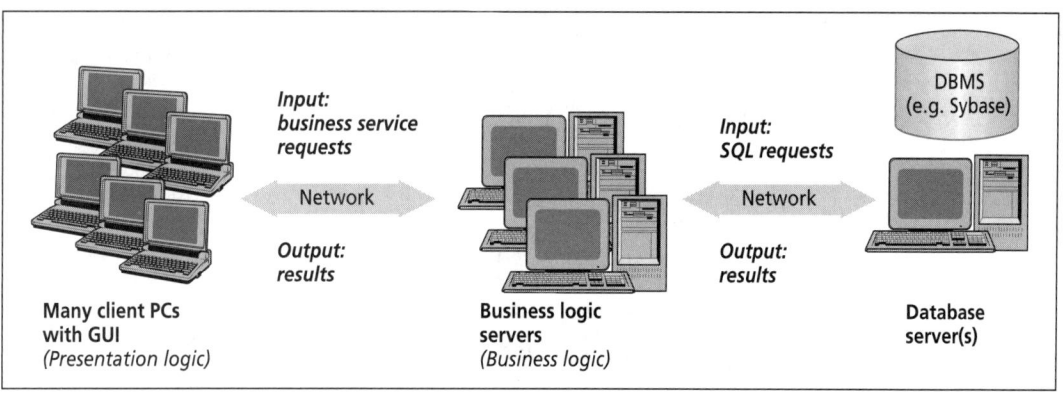

A three-tier client–server system **Figure 1.3**

client concentrates on user interaction and displaying results, and sending logical requests for data manipulation to the middle tier. The middle tier provides the logical business functions, accessing the database tier on behalf of clients and returning the results of user queries. Modifications to presentation or business logic can be carried out independently, reducing software maintenance and upgrade costs. Client code is completely isolated even from radical but not uncommon changes such as a new database structure (or vendor).

This is, of course, where middleware becomes necessary. In its most simple form, middleware technology provides a high-level, consistent and reliable mechanism for servers to offer services to clients. Clients communicate requests to servers by calling named functions that the server supports, and passing the necessary parameter values. To the client, calling these functions is very similar to calling local functions in the client program. In reality, the functions the client calls are the hooks into the middleware layer. The middleware on the client will use the underlying network protocols to send the data associated with the request to a server who can execute that service. When the service is complete, any results are passed to the middleware on the server, and the middleware returns these to the client program. Figure 1.4 illustrates part of this scheme. Be aware that lots of detail is skipped over here: this will become apparent in later chapters.

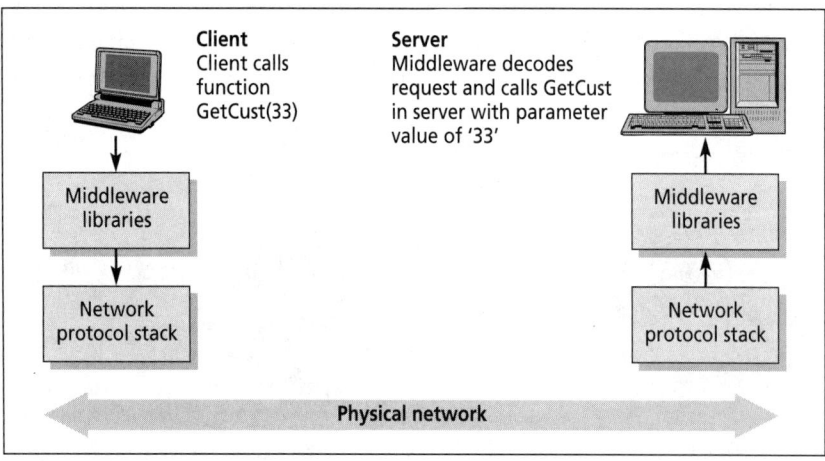

Figure 1.4   **Sending a request to a server**

Once middleware is in place, by using powerful server machines in the middle tier, one business logic server can support many simultaneous users. This also reduces database connections, as many user requests can be multiplexed over fewer connections. Crucially, by replicating the middle tier, hundreds and potentially thousands of users can be supported, providing excellent scalability. Having many business logic servers not only improves performance, but also provides enhanced reliability. If one middle tier server fails (process or machine), clients can simply reconnect to any of the other available servers. All in all, this is a very attractive, flexible architecture.

The middle tier also becomes the integration layer. Departmental systems can create middle-tier services that offer the required functionality for integration with other departmental systems. For example, the Payroll system can offer a service to the Human Resources system to update an employee's annual salary. The HR system can then simply use this service, and it remains completely oblivious to the exact technological details of the Payroll system. Even better, if all departmental systems across the organization use the same middleware technology to offer services, programmers quickly become familiar with the technology. This makes the integration task much less costly.

Still, a number of key technical issues desperately needed commercial-strength solutions before three-tier architectures could be deployed as high-performance, business-critical systems. Again, in no particular order, these were:

- A simple, reliable and efficient method for passing requests and returning results between presentation and business logic.
- A consistent and high-performance technique for clients to find given services in the network, and to spread client load across replicated services.
- Some way of implementing and managing security for users and processes.
- Tools for monitoring, administering and managing the components of the system, and reporting errors and failures.
- A method of coordinating transactions across multiple databases to ensure data remains consistent and recoverable.

Not surprisingly, all of these features can be found to varying degrees in today's middleware technology. We can now design and build wide-scale distributed information systems with high performance and reliability and the ability to scale to higher loads in the future. Some systems today support many thousands of globally dispersed users, processing thousands of transactions per second, and have no unplanned downtime (so-called $24 \times 7 \times 365$ systems). These are impressive feats of technological and human endeavor.

Make no mistake though, three-tier distributed systems are not easy to build, despite the availability of excellent middleware products. Fundamental distributed system issues – for example, handling concurrency, failure-scenarios and scalability – require skilled professionals to devise workable solutions. Product complexities (unfortunately, it's true!) require software engineers who have product experience and insight. There's no doubt that in the late 1990s, such architects, designers and developers are in short supply.

▶ THE STATE OF THE MARKET

Making predictions in this industry is a notoriously hazardous and foolhardy activity. So here, we'll just briefly mention the major products that exist in the OTM arena as of the time of writing (late 1999), and indulge in a little speculation about where things are moving.

One collection of OTMs has evolved from the TP monitor products. The two leading products in this area are BEA's WebLogic Enterprise and IBM Transarc's Encina++. The key attraction of both is the fact that their core transaction processing capabilities have been well proven over many years of operation in the field. They have been used to build some very large, complex applications which scale well. Essentially these products have bolted on an object-oriented application programming interface (API) which, under the covers, maps to the procedural API that the underlying products (Tuxedo and Encina respectively) have always supported. The object-oriented API fully implements the CORBA OTS specification. Some will call this 'window dressing', rebadging old technology as new. Personally I don't really think it matters whether this is true or not. What matters is being able to successfully build quality distributed applications using object-oriented approaches. In this respect, WebLogic Enterprise and Encina++ seem to match up to any OTM technology.

Another set of OTM products has grown from the CORBA world. The two major examples are Iona's OrbixOTM and Inprise's Visibroker ITS. Both fully support the CORBA OTS standard and associated

CORBAServices to create a fully featured OTM package. While both products are relatively new, released in 1998, they are attracting much interest, and application experience is being gained through a number of successful deployments. New versions of both these products were due in late 1999.

A further set of OTM products is built upon proprietary middleware technologies. A number of products fit in to this category, but debatably the major two are Microsoft's COM+ and Forte. COM+ extends Microsoft's COM technology with what was formerly known as the Microsoft Transaction Service (MTS) to support distributed transactions. Forte is a product that includes its own development language (TOOL) and environment, plus tools for system deployment and management. A major attraction of both is their close integration with development languages and tools. This lessens the development complexity and reduces the number of third party tools required.

If this represents a very broad statement of where the market currently is for OTMs, what is likely to happen in the short term? I expect there to be developments in the following three areas:

1. **Product evolution**: Existing products will become more fully featured, easier to use and more reliable.

2. **Product interoperability**: Bridges between products will become commonplace, enabling for example a CORBA client to communicate transparently with an MTS server and an Encina++ server running on DCE. This bridging technology is already a part of some OTM products.

3. **Java and EJB**: Nearly all the major players in the OTM market are producing Enterprise Java Beans (EJB) OTMs. Currently, most OTMs do not fully support Java on the server, but by the time you read this I suspect the situation will have changed radically. In addition, EJB and the emerging CORBA component model will be very closely related, promoting interoperability.

The emergence of EJB is potentially the greatest influence on OTM technology directions in the next few years. It's important to realize however that there is very little actual application experience with deploying EJB technology in real application domains. This will undoubtedly be an interesting exercise for all involved. What is more certain is that EJB products, like any complex distributed technology, need time to mature. So don't write off all today's dinosaur TP monitors and OTMs just yet!

▶ SUMMARY

The transaction processing world has changed a lot recently. While large mainframes still crunch through huge amounts of transactions daily, they are complemented by heterogeneous, distributed transaction processing systems built on Unix and NT servers running TP monitor products. OTMs are strategically important new technologies that promise to combine the best of TP monitors with the best of object-oriented middleware technologies. Different vendors have taken radically different approaches to building OTM products. Some have enhanced their TP monitors to support the OTS specification, while others have enhanced their Object Request Broker (ORB)-based or proprietary middleware to support transactions.

Regardless of the underlying architecture, OTMs allow TP systems to be built using object-oriented principles and techniques. This is attractive to many development organizations that have invested heavily in OO over the last decade. Today's generation of OTMs still predominantly support C++ only on the server. The emergence of Java and Enterprise Java Beans is fuelling the development of the next generation of OTMs. Java promises much, but is still largely unproven technology in business-critical enterprise systems. Perhaps the long term OTM future belongs to Java, but the present and the short term are likely to be dominated by the evolution of existing OTMs.

FURTHER READING

A reasonable and recent high-level overview of some OTM products is:

Essential Guide to Object Monitors, K. Boucher and F. Katz, John Wiley & Sons, 1999.

Beware though, the product information in this book will date very quickly!

A much more comprehensive and technical coverage is provided in:

Enterprise CORBA, D. Slama *et al.*, Prentice Hall, 1999.

This book contains an excellent discussion of CORBA-related services and topics and design approaches applicable to distributed object-oriented systems. Much of this is applicable to distributed transaction processing applications.

Chapter 2

Distributed transaction processing fundamentals

Introduction	*18*
What is a transaction?	*18*
Two-phase commit	*21*
Transaction demarcation	*24*
Resource manager access using XA	*26*
Transactional remote procedure calls	*29*
Heuristic outcomes	*30*
Nested transactions	*32*
Transactional queuing technology	*35*
Locking	*37*
Recovery	*39*
System administration and monitoring requirements	*40*
Summary	*41*
Further reading	*41*

▶ INTRODUCTION

This chapter lays the foundations for the rest of the book by describing the fundamentals of distributed transaction processing. It defines the necessary properties of a transaction, and illustrates how a transaction processing (TP) monitor maintains these properties using two-phase commit protocols, logging and recovery. In addition, the XA protocol for coordinating transactions with resource managers is explained, and methods for programmatically defining the boundaries of a transaction are described. This discussion leads to a definition of the behavior and semantics of subtransactions. Finally, the use of recoverable queuing mechanisms to support off-line transactions is then described along with resource locking and server recovery, and an overview is given of the system administration tools required with a TP monitor.

The chapter should give the application developer most of the information needed to begin constructing distributed TP systems. Advanced projects will need more detailed knowledge of the internals of such systems. The references at the end of the chapter, especially the books by Jim Gray and Phillip Bernstein, provide much more detailed coverage of these issues. Both are highly recommended for readers who need to know more.

▶ WHAT IS A TRANSACTION?

The essential aim of a transaction is to move a system from one consistent state to another. The group of operations, the transaction, which carries out the state transition must either all succeed or all fail. This ensures the system state remains consistent. Hence a transaction can be viewed as an indivisible, logical unit of work. Transactions typically update records in one or more databases, and ensure all the changes become permanent, or all fail.

The classic transaction example is a transfer of money between two bank accounts. The transfer transaction must successfully perform the withdrawal operation and the deposit operation. If for example the withdrawal succeeded and the deposit failed, we'd have a very happy bank and somewhat dissatisfied customers!

A more contemporary example would be purchasing products over the Internet. Imagine for example a WWW site that offers wine sales to customers. The customer can browse the WWW site selecting bottles of wine to purchase, and adding these to their virtual shopping cart. When the user has completed their selection, they go to the payment and delivery page. Here they enter their credit card details, delivery address and instructions. When these have been completed, the customer hits the submit button. This scheme is depicted in Figure 2.1.

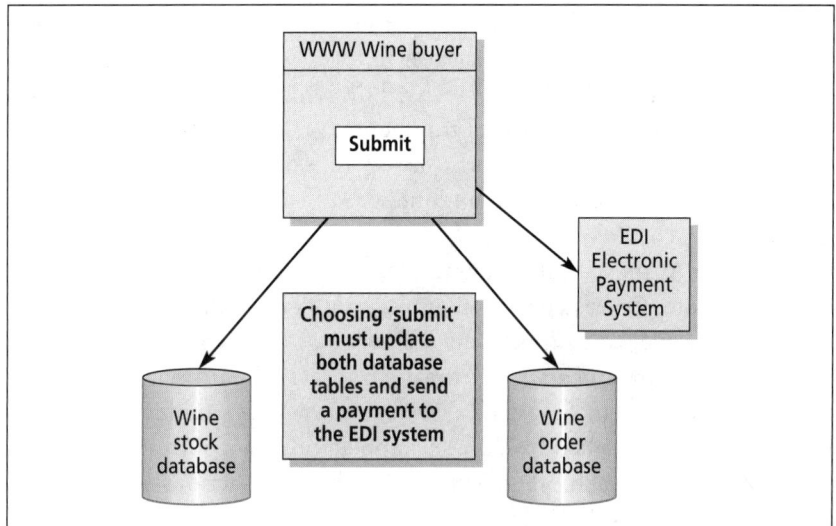

A transaction example: Internet purchasing   **Figure 2.1**

The wine purchasing system must correctly update the two databases to reflect the contents of the order. It must also submit a request to authorize the customer's credit card transaction to a standard Electronic Data Interchange (EDI) system. Finally, the customer should be informed of the outcome of the order. All these must occur for a successful transaction to take place.

Of course, the customer's expectations are that:

1. They will soon receive a delivery of the wine they have ordered.

2. The cost of their wine purchase will appear on their next credit card statement.

While a customer may not complain if (1) occurs and (2) doesn't, the WWW site operator certainly won't remain in business very long! Therefore transactional semantics are needed to ensure that a partial failure cannot occur, and both customers and the wine sales business get what they expect.

More formally, a logical operation is said to be transactional if it adheres to the **ACID** properties of **Atomicity, Consistency, Isolation** and **Durability** mentioned briefly in Chapter 1. These are explained in more detail below:

Atomicity: All the operations that a transaction performs which involve updates to any kind of resource are treated as indivisible, or atomic. The entire transaction is either completed or not completed. Any partial completion due to system or application failures will be rolled back. This means we don't get bank account withdrawals without a deposit in a transfer transaction. A successful transaction is said to commit. An unsuccessful transaction is said to abort. Any operations and updates carried out by an aborted transaction are undone, or rolled back, so that its effects have not happened.

Consistency: At the end of a transaction, all updated resources will be in a consistent state. Consistency is an application-defined quality. In the bank transfer example, this means that the totals of the two accounts should be the same before and after the transfer transaction has occurred.

Isolation: Concurrent access to shared resources by simultaneous transactions being performed by different applications is coordinated so that they do not affect each other. This means that transactions that compete for resources are isolated from each other, and the results of a transaction are not made visible to other transactions until successful completion has occurred.

Durability: All updates to data and other resources that have been performed by a transaction will be permanent, or durable. This means that a later failure such as abnormal program termination, network failure or machine failure does not cause the updates performed to be lost.

There are of course a number of places in a transaction where failures can occur. In the wine-purchasing example, once the user submits an order for processing, the following problems might happen:

1. The user's link to the subscription service might fail during submitting the order.

2. Updates to either of the two databases may fail.

3. The EDI payment message may fail. It may not arrive at the EDI system or it may not be authorized.

4. The return message to the user informing them of the transaction outcome may not arrive, due to client or network failure.

Any one of these failures could and almost certainly would affect the integrity of the transaction outcome. A distributed TP monitor is therefore responsible for ensuring that groups of operations that should behave transactionally adhere to the ACID properties. It does this by coordinating the actions of all the processes that participate in the transaction, including the databases and external data sources.

From an application developer's perspective, possibly the simplest way to think of transactions is as a tool to simplify failure scenarios in distributed systems. The application simply defines which operations must be carried out with ACID properties, and the TP monitor does the rest. This greatly reduces the application complexity, as the code can ignore subtle and numerous failure possibilities. It just waits for the TP monitor to inform it of the transaction outcome, commit or abort, and behaves accordingly.

▶ TWO-PHASE COMMIT

Major problems can occur in TP applications when updates are made to more than one database or resource. In the wine purchasing system, updates to the two databases and the EDI system must all occur, or none must occur. A partial failure, say one that causes the *Wine Order* database update to fail, causes the system to behave incorrectly. Without a TP monitor, the application programmer would effectively have to break the transaction down into three individual updates. This would mean:

- performing each update separately, and checking that each succeeds; and
- if any fail, the updates already carried out must somehow be undone.

As transactions are inherently permanent, and hence not undo-able, the latter requires a compensating transaction to be performed to restore the old state. This of course, may or may not succeed. By now, it should be pretty clear that this isn't simple code to write! Fortunately, this is what TP monitors are designed to do. TP monitors employ a two-phase commit protocol to coordinate updates to resources within a transaction.

In order to understand the two-phase commit protocol, it's useful to briefly review the X/Open's[1] reference model for distributed transaction processing. As Figure 2.2 shows, it defines the roles and application programming interfaces that comprise a distributed TP application.

[1] X/Open is part of the Open Group.

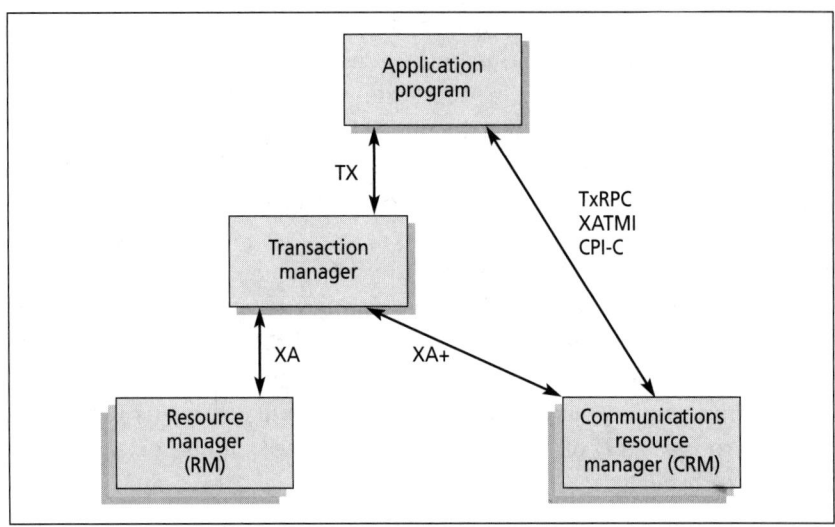

Figure 2.2 X/Open distributed TP reference model

The major components are:

Resource manager (RM): The RM role includes any components that manage persistent resources. This includes databases, file systems and message queuing systems.

Transaction manager (TM): The TM maintains the state of a transaction, and drives the two-phase commit protocol. The TM is a recoverable process. This means it logs its actions and can return to a previous state if it fails and subsequently restarts. All recoverable processes must store transaction state information.

Communications resource manager (CRM): The CRM provides an application-programming interface (API) to a communications system that can be used for distributed transactional systems. The reference model has adopted three variants. These are TUXEDO's XATMI, TxRPC (based on Transarc's model), and CPI-C (based on IBM's CICS and LU6.2).

XA: XA defines the API between the TM and the RM. For a TM and RM, such as a database, to participate in a distributed transaction, both must implement the XA API. Most TP monitors and major database vendors support XA.

TX: TX defines an API for application programs to begin and end transactions, and enquire about their status.

XA+: XA+ is a superset of XA, allowing the CRM to communicate with the TM about new nodes that join a distributed transaction.

When a transaction begins, the TM allocates it a unique transaction identifier, usually known as the *tid*. The *tid* identifies a data structure maintained by the TM that is known as the transaction context. The transaction context records among other things the processes or participants who take part in the transaction. The TM also writes state information to the transaction log. The log is crucial since, if the TM fails, it can be restarted and made to read through its log to discover which transactions were unfinished, or in-flight. These transactions can then be completed, typically by aborting the transaction.

When the client requests that the transaction is committed, the TM begins the two-phase commit protocol (*see* Figure 2.3). This involves the following phases:

Prepare phase: Sends a message to all RMs to tell them to prepare to commit the transaction. When an RM prepares, it guarantees that it can commit the transaction and makes a persistent record of the updates the transaction performed. After this, it can no longer unilaterally decide to abort the transaction. If an RM cannot prepare (that is, if it cannot guarantee to commit the transaction) it must abort. Each RM informs the TM about its decision to commit or abort by returning a message that contains its decision.

Resolution phase: When all the RMs that participate in a transaction have replied to the prepare phase, the TM examines the results. If all the RMs can commit, the whole transaction can commit, and the TM sends a commit message to each RM. The RMs acknowledge this when they have successfully ended the transaction. If any RM has decided that it must abort the transaction, or doesn't reply to the TM within a specified time period, the TM sends an abort message to each RM.

So, the two-phase commit protocol is needed to guarantee the ACID properties of a transaction when more than one RM participates in a transaction. In such circumstances, the application designer really has no choice if they want a *correct* system. There is however a cost in using two-phase commit. This is because of the extra set of messages that must be sent to implement the protocol. While TP monitors do their best to optimize the interactions, including using a one-phase commit protocol when a transaction has only one RM, the cost can be significant.

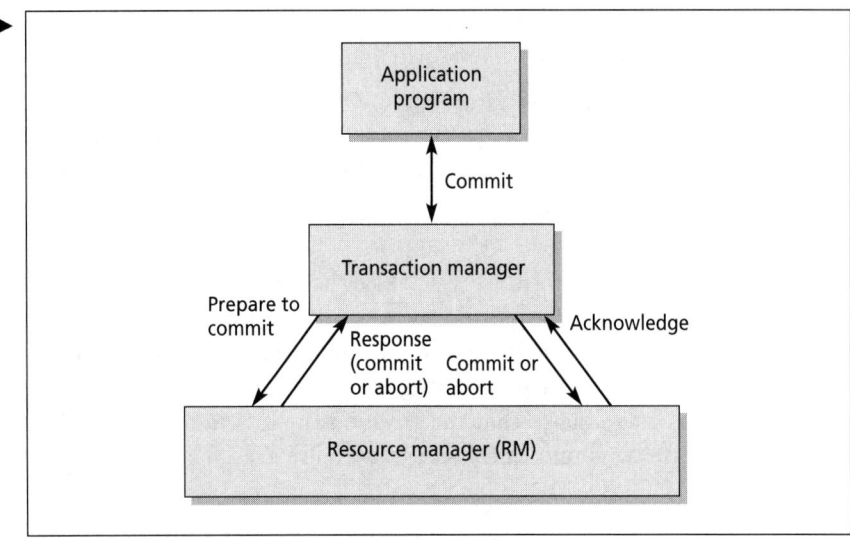

Figure 2.3   **Two-phase commit**

▶ TRANSACTION DEMARCATION

X/Open defines the TX API for controlling transactions in applications. The TX API can be used to open and close resource managers, begin and end transactions, and obtain information about the status of transactions. For example, the Encina TX API has the following functions:

- `tx_begin`: Starts a transaction and associates it with the current thread.
- `tx_commit`: Tries to commit the transaction associated with the current thread. Only the thread that called `tx_begin` for this transaction may perform this operation.
- `tx_rollback`: Aborts the transaction associated with the calling thread.
- `tx_open`: Initializes the XA interface.
- `tx_close`: Closes any RMs that have been opened by this application.
- `tx_info`: Obtains information about the current transaction.
- `tx_set_commit_return`: Sets the point at which a call to the `tx_commit` function returns in a two-phase commit protocol: this may be either when the commit is completed or when the commit is logged by the TM.

`tx_set_transaction_timeout`: Configures the maximum amount of time a transaction is allocated to complete before it is rolled back by the TM.

Using TX, applications bracket the operations that must occur in a transaction between calls to `tx_begin` and `tx_commit`. Calling `tx_commit` tells the TM to drive the two-phase commit protocol.

TP monitors typically define a higher-level API for applications to utilize. Encina has Tran-C and Tran-C++ and, in object-oriented applications, the OMG's CORBA Transaction Service defines an IDL interface for transaction control. The most commonly used interface is depicted in Figure 2.4. As can be seen, it has a strong functional resemblance to the TX API. Later chapters include many code examples of using transaction demarcation syntax.

```
interface Current {
    void begin ()
        raises (SubtransactionsUnavailable);
    void commit (in boolean report_heuristics)
        raises (
            NoTransaction,
            HeuristicMixed,
            HeuristicHazard
            );
    void rollback()
        raises (NoTransaction);
    void rollback_only()
        raises (NoTransaction);

    Status get_status();
    string get_transaction_name();
    void set_timeout (in unsigned long seconds);

    Control get_control();
    Control suspend();
    void resume (in Control which)
        raises (InvalidControl);
};
```

CORBA IDL for the transaction service   **Figure 2.4**

It's worth noting that some TP monitors have alternative, non-programmatic ways for applications to bracket transactional operations. Microsoft's MTS and Java's Enterprise Java Beans allow programmers to define transactional attributes for application objects. These attributes define whether an object, for example must be called in the scope of a transaction; will join any transaction within whose scope its operations are called; or cannot participate in a transaction.

▶ RESOURCE MANAGER ACCESS USING XA

TMs use the XA protocol to communicate transaction context to RM. Each time the TM performs a start, end or commit operation, it informs RMs of its actions. In order for TMs to use an RM's XA protocol, the RM must provide its RM-specific library for the TM to call. This is known as the XA Switch, and its structure is depicted in Figure 2.5.

```
struct xid_t {
long formatedID;
long gtrid_length;
long bqual_length;
char data [128];
};

type struct xid_t XID;

struct xa_swith_t {
char name[32];
long flags;
long version;
int (*xa_open_entry) (char*, int, long);
int (*xa_close_entry) (char*, int, long);
int (*xa_start_entry) (XID*, int, long);
int (*xa_end_entry) (XID*, int, long);
int (*xa_rollback_entry) (XID*, int, long);
int (*xa_prepare_entry) (XID*, int, long);
int (*xa_commit_entry) (XID*, int, long);
int (*xa_recover_entry) (XID*, long, int, long);
int (*xa_forget_entry) (XID*, int, long);
int (*xa_complete_entry) (int*, int*, int, long);
};
```

Figure 2.5   **XA switch definition**

The application programmer must tell the TM which XA-compliant RMs it can use. It does this by registering each RM with the TM, and passing the TM a structure called an open string and a pointer to the RM's XA library routines. The open string is used to establish a connection to the RM, a function performed by calling the RM's `xa_open` library routine. A close string can also be specified to use when the RM connection is closed using `xa_close`. The basic interactions between the TM and RM for each transaction comprise the following (*see also* Figure 2.6):

`xa_start`	Tell the RM that it is being accessed in the scope of a new transaction
`xa_end`	Tell the RM the transaction has completed
`xa_prepare`	Ask the RM to vote on whether it wishes to commit or abort the transaction
`xa_commit`	Tell the RM to commit the changes made by the transaction
`xa_rollback`	Tell the RM to undo changes made by the transaction
`xa_recover`	Gets the set of *tids* which a RM is waiting to know the outcome of. This is called by a TM after it has failed and is subsequently restarted

It's important to note that these calls are rarely made by the application programmer. All that is necessary is that the application that accesses the RM registers the resource correctly. The TM will then make the XA calls at the appropriate times, and drive the RM through the two-phase commit protocol using its XA calls.

Most widely used databases support XA, along with message queuing systems like IBM's MQ Series. It is important to check if the RM's XA library is thread-safe. If the library is thread-safe, it means that multiple threads in a process can be associated with the RM at any given time. This means the application can have many threads with RM connections open and can be performing work within calls to `xa_start` and `xa_end`. If the XA library is not thread-safe, this requires an application to only have one thread (and hence one transaction) associated with the RM at any given time. Essentially the TM will acquire an XA lock whenever `xa_start` is called by a thread, and will release this only when `xa_end` is called.

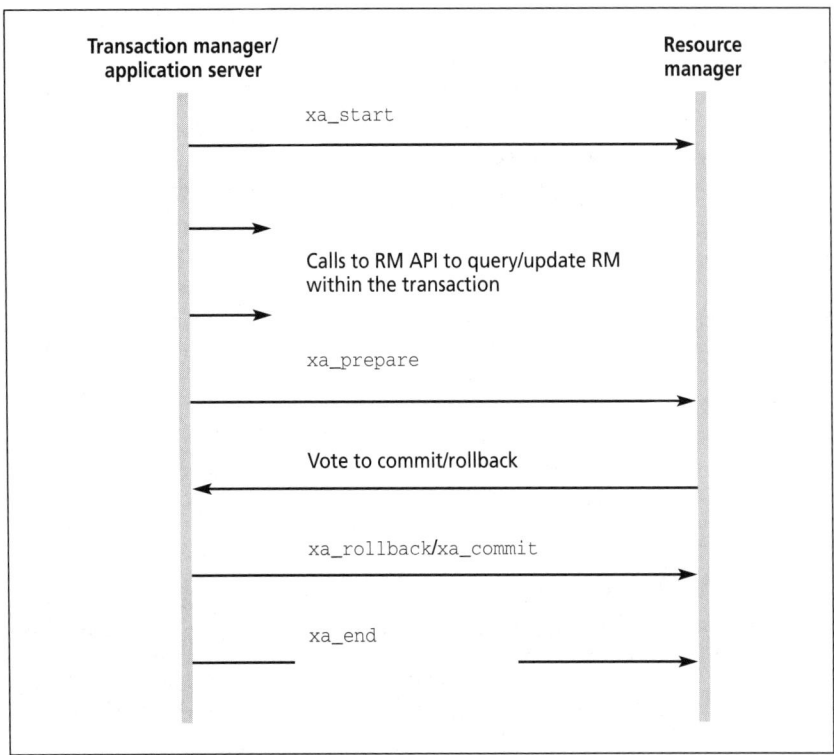

Figure 2.6 Typical interaction between a transaction manager and resource manager using XA

Using a non-thread-safe XA library with multiple concurrent threads will lead to deadlocks. This is obviously not a good thing. It is caused by lock contention between multiple threads, as shown in Figure 2.7. Two threads can begin simultaneous transactions, and access entries in the RM. To update these, they must acquire RM locks. Their RM accesses are serialized, as each thread has to acquire the XA lock before querying or updating the RM. In Figure 2.7, thread 0 acquires some locks to data in the RM, performs some updates, and then releases the XA lock. Thread 1 immediately acquires the XA lock, and attempts to acquire locks to the same data in the RM that thread 0 still holds locks on. This causes thread 1 to block. Thread 0 then attempts to acquire the XA lock, but as this is held by thread 1, it too blocks and a deadlock occurs. Other threads are also blocked when attempting to acquire the XA lock. This situation will persist until the RM times out on the lock and selects a transaction to abort and free the deadlock.

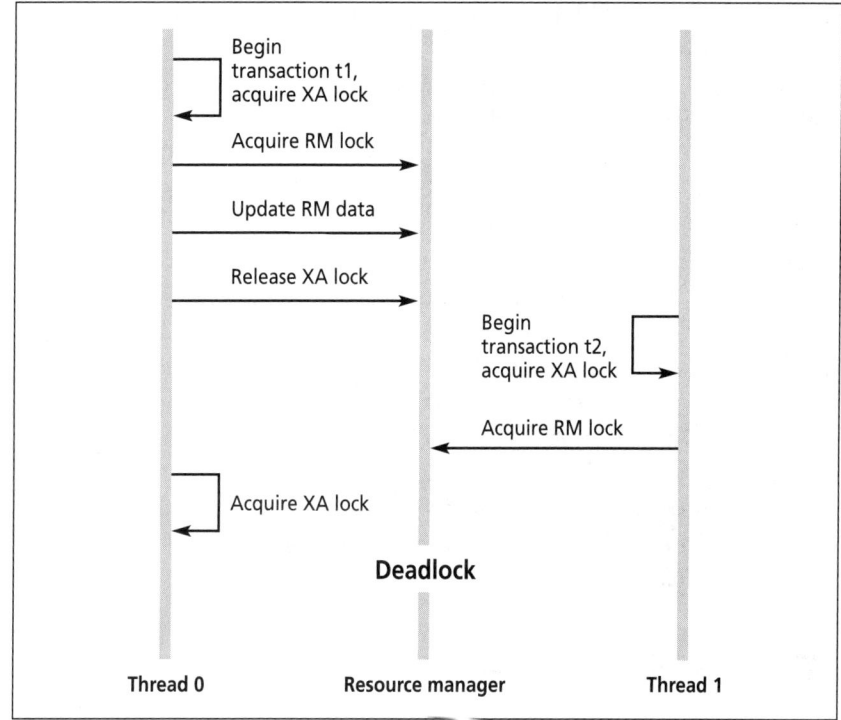

Deadlocks using non-threaded-safe XA libraries   **Figure 2.7**

The application programmer has no choice in this case but to implement single-threaded processes that access the RM. In general, most RMs now provide thread-safe libraries. This allows processes to maintain multiple RM connections and achieve concurrency using lightweight threading mechanisms instead of heavyweight process replication. For this reason, multithreaded processes are generally more efficient.

▶ TRANSACTIONAL REMOTE PROCEDURE CALLS

Remote procedure calls (RPCs) are well understood and used widely for distributed systems programming. The basic idea is to allow one program to make calls to remote abstract interfaces defined by other programs in the system. The RPC service makes the communication of parameters and return values across the network transparent to the programmer.

When RPCs are used for remote communications in a TP system, they must be augmented to convey transaction-related information. A basic

RPC only identifies the host system and port from which the RPC was issued. In transactional systems, it is also necessary to identify which transaction the RPC is performing work on behalf of. This is achieved by adding the transaction id (*tid*) and accompanying transaction context information to the RPC as extra parameters. This is normally performed invisibly by the transactional RPC service and the interface definition language (IDL) processing tools.

In addition, transactional remote procedure calls provide stronger guarantees of success and failure than RPCs. Unlike basic RPCs, transactional RPCs provide *exactly-once* semantics. This means that if a transactional RPC returns successfully, the remote procedure is guaranteed to have been executed once and only once in the remote process. This supports transactional semantics, ensuring the work carried out on behalf of the transaction occurs once if the transaction commits and not at all if it aborts. A basic RPC does not provide this guarantee. In fact, an RPC that a client believes has failed (due perhaps to a lost return message) may actually have partially or fully completed.

▶ HEURISTIC OUTCOMES

Like any software component, the TM can fail at inconvenient times. One of the most inconvenient of these is during the two-phase commit protocol. When all the participating RMs in a transaction have completed the prepare phase of a transaction, they are obliged to await the TM's decision on whether to commit or abort. The RMs must hold any locks and resources so they can perform the necessary actions dictated by the result of the commitment protocol and maintain the ACID properties.

If the TM fails after preparing one or more RMs, or the network connection fails, the participating RMs have two options:

1. Wait for the TM to restart and re-establish contact to complete the transaction.

2. Make a local, heuristic decision about the outcome of the transaction.

This problem is illustrated in Figure 2.8.

The first option can lead to unacceptable delays at the client, and impact on other transactions due to the locks being held for long periods. In most cases, a heuristic decision after a time-out period is therefore preferable, although it can cause problems of its own, as we will see.

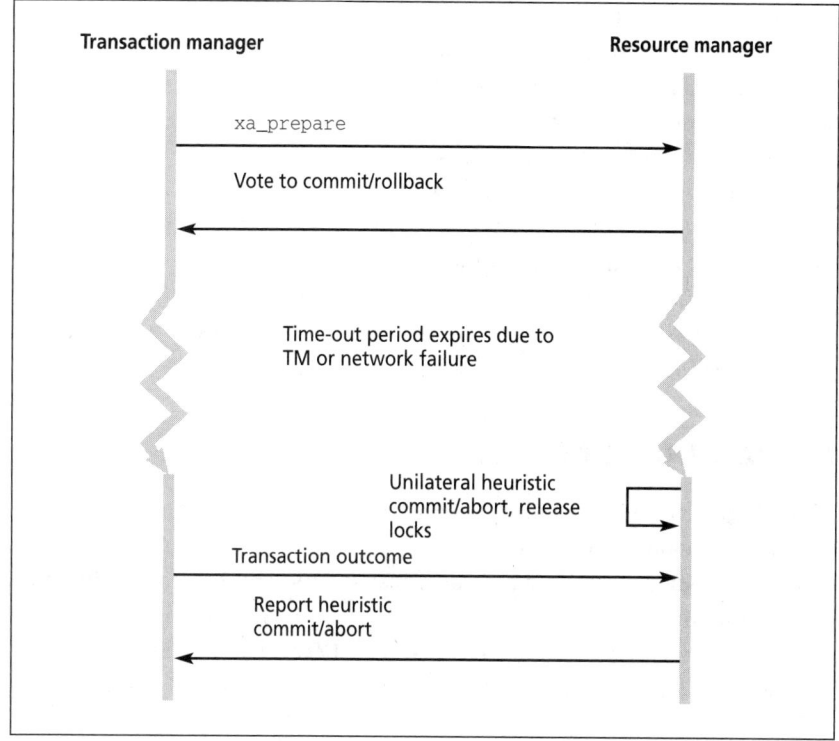

Heuristic transaction outcomes **Figure 2.8**

In general, heuristic outcomes result in the RM either performing a local commit or abort for in-doubt transactions.[2] The RM records this outcome in its log as heuristically completed. Some time later, the failed TM will contact the RM to tell it to commit or abort the transaction based on the result of the two-phase commit. It's at this stage things get interesting!

Obviously, if the heuristic outcome agrees with the result of the distributed transaction outcome, then there are no problems to resolve and everything proceeds as normal. However, if the RM's heuristic decision disagrees with the TM's, the RM will inform the TM that there is a mismatch between the two outcomes. This of course means that the ACID properties of the particular transaction may have been violated. All that can be done at this stage is to report the problem to the system administrator, and leave it to human intervention to clear up.

[2] The CORBA OTS specification also allows for *mixed* outcomes, in which some resources are updated and others are rolled back.

Heuristic outcomes also occur when a transaction is forced to complete by the system administrator. This occurs when errors are encountered in the application or the TP monitor itself (yes, like all software, TP monitors have errors!). The TP monitor will provide management tools that enable system administrators to watch the progress of transactions, and note when particular transactions remain in doubt for long periods. The management tools will allow the administrator to force a transaction to commit or abort, thus freeing up any locks. Still, the administrator's decision may in fact conflict with the TM's eventual decision and, if this happens, again a diagnostic must be raised and the problems resolved manually.

▶ NESTED TRANSACTIONS

Nested transactions, or subtransactions, provide a programming model for hierarchically decomposing the work carried out by a single transaction. An existing parent or *top level* transaction can create one or more subtransactions to carry out work on its behalf. In turn, subtransactions may create their own subtransactions, with nesting allowed to any depth. The set of nested transactions created from the parent transaction are known as a transaction family.

Subtransactions adhere to the ACID properties. This means that in the process of executing a subtransaction, any resources it updates are hidden from its parent and other subtransactions. If a subtransaction commits, the resources it has updated are made available to other subtransactions. The updates are not however made permanent at this stage. If a subtransaction aborts, all its updates, and all the updates performed by any of its subtransactions, are rolled back. The subtransaction abort does not force its parent transaction to abort. The parent is simply notified of the outcome of the subtransaction and behaves accordingly.

Importantly, nested transactions commit with respect to their parent. If the parent and its subtransactions all commit, then the updates of the subtransaction and the parent are committed. If the parent aborts, the subtransaction's updates are rolled back, even if it committed independently. An example of this is shown in Figure 2.9 using Encina's Transactional-C constructs for transaction bracketing.

The top level parent transaction begins at the `transaction` statement. After doing some (unspecified) work in the transaction, the parent

```
transaction {
    cout << "Parent transaction begins" << endl;
    // do some work...
    transaction {
        cout << "Child transaction begins" << endl;
        // do some work...
    } onCommit {
        cout << "Child transaction comitted" << endl;
    } onAbort {
        cout << "Child transaction aborted" << endl;
    } // end child transaction
    // optionally do some more work in parent transaction
} onCommit
    cout << "Parent transaction committed" << endl;
} onAbort {
    cout << "Parent transaction aborted" << endl;
} // end parent transaction
```

Nested transactions in Encina's Transactional-C   **Figure 2.9**

creates a subtransaction automatically at the nested `transaction` statement. The code within the nested transaction executes sequentially and eventually commits or aborts. After this, the top level transaction resumes, and it then either attempts to commit or abort.

Let's assume the nested transaction commits, and the parent transaction also commits. The output produced by the code would be:

```
Parent transaction begins
Child transaction begins
Child transaction committed
Parent transaction committed
```

Now let's assume the nested transaction aborts, but the top level transaction commits. The output produced by the code would be:

```
Parent transaction begins
Child transaction begins
Child transaction aborted
Parent transaction committed
```

This therefore illustrates that even if the child transaction aborts, the parent can commit its work independently. Finally, if the nested transaction commits but the top level transaction decides to abort, then the following output is produced:

```
Parent transaction begins
Child transaction begins
Child transaction committed
Parent transaction aborted
```

Note the output here is somewhat misleading. The `onCommit` clause of the subtransaction is executed when the subtransaction decides to commit. However, the subtransaction cannot decide to independently make its updates permanent, as it must await the outcome of its parent transaction. In this case, the subtransaction will actually be aborted because the parent aborts. Consequently, any behavior performed when a subtransaction commits should be viewed as an indication of the eventual outcome of that transaction family, and certainly not as concrete evidence that the subtransaction has committed.

Nested transactions are useful in scenarios where a transaction needs to perform an operation that may fail, but which should not cause the overall transaction to fail. For example, a transaction, in the course of updating resources, may wish to also update a shared transactional (local or remote) cache to reflect the changes it has made. Although an immediate update of the cache is preferable, delays may occur because another transaction may hold locks on the cache or, if the cache is remote, the remote object invocation may fail.

This makes the cache update operation a candidate for encapsulating in a subtransaction. If the cache update succeeds immediately, then all is fine and the subtransaction commits. If it fails, the parent transaction can perhaps log the necessary cache updates in a file or queue, and defer the operation to a background thread whose job it is to update the cache in such situations. The parent transaction can then decide to commit or abort. If it aborts, it also rolls back any changes the subtransaction made to the cache.

One restriction of subtransactions is that the X/Open DTP model does not include the concept of the subtransactions. This essentially means that XA resource managers do not support nested transactions and therefore don't allow nested transactions semantics to be directly implemented. For this reason, using nested transactions with XA resources is difficult. The Encina and OrbixOTS transaction services do allow the programmer to decide how to map subtransactions to XA transactions. However, the mapping approach taken has subtle implications on the ACID properties of the transaction family. Interested readers should consult the product documentation for details. In practice, most people will avoid this feature!

▶ TRANSACTIONAL QUEUING TECHNOLOGY

Sometimes a transaction needs to perform some updates that may take a long time. A *long* time is a very application-dependent attribute, but might include functionality such as:

- accessing resources across a slow and/or unreliable network; or
- performing off-line processing, such as printing an invoice for an order that has been placed by a customer.

In these situations, waiting for all aspects of the transaction to complete will most likely give unacceptable performance for system users. At the same time, performing slow operations outside the scope of the transaction is not an option, as the ACID properties may be violated.

Queuing technology is designed for circumstances such as these. A transaction is able to transactionally write messages to a message queue, and these messages are committed to the queue when the transaction commits. At this stage, the transaction has logically completed its work, as it can be assured that the message it placed on the queue will not be lost. Another application process will be responsible at some later time for transactionally retrieving messages from the queue and processing them. This actually completes the work associated with the transaction.

Consequently, queues allow transactions to safely delegate the completion of portions of the transaction's work that are not time-critical to later processing by another part of the application. This is ensured because writes and reads of messages to and from queues are performed within transactions. Once a message is committed to a queue, it is reliably stored until it is removed by a new transaction.

Figure 2.10 illustrates a simple use of a queue in a transaction. The first transaction updates the database and places a message on the queue. When the transaction commits, the database updates become permanent and the message is guaranteed to be placed persistently on the queue. Should the transaction abort, the TM would ensure the updates are rolled back at both the DBMS and the queue.

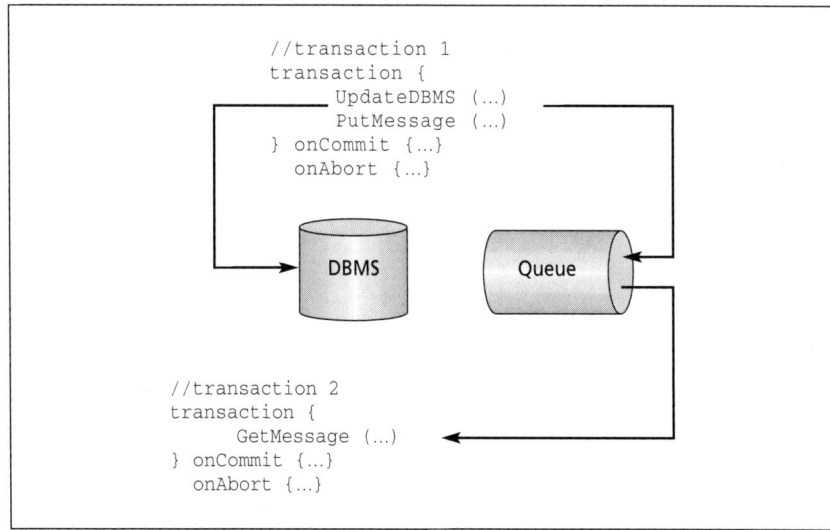

Figure 2.10 Using transactional queuing systems

The second transaction removes messages from the queue and processes them. Typically, this transaction will be performed in a loop, repeatedly removing messages and processing them accordingly. If there are no messages on the queue, the usual semantics are to block the process until it times out or a message arrives. Again, should this transaction commit, the message is removed from the queue. If it aborts, the message remains on the queue for later processing.

The method used for the TM to coordinate transactions with the queue is queuing-system dependent. For example, IBM's MQ Series has an XA interface, just like any resource manager. Others are more tightly coupled with particular transaction processing monitors, and have proprietary commit protocols.

Queuing technologies have many advanced features that can be used by applications. Typical features are:

- priority queuing mechanisms;
- logical queue clusters to promote load balancing across clients;
- non-FIFO access; and
- message browsing facilities.

Interested readers should consult individual product documentation to delve more deeply into these topics.

▶ LOCKING

Isolation is one of the key properties of transactions; it is in fact the I in ACID. If concurrent transactions are isolated, this means they behave as if they were executed serially, one after the other. The most common way to achieve isolation of concurrent transactions is by locking. When a transaction accesses some data items that could be potentially accessed simultaneously by other transactions, it acquires locks on the data. This prohibits other transactions from accessing this data until the transaction that owns the locks terminates.

There are two types of locks. A transaction acquires a *read* lock before it reads a data item, and a *write* lock before it updates a data item. A transaction may acquire a lock on a data item according to the following rules:

- A transaction can obtain a read or write lock on a data item if no other transaction has any locks on the data.
- A transaction can obtain a read lock on a data item if no other transaction has a write lock on the data.
- A transaction can obtain a write lock on a data item if no other transaction has either a read lock or a write lock on the data.

Hence read locks are said to *conflict* with write locks, and write locks conflict with other write locks.

In order to ensure isolation of transactions, and thus serializability, transactions must obey a two-phase locking rule. This states simply that transactions must acquire all their locks (the first phase) before they release any locks (the second phase). This means that as a transaction executes, it acquires locks as it touches (reads/writes) data items, and then once it releases any of these locks, it cannot acquire any more.

In a transaction processing system which interacts with resources managers (databases, file systems, queues) it is the responsibility of resource manager to handle locking on the data items it controls. The programmer simply brackets the operations that comprise a transaction, and the transaction manager and the resource manager coordinate to do the rest. When an operation in a transaction performs a read or write, the locks are acquired automatically on the transaction's behalf. The resource manager ensures all locks are held until the transaction manager commits or aborts the transaction.

This is one the most powerful features of TP monitors, as it hides the complexity of locking from the developer. However, there are some aspects of locking that are important for TP system designers to appreciate, as they affect a system's performance and behavior. These are lock granularity and deadlocks.

Lock granularity refers to the amount of data a resource manager locks when a transaction accesses a data item. Resource managers typically contain a lock manager component that maintains locks on data. When a transaction wishes to acquire a lock, it requests the lock manager to add the locks to the lock table it maintains. Lock granularity affects the performance of the lock manager. If *fine-grain* locking is used, the lock manager has to record locks for every data item individually. Potentially this could be a very large number of locks for each transaction, and this increases the overheads of acquiring and releasing locks. Fine-grain locking typically refers to record-level locking in a database.

Alternatively, *coarse-grain* locking means that when a transaction wishes to acquire locks, it locks the whole file, database table or database page in which the data items reside. In this case, the amount of work required by the lock manager is reduced. It maintains a single lock on whole regions, which effectively locks all the individual data items that exist in the region (page, table, file, etc.).

The problem with coarse-grain locking is that it inhibits concurrency in the application. A transaction may only access one row in a database table, but the lock it acquires stops other transactions from accessing some other rows in the table while it holds the lock. This will cause simultaneous transactions to wait until the lock is released, reducing transaction throughput and increasing response time. This is not desirable in high performance transaction processing systems, in which many concurrent transactions require rapid access to data items in the same table or database page.

It is therefore important to understand how a resource manager handles locks. Fine-grain locking is usually preferable. Still, transactions should be designed so that behavior which would cause thousands of locks in a single transaction is minimized, especially if performance is a key criterion.

Deadlocks occur in resource managers when concurrent transactions attempt to access the same locks, and each holds a lock that the other requires. An example of this is depicted in Figure 2.11.

In this example, the two transactions deadlock because they require access to data items that the other has already locked. The only possible outcome here is that the resource manager will detect the deadlock and

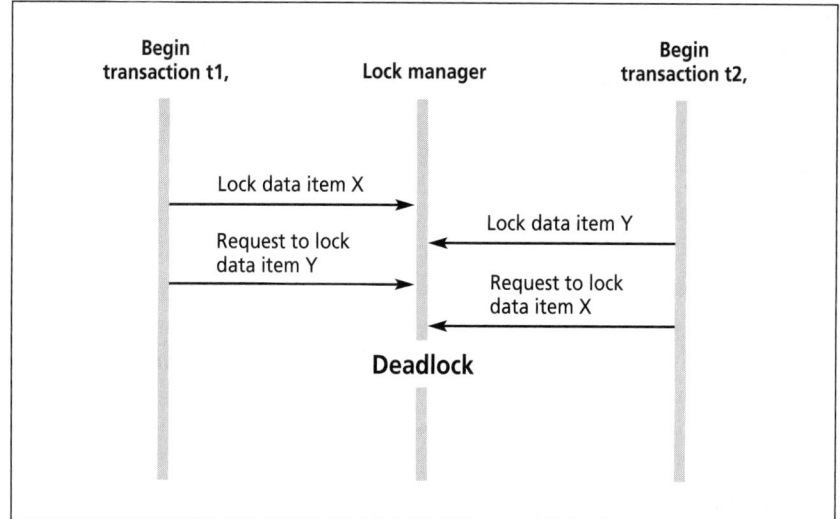

A deadlock with resource manager locking   **Figure 2.11**

choose one of the transactions to abort. This is typically known as the deadlock victim. The resource manager API will also report back to the application program that a deadlock occurred and this caused the transaction to fail.

The essential problem here is that the transactions have acquired locks to different types of data in different orders. If every transaction was mandated to acquire a lock to data item X before it could acquire a lock to data item Y, then transactions would only be delayed, not deadlocked. Typically then, applications must define a locking order for transactions. This should alleviate the deadlock problem.

▶ RECOVERY

Transaction managers and resource managers must be recoverable processes. Recoverable processes are able to restore their state on restart if they fail unexpectedly. In order to recover state, this means:

- the transaction manager must log transaction state to a persistent store known as the transaction log; and
- resource managers must also have a persistent transaction log, and record transaction state and the modifications that a transaction has performed to data in this log.

When a transaction manager crashes and restarts, it reads through its transaction log to recover the state of all in-flight transactions, that is, unresolved transactions at the time it failed. This is known as replaying the transaction log. It then resolves these transactions by continuing the two-phase commit protocol for each transaction.

When a resource manager fails, it too must replay its log to discover which transactions were not resolved at the time it failed. If an outcome for a transaction was reached and logged (i.e. commit or abort), the transaction can be completed and the acknowledgement sent to the transaction manager. If the transaction is logged as prepared, but no outcome was received from the transaction manager, the resource manager must re-establish a connection with the transaction manager. Typically it will re-send its vote in response to the prepare message. When the transaction manager receives this, it knows the resource manager hasn't received the commit or abort decision, and can simply re-send the transaction outcome. Finally, if no prepare decision has been logged, the transaction cannot have committed, as this participant hasn't voted. In this case, the resource manager can simply abort and inform the transaction manager of its decision.

The beauty of all this is that recovery is performed automatically by the components of the transaction processing system. The programmer is absolved of the responsibility of handling these complex situations. This is one of the most powerful aspects of transactions processing monitors.

▶ SYSTEM ADMINISTRATION AND MONITORING REQUIREMENTS

A TP monitor must provide a set of administration and management tools to allow the application to be monitored and controlled. The actual features provided by different products vary considerably, but the following are essential:

- Set application configuration parameters.
- Start and stop application servers.
- Monitor and automatically restart failed application servers.
- Report transaction exceptions, transaction rates and transaction progress.
- Administratively force the commit or abort of blocked transactions.
- Set and manage application server security, such as access control lists.

We'll look at some of the specific administration features of OrbixOTM and Encina in later chapters.

▶ SUMMARY

Transactions are one of the great successes of the software industry. They encapsulate much complex behavior in a simple programming model. Some of the complexity in managing transactions is explained in this chapter. The discussion has covered:

- the ACID properties that transactions must adhere to, and the way in which transactions are defined in programs;
- the two-phase commit, explaining how it works, and how X/Open standards such as XA allow for interoperability between transaction managers and resource managers;
- the basics of transactional queuing technologies such as MQ Series;
- the semantics of nested transactions;
- how transactions lock data in resource managers, and why deadlocks occur;
- how transaction managers utilize transaction logs to recover from failures; and
- an overview of the facilities that are needed for managing distributed transaction processing systems.

The aim of this chapter has been to provide coverage that is adequate for application developers to gain some understanding of what happens underneath the covers of a TP monitor. Armed with this knowledge, it should be possible to make more intelligent design decisions and have considerably more insight into the problems that will inevitably arise in building complex distributed transaction processing applications.

▶ FURTHER READING

Principles of Transaction Processing for the Systems Professional, P.A. Bernstein and E. Newcomer, Morgan Kaufmann, 1997.

Transaction Processing: Concepts and Techniques, J. Gray and A. Reuter, Morgan Kaufmann, 1993.

Chapter 3

Distributed transaction processing system architectures

Introduction	*44*
The need for software system architecture	*44*
A general transaction processing system architecture	*46*
Application server architectures	*49*
Summary	*65*
Further reading	*66*

▶ INTRODUCTION

Before we discuss any specific TP monitor technology, this chapter introduces some typical architectures for TP systems. These system architectures are essentially technology-independent. The architectures described have been deployed in many real systems, and hence they will give the reader an instant appreciation of solutions that work satisfactorily in production environments. For each approach, the advantages and disadvantages will be outlined, along with the design trade-offs that need to be considered.

▶ THE NEED FOR SOFTWARE SYSTEM ARCHITECTURE

It makes sense to first clarify what's meant by software system architecture in this chapter. Architecture means many things to many people so, for the purpose of clarity, the following definition from the Software Engineering Institute has been adopted:

The software architecture of a program or computing system is the structure or structures of the system, which comprise software components, *the externally visible properties of those components, and the relationships among them.*

In distributed transaction processing systems, the architecture mainly comprises:

- the client, application server and resource manager components that implement the application's behavior;
- the TP monitor components that the application relies upon to provide key functionality, including directory services, replication and fault tolerance; and
- the interactions between these components.

The architecture of the system is vital in software engineering. It gives the highest level view of a solution. This enables the following issues to be addressed, as depicted in Figure 3.1:

While a detailed coverage of most of the topics in this diagram is beyond the scope of this book, let's just touch briefly on each area.

Transactions: Where do transactions begin? Which components are aware of transactions? How do application servers interact transactionally with resource managers and other legacy components?

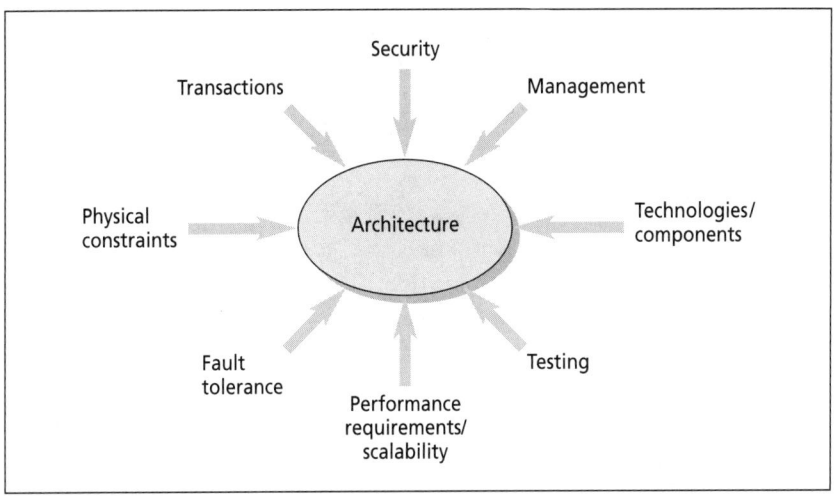

Figure 3.1 Architectural issues in distributed transaction processing systems

Security: How do users identify themselves to the application? How are application services and transactions authorized for various groups of users such as administrators and customers? Is any level of encryption required? What is the cost of providing these services?

Management: How will the components of the system be managed? Will components automatically restart when they fail, or is manual intervention required? What sorts of tools or scripting facilities are there for configuring and administering the system?

Technologies/components: What technologies are to be used to implement the various components? How do these technologies integrate?

Testing: What are the key system scenarios that should be used for testing the system? What test monitoring and debugging facilities are available or need to be built?

Performance/scalability: What are the performance requirements for the system? How will these change over time? Are there any bottlenecks in the architecture that could impede scalability?

Fault tolerance: What happens when components fail? What are the implications of component failure for users and administrators? Can the architecture support graceful degradation of performance while there are failures? What support does the middleware technology have for fault tolerance?

Physical constraints: Must certain components be physically located at certain places, such as remote sites? Does the system span a small geographical area or a wider area? What are the implications of this on network performance, time-outs, failures and so on?

As in any complex system, resolving some of the above issues requires design trade-offs. For example, increasing security levels may adversely impact on performance, or providing advanced fault tolerance capabilities may increase the testing burden. This is where the role of the architect becomes difficult. Architectural decisions are often made before any concrete artifacts of the system exist. This is because, by necessity, the architecture must start to evolve early in the system's life cycle. This is also a time when the system requirements are often not fixed, and sometimes changing daily. To quote Phillipe Krutcheon from Rational: "The life of a software architect is a long and rapid succession of design decisions taken partly in the dark".

The most common way of shedding light on the process of designing architectures is to build proof-of-concept and proof-of-technology prototypes. These enable the proposed system architecture to be validated and the various issues explored in some detail. In turn, the prototype can reduce the risk inherent in making these decisions.

Proof-of-technology prototypes validate that the chosen middleware and component technologies can actually do what they say they can do. TP monitors and distributed technologies in general are complex. It's important that the many issues of concern are explored in a controlled and concrete way. Again, the aim is to rapidly remove as much uncertainty as possible from the design process. A running prototype of the skeletal system can go a long way in this respect, as well as help to mitigate technology integration risks, jump-start the testing effort, and run-in development tools.

▶ A GENERAL TRANSACTION PROCESSING SYSTEM ARCHITECTURE

Figure 3.2 gives a simplified high-level view of a typical TP system architecture. This architecture is essentially product- and technology-neutral, and can be constructed using almost any transaction processing middleware product. It is designed to allow client access via standard WWW browsers and/or dedicated application clients written in a standard programming language.

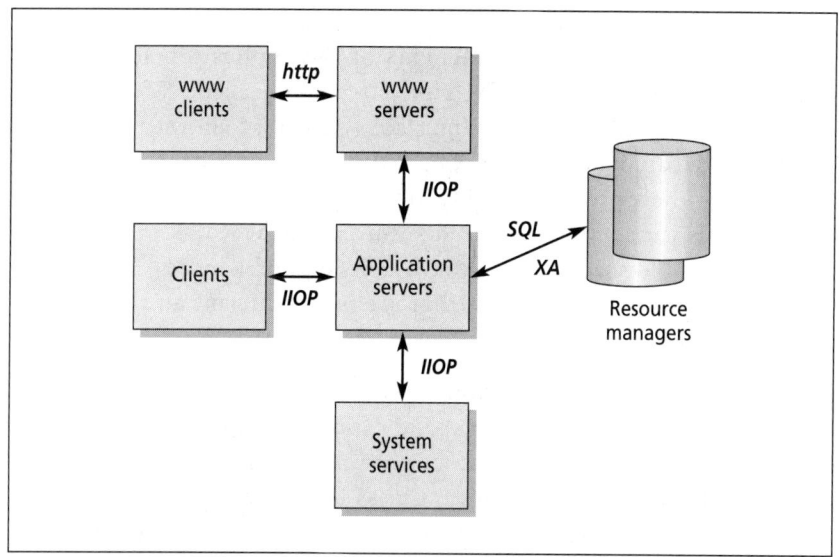

General distributed transaction processing system architecture Figure 3.2

The components of this architecture are:

WWW clients: WWW clients enable access via standard Internet protocols (i.e. HTTP) to the TP application. The WWW clients will typically have a form-based HTML interface. This will allow users to navigate through the application, enter data and submit queries. Results from queries are returned as formatted HTML pages. The major advantage of supporting WWW clients is that anyone with a WWW browser can gain access to the application. This is essential in WWW-based e-commerce environments.

Clients: Standard application clients are typically deployed in intranet-based application environments. The clients are written in a standard programming language such as C++, Java or Visual Basic. They communicate with the TP application using native middleware product protocols like CORBA's IIOP or DCE's RPC. Clients may begin transactions or make non-transactional requests to application servers who take on the responsibility for transaction bracketing.

WWW servers: WWW servers handle requests from WWW clients. They receive HTTP requests and execute scripts associated with the addresses in the HTTP request (in fact the URL). In this mode, the WWW server is a gateway into the TP application. The scripts executed in response to the HTTP requests become the clients of the application servers, and format the query results in HTML for return to the client. WWW servers support the Common Gateway Interface (CGI) that allows scripts written in standard languages (e.g. C/C++/Perl) to call other applications. Using CGI, a new process is created by the WWW server for each client request. This is an expensive mechanism. Hence WWW servers such as those from Netscape and Microsoft support more lightweight approaches (e.g. NSAPI, ISAPI) that are more efficient and scalable in high-performance TP systems.

Application servers: Application servers accept requests from clients (standard or WWW server scripts) and execute the application's business logic. The servers act as host processes for one or more server objects that implement the application's business logic. Application servers are usually replicated to spread client load across multiple concurrent processes running potentially on more than one server machine. This provides improved performance, scalability and fault tolerance, as the failure of one server process doesn't overly impact on the overall application performance.

Resource managers: These manage the application's persistent data. Relational database resource managers are normally accessed by application servers using embedded SQL, with transactions being coordinated using XA. One application may comprise one or more databases and/or queuing systems which all play the role of resource managers.

System services: Distributed systems require a set of supplementary services required for efficient system functionality. These include a directory or name service, security service and system management services. A name server allows objects in the system to be located by a logical name independently of their physical location. A security service allows user profiles and security information to be created and managed, and used for authorization and authentication purposes. Management services allow the application's components to be monitored and controlled, and to report exceptional conditions to system operators.

Of all these components, the application servers are usually the ones that require the most careful and thoughtful design. The following sections go on to look at some of the important issues involved in designing scalable, reliable transaction processing architectures.

▶ APPLICATION SERVER ARCHITECTURES

The need for load-balancing

An application will replicate the server objects in application server processes. This essentially provides multiple instances of the application services for client utilization. The replicated server processes have two main purposes:

1. They provide a measure of fault tolerance, since if one server process fails, clients can utilize objects hosted by replica servers. This is especially true if replicas run on physically different server machines in order to provide additional tolerance of hardware failure.

2. They provide scalability, as multiple clients can connect to replica server processes. Each replica has its own resource manager connection. This increases the processing capacity of the application.

The scalability issue is crucial. Replication increases the application's processing capacity, as long as this capacity is effectively utilized. This requires that client requests be spread as evenly as possible across replicas. The key to this is load-balancing. Application objects and servers that lie totally or partially idle are a waste of resources.

As a simple example, Figure 3.3 depicts three application server processes to which clients may connect.

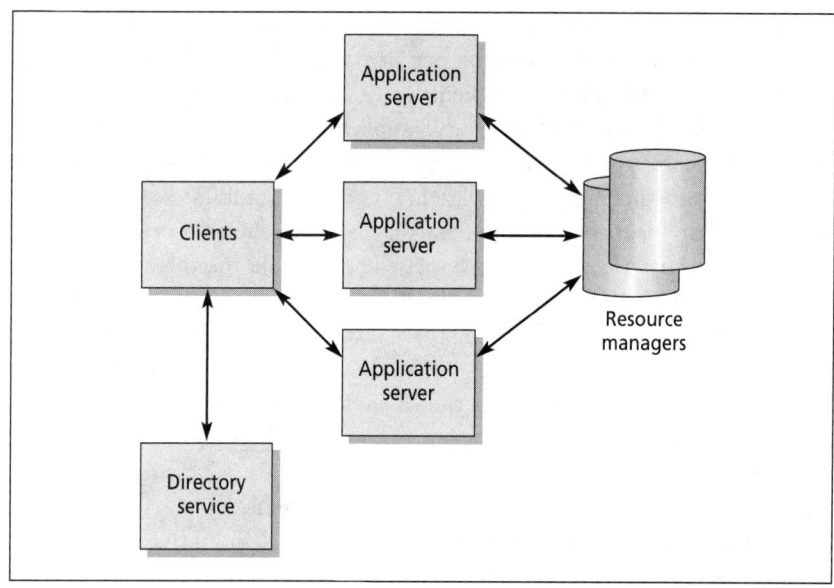

Three application servers with multiple clients   Figure 3.3

When a client starts up, it must find a server object to perform the transactions it requires. The most flexible mechanism to achieve this is by using a directory or name server. The general steps in the process are as follows:

1. When an application object comes to life, it contacts the directory service and stores its address at a well-known entry in the directory. This effectively advertises the existence of the object. The object's address can be viewed simply as a reference to the object in the distributed application. The address typically contains the host IP address on which the server object exists, the name of the server process that the object executes in, and a unique object identifier or marker. Different types of server objects store their references in different places on the directory.

2. When a client application starts, it contacts the directory server to obtain a reference for a server object of the desired type to communicate with. This requires the client to know the name of the entry in the directory where server objects advertise themselves. The directory server returns an object reference to the client, and the client uses this to contact the server object and perform transactions.

Once a client has a valid object reference, it is free to continue using this object for as long as it likes, with the option of performing multiple transactions.

The first issue in this scheme is the initial handing out of object references to clients by the directory service. It would generally be a bad idea to *hardwire* or pre-designate each client to use a particular server object. This would only work in a fixed and stable application configuration. Few transaction processing applications can guarantee which clients will be alive at any given time, and that they will generate a given amount of requests. So in most real applications, a more flexible, dynamic scheme is needed.

A simple but effective improvement is to enable the directory service to use some algorithm to hand out object references of the same type to clients. If all the object references for a given type of object are stored in the same entry in the directory, then they can be distributed in some known way. The location of all the objects in the directory is known as an object, or name group, as shown in Figure 3.4. A common approach is to return members of the group randomly to successive client requests. Alternatively, the directory server may implement a round robin approach, or even something more sophisticated including weightings for each reference.

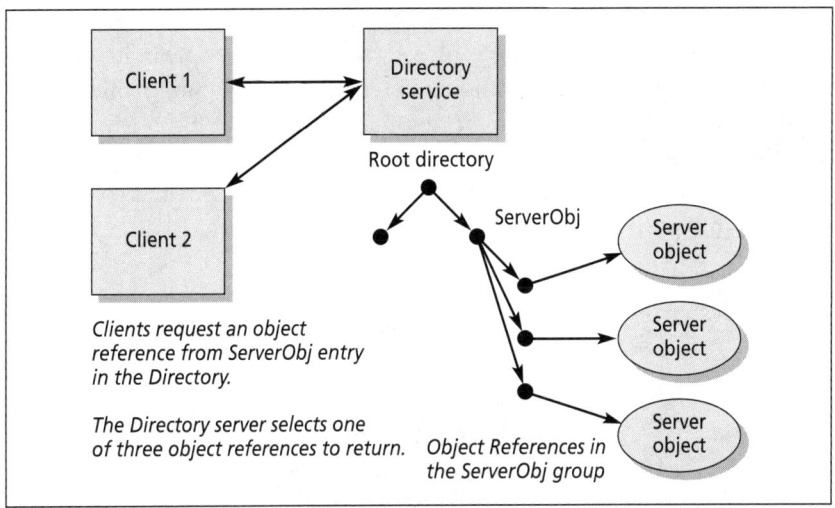

Grouping object references in a directory server **Figure 3.4**

Using this approach, a reasonable attempt at load-balancing is possible. Let's take a simple example. Five replicated server objects of the same type start and advertise themselves in the same object group. At 9 am, 500 employees come to work, start up their clients, and request a server object reference from the object group. The directory service hands out object references from the group in a round robin fashion. Exactly which client gets which object reference depends on the precise order the client requests reach the directory but, as shown in Figure 3.5a, the clients are guaranteed to be distributed evenly across server objects. Assuming each client exerts a similar amount of load on its server object, then we have achieved a good degree of load balancing at very low cost.

Sever object reference	Client numbers	Total clients per server object
1	1–100	100
2	101–200	100
3	201–300	100
4	301–400	100
5	401–500	100

Load-balancing with a round-robin initial allocation **Figure 3.5a**

At lunchtime however, 300 part-time employees close down their clients and go home. They are replaced by 300 new people, who start up clients that request a server object reference. Let's assume for illustrative purposes that the users for client numbers 201 to 500 log off and leave, and they are restarted by new users, who request new object references. Using the round robin allocation for the object group, the new load is depicted in Figure 3.5b.

Sever object reference	Client numbers	Total clients per server object
1	1–100, 201, 206, 211, ..., 496	160
2	101–200, 202, 207, 212, ..., 497	160
3	203, 208, 213, .., 498	60
4	204, 209, 214, ..., 499	60
5	205, 210, 215, ..., 500	60

Figure 3.5b   **Cient allocation after restart**

This simple and somewhat contrived example shows the problem with round robin allocation. The round robin method has worked as expected, but as clients disappear and new ones start up, the load across servers inevitably becomes uneven. This is because there is no dynamic adjustment to rebalance the client load as the system's configuration evolves. Two server objects are loaded with 160 clients, and three only have 60 clients. This means clients of the heavily loaded objects will experience longer response times, and the three lightly loaded objects may be partially idle, wasting processing and database connection resources. So, a really effective load-balancing mechanism must build upon the basic facilities offered by the directory service. It must then adapt as the system configuration evolves. One simple approach would be as follows:

1. Clients start up and obtain initial object references from the object group, using a random, round robin or some other mechanism (as above).

2. At *some time* in the future, all clients discard their object reference, and ask the directory service for a new one.

Some time is something that is application-specific. It might be every ten minutes, every minute or every 20 transactions. The important thing is to ensure that clients regularly obtain a different object reference. At the same time, the cost of many clients accessing the directory service more regularly must be considered. This is unlikely to be extremely expensive (e.g. the order of a few milliseconds) but may become significant as it will place load on the directory service and the network. As usual, this is a design trade-off.

To illustrate the effectiveness of this approach, let's look at the results of a simple experiment in Figure 3.6. The application was an implementation of a relatively complex transaction processing example.

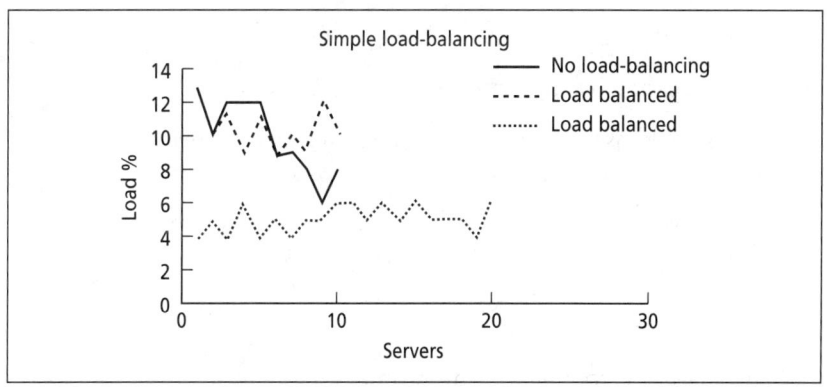

A load-balancing experiment **Figure 3.6**

An initial test with ten server objects selected on start-up by 200 clients from a random object group gave a maximum application load on a server object of 13%, and a minimum of 6%. Each server object executed in its own process. In this case, the load was calculated by recording how many transactions each server object executed from the total transactions executed in the test. Each client performed exactly the same set of several hundred transactions, and did not get a new object reference once it had initialized. Effectively, some server objects were performing twice as much work as others, and the client load was distributed unevenly. Not surprisingly, some fell idle towards the end of the test several minutes before the other, more heavily loaded servers.

The clients were then modified to get a new server object reference from the directory after every 20 transactions. Two more identical sets of 200 clients were then run and the percentage load on each server recorded. A test with ten server objects showed a maximum load of 12% and a minimum load of 9%. Crucially, the test completed in 10% less time than the identical test executed without client load balancing. This shows the server resources were being more effectively utilized. The same 200 client load was then run against 20 server objects, and the load on each was between 4 and 6%. Again the overall test execution time fell significantly.

The results from these experiments show that the additional cost of accesses to the directory service was amortized across the 20 transactions each client performed in between directory service access. In some applications, this may not be the case. Regular name server requests may be too expensive. A solution can be found along the lines of the following:

1. Clients start up and obtain all object references from the object group.

2. They store the object references in a local cache.

3. After each transaction or set of transactions, they select a new object reference from the local cache.

4. After a given period, the client refreshes the cache to obtain object references to any new server objects that have started up since the last cache refresh. The refresh period can be relatively long, for example 20 minutes or one hour.

This is a more complex solution, but is likely to provide even better load-balancing at lower cost. It requires less remote access to the name server, reducing latencies and network load. Of course, should a server object fail, the client must mark this as unusable in the cache, and the client must continue to operate if the directory service fails. Also the cache accesses should be thread-safe to support multi-threaded clients.

Load-balancing is a key feature of successful distributed transaction processing systems. Without effective load-balancing, system resources can be wasted, and the application throughput and response time can quickly fall to unacceptable levels.

Service partitioning

The load-balancing discussion in the previous section has one unstated assumption. Essentially it treats the load-balancing problem as one of distributing *all* transactions evenly across servers. For this to be completely effective, it assumes that each different type of transaction exerts a similar demand on system resources. This is often not the case. Let's see why and how this complicates the load-balancing in a system.

For example, a bank's call centre application may contain a simple query transaction that returns a simple value, such as account balance, from a database. Another transaction may retrieve a given customer's full details, including information from all of their account records and recent transaction history. Obviously, the resources used by these two transactions in terms of database query time, application server processing time and network bandwidth will vary considerably. The balance query may have an average server processing time of 10 milliseconds, while the full customer account query may have an average server processing time of 500 milliseconds.

Now, let's assume that an analysis of the application's transaction profile results in 50% of the transactions being account balances, and 20% being retrieving customer details. (The remaining 30% are other transactions that are not important in this example). In addition, the two transactions are supported by the same object type, which is replicated many times and in many processes to service the client demand. The object interface might look like this:

```
interface CallCentre {
   //....other transactions
   float GetBalance (in AccountKey key) ;
   void GetFullCustInfo ( in CustKey key, out CustInfo cust) ;
}
```

Now, assume two clients have an object reference to the same server object. Simultaneously, one client requests an account balance, and the other requests a customer's information. These requests are handled by the middleware and network, and arrive at the server process that the server object belongs to. Of course, the order they arrive in is non-deterministic. If the balance enquiry arrives first at the server object, the customer details query has a typical wait time of 10 milliseconds until it is processed. This adds little, around 2% in fact, to the latter's overall transaction processing time due to the delay in processing. However, if the server object sees the customer details query first, the account balance transaction must wait on average 500 milliseconds. This increases the transaction processing time for the query by 500 milliseconds, which is extremely significant indeed.

This simple example highlights a common design issue. Fast, lightweight transactions are often blocked for relatively long periods waiting for heavyweight transactions to complete. This can add unacceptable delays to the response time for a transaction, and severely decrease an application's throughput. The solution is to partition short and long duration transactions into different types of server objects. For example:

```
interface CallCentre {
   //….other transactions
   float GetBalance (in AccountKey key) ;
}
interface GetFullCustInfoTrans {
   //….other transactions
   void GetFullCustInfo ( in CustKey key, out CustInfo cust) ;
}
```

Server processes can now create the two different types of objects, and adjust the numbers of these accordingly to suit client demand. At the very least, this will mean that fast transactions will not be significantly held up waiting for long duration transactions to finish. And if a long duration transaction holds up another long duration transaction, then the delay is proportionally considerably less of an issue.

Service partitioning is an extremely application-dependent design activity. A typical methodology requires insight into the duration of individual transactions and the likely transaction mix. With this information, services can be allocated to different object types and these deployed in sufficient numbers to handle the simultaneous client demand. Like many design issues in distributed transaction processing, this is an experimental exercise requiring repeated adjustments and optimizations. The key is to keep the server object designs as flexible as possible so that early, and possible poor, design decisions are not difficult and expensive to fix.

Multi-process versus multi-threaded servers

The discussion so far has described how application server processes can be replicated to increase server availability and application scalability. Individual server objects execute in servers, and these objects implement the business transactions that clients call. Servers may create and host many server objects.

Threads are a mechanism provided by operating systems to implement lightweight multitasking within a process. An operating system process can be made up of many threads, each of which has its own stack and execution context. The operating system typically views threads as the unit of scheduling on a system.[1] This means threads can be allocated a time slice to execute in, and can block and/or be pre-empted by threads of higher priority. Threads and objects are orthogonal concepts. This means that:

- A thread of execution may call the methods of many different objects. Each object method executes in the context of the calling thread.
- One object may have active methods executing in the context of many different simultaneous threads.

With middleware technology that supports multi-threaded applications, the implications of this are as follows (*see* Figure 3.7):

- A server process has by default only one application thread. It creates many server objects that clients simultaneously make requests to. However, the client requests are effectively serialized, as only one request to one object executes at any given time. This means a single

[1] *Operating systems with kernal thread implementations schedule work on a thread-by-thread basis. Thread packages implementated in user space must implement their own thread scheduling within the encompassing process.*

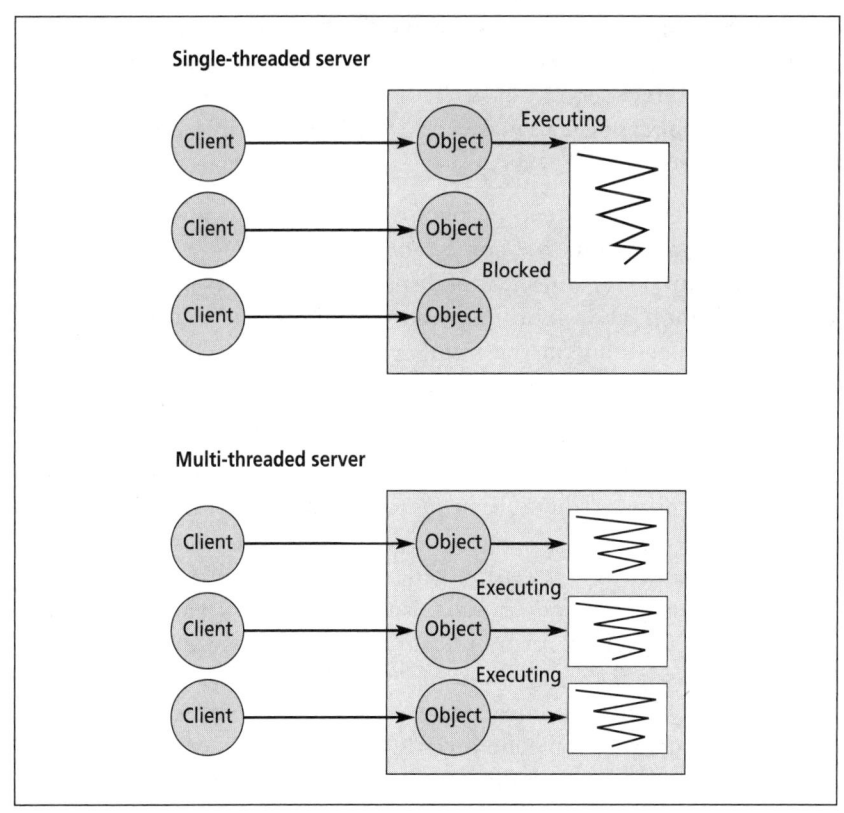

Single and multi-threaded servers   **Figure 3.7**

threaded server accepts one client request at a time and processes each request to completion before accepting the next. This is regardless of how many server objects and client connections the server process has.

◆ A server process creates many server objects that clients simultaneously make requests to. For each incoming request, the server creates a new application thread and dispatches this thread to execute the client's request. This means that the processing for clients' requests is effectively overlapped and, from the client's perspective, proceeds in parallel.

Three common approaches to implementing multi-threaded servers are as follows:

Thread-per-client: In this approach, a new server thread is created for each client process that connects to a server. This thread handles the incoming requests from one client process only. If multiple clients connect to the same server object, then each client has its own thread and effectively shares the server object's state.

Thread-per-object: A thread is created for each server object. When a request arrives for a server object, it is dispatched to the thread that executes for the target server object. This means if multiple clients connect to the same object, their requests are effectively multiplexed through the same thread.

Thread pool: A server creates a pool of threads at start-up. Each thread is initialized and waits for some work to do. When a client request arrives for any server object, it is dispatched to any available thread in the thread pool. The thread pool is typically fixed in size, and hence places an upper limit on the number of application threads a server process may have concurrently executing.

Thread pools are commonly used in transaction processing systems. They only have thread creation overheads when the process begins, and tend to give more predictable behavior in terms of response time and throughput.

Multi-threaded servers are in general preferable as they exploit the operating system's threading mechanism to increase application throughput. This is especially pronounced when an operating system can schedule individual threads to different physical processors in a multi-processor machine. This achieves true concurrency in the server.

Another important but often overlooked advantage of multi-threaded servers is a lower administration cost. If a fixed size thread pool is used, each thread can have its own resource manager connection. A resource manager may for example allow fifty simultaneous connections. For single threaded servers, this would require fifty replicated server processes to be individually created, started, monitored and managed. If multi-threaded servers are used with a thread pool of size ten, then only five server processes need to be of concern to the system administrator. However, for multi-threaded servers accessing resource managers using XA, this will only work if the resource manager's XA library is thread-safe.

The downside of all this (there always is one) is that multi-threaded servers are more complex to write and debug. Objects that can be correctly executed in a multi-threaded server must be thread-safe. This means that all accesses to the object's shared state must be serialized. So, if an object has a *count* data member that it uses to record the number of requests it receives, it must ensure all modifications to this data member are serialized. This is normally achieved by using a lock (often known as a *mutex* lock) to ensure exclusive access to the shared data. For objects with many data members, this can result in complex and error-prone code.

Stateless versus stateful servers

Many existing transaction processing monitors do not allow middle tier application servers to maintain any state after a transaction completes. Any persistent application state is maintained only in resource managers. In this case, each transaction is responsible for initializing any state data it requires from the resource manager, and returning the desired results to the client. When the transaction completes, the TP monitor flushes the state. Such application servers are known as stateless.

The advantages of stateless servers are that:

- any client can always use any application server, which enhances availability and scalability; and
- application servers do not have to log or remember any state. If they fail in the middle of a transaction, they simply restart and wait for a new transaction to arrive. The transaction manager and the resource managers will ensure that the failed transaction is aborted.

So, stateless servers are simple as they do not have to worry about state recovery code, and are easily scalable. This is proven by practice. Many of the successful distributed transaction processing systems in existence today employ stateless servers. Still, a software component that is stateless is unusual in the object-oriented world. One of the raisons d'etre of objects is that they encapsulate and maintain their own state.

Not surprisingly then, as object technology is increasingly used for transaction processing, opportunities for servers that maintain state, known as *stateful* servers, are being explored thoroughly.

In a stateful server, clients connect to an application server and are allocated their own exclusive server object. A *factory* object performs the object allocation for the client. The factory object is responsible for creating objects on the server at the request of clients, and deleting server objects when a client tells the factory it has completed its work. Once the factory has passed the client an object reference for the server object, the client can utilize this object to perform one or more transactions. When the client is finished, it informs the factory, and this terminates the server object. Figure 3.8 illustrates this scheme.

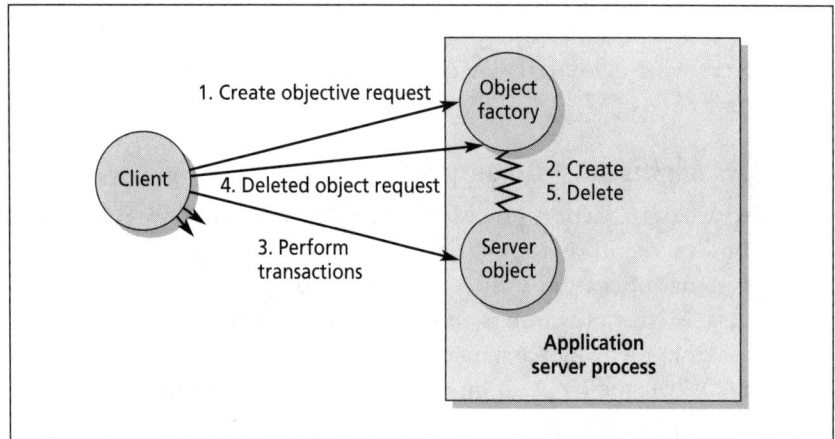

Figure 3.8 Stateful server objects

Stateful servers have several potential advantages:

- The client needs only to establish a connection to a server object once. It then uses that object for the duration of the work it wishes to perform.
- The server object can maintain state information on the identity of the client. For example, it may validate the client's security credentials, and keep the client's permissions available. In a sense, the server objects can exploit the fact that they *know* who their client is.

- The server object can cache client-related information. For example, when a customer's information is retrieved from a database in an initial query transaction, the server may read additional data from the database so that future requests for additional customer-related details can be satisfied from objects in memory. This is known as read-ahead caching, and can considerably improve transaction response times in certain types of applications. Typically these include applications with well-understood and consistent navigation paths.

These advantages are attractive, and are leading to this approach being adopted in modern object-oriented transaction processing systems. As always, however, some additional concerns need to be addressed before these advantages can be fully realized.

First, stateful server objects must be able to deal with unexpected failures. There are two main scenarios here, client failure and server failure. Assume a client is in the midst of carrying out a series of transactions with a server object. For some reason (machine/program crash, user becomes ill, turns off machine and goes home etc.) the client fails. Importantly, the client does not get the chance to inform the server that it is terminating. In this situation, the server object does not know that its client has gone. If the client does not re-establish contact, this object will live forever, taking up system resources, unless the system takes some remedial action.

One solution often adopted is for servers to *ping* their clients at a given interval if inactivity is detected. This obviously incurs overheads and complications such as the client must be able to receive requests from other objects.[2] Alternatively, the server could require the client to send a heartbeat message at certain intervals. If a sequence of heartbeats is not received when expected, the server assumes the client has gone away. In either case, the server object needs to be garbage collected. In long running servers in systems which require 24×7 performance, this is a critical issue that needs an appropriate and efficient solution.

Second, if the server object should fail unexpectedly, the client's object reference will be invalidated. The client must therefore adopt a strategy to create a new server object and continue with its series of transactions. In this case, applications need to be designed carefully to ensure that the state lost when the server object failed does not adversely affect the user's intentions.

Third, stateful objects severely complicate load balancing. Each server process will have its own factory object to which clients connect and

[2] *In practical terms this usually means the client has to be linked with server libraries.*

request a server object. It's easy to use standard load-balancing strategies to spread client requests evenly across the replicated factory objects. Assuming each factory creates server objects locally (i.e. in the process it is running), this will lead to an initially well balanced system. The problem, though, is that clients will typically use server objects for different periods of time. As clients appear, creating new objects, and disappear, destroying their server objects, the overall system load is most unlikely to remain evenly spread across server processes. All we can guarantee is that each server process will be asked to create an even number of objects. There's no guarantee that, for example, the clients connected to one process will be short-lived and inactive, while the clients connected to another process will be long-lived and active. In reasonably static applications in which clients do not dynamically appear and disappear with a high frequency, this may not be a problem. In systems without these attributes, load is unlikely to be shared effectively.

A possible solution to this is to allow factory objects to collaborate and create server objects remotely. Factories know how many server objects are active locally. When a request to create a new server object arrives, a factory in a heavily loaded process could delegate the request to a factory in a more lightly loaded process. The remote factory would create the server object and arrange for its object reference to be returned to the client. Factories would need to periodically broadcast their load information to other factories so that sensible and timely decisions could be made. This introduces more complexity and overheads into the factory's behavior, but the potential gains may be worth the effort.

Caching

Another aspect of stateful servers is caching. Let's explore this with an example. A warehouse system can issue orders for 10 000 stock items. As order transaction rates are high, the architects decide that it might be possible to cache stock item information in each server process. This would then mean each order transaction could get the stock information it requires from memory, thus eliminating the time involved in going to the database. As the 10 000 stock item records are not large, it's feasible to keep them in memory. The basic solution is illustrated in Figure 3.9.

Now, transactions that just need to read stock item data can do this using the cache. This is fast and efficient. Transactions that need to alter stock item data are somewhat more complex. Essentially this requires a three-step process:

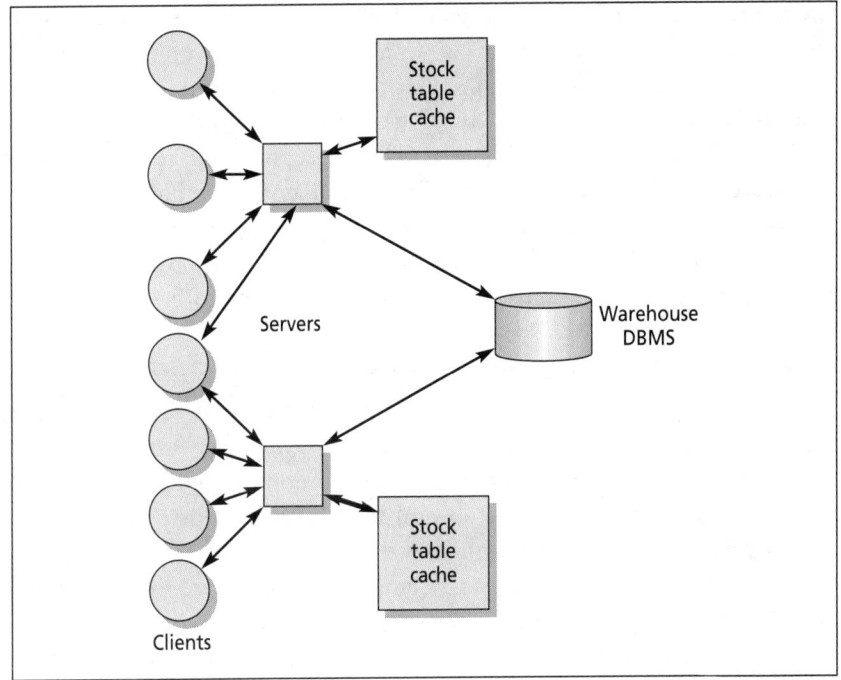

A data caching example   **Figure 3.9**

1. Update the stock item data in the database, commit the update and return the results to the client.
2. Update the stock item data in the local cache.
3. Tell all other server processes to update their cache to obtain the updated stock item data.

Steps 1 and 2 are no problem. Step 3 is not simple, however. First, the server needs to know the identities of all other server processes that maintain the cache. This must be performed dynamically to handle server processes failing and new ones starting. Second, it must communicate the update to all these processes. If there are many updates, this will create overheads in terms of application performance. In some cases, this may introduce unacceptable performance penalties.

The two actions in step 3 are not enormously difficult to implement, although some thought is required to reliably and efficiently ensure that all messages are always communicated to all other processes. The problem is that there is a delay during which server processes have a stale data for the updated stock item in their local cache. This means that while steps 2 and 3 are being carried out, other transactions in other processes may be reading out-of-date data from their cache for the updated stock item. In some applications, this may be totally unacceptable.

It should be clear from this example that such caching strategies can introduce complexity and, worse, potentially incorrect behavior. Caching works best when the cached data is mostly or only used for read accesses. If the cached data can be altered, the business rules must be able to accept situations when the data retrieved from the cache may not be current.

Information brokers: publish–subscribe architectures

In many classes of business applications, core business scenarios often require information to flow from a potentially large number (100–10 000+) of source objects to a smaller set of monitoring and controlling objects. In addition, the existence and information needs of monitoring and controlling objects are typically dynamic, and hence information flows must adapt dynamically to demand. Also, the application must scale to potentially high loads and be fault-tolerant.

A well-understood approach to handling this scenario is an application architecture based around a *publish–subscribe* mechanism. Publish–subscribe architectures are designed to resolve the following design problems:

- One or more subscriber components must be notified, with given quality-of-service, about events that occur at one or more publishing components.
- The number and identities of interrelated components is not statically configurable and changes with time.
- Explicit polling of events from publishing components is not feasible.
- Event publishers and dependent subscriber components should be highly decoupled, in order that publishers need have no knowledge about the identity of subscribers.

Publishers and subscribers typically exist in different processes. A publish–subscribe infrastructure enables event sources to publish their events at known locations, and subscribers to register their interest in receiving events from various publishing sources. The publish–subscribe communications infrastructure itself usually exists in its own process, and has the potential to provide publishers and subscribers with various quality-of-service levels, such as best-effort or guaranteed delivery. This is depicted in Figure 3.10.

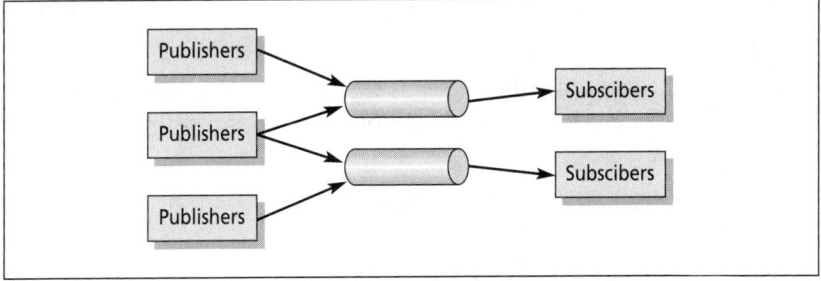

A publish–subscribe architecture **Figure 3.10**

To ensure the architecture doesn't suffer from a performance bottleneck or single point of failure, the publish–subscribe components can be replicated to enhance performance and reliability. A key component in realizing such flexibility and scalability in the architecture is a directory service. For example, publishers and subscribers use the directory service to locate the communications infrastructure components needed to successfully communicate events. Specifically:

- publishing components advertise the identity of the location to which publishers must subscribe in order to receive events; and
- subscribers query the directory service to locate the identity of the communications infrastructure that a publisher is currently using.

This scheme caters for the failure or overload of a given communications infrastructure process. It enables publishers to inform subscribers of a change of subscription location simply by updating their entry in the directory service.

Publish–subscribe technologies are not always transactional, although their concept of guaranteed delivery is close to being transactional. Some technologies, however, are built on top of transactional message broker systems, and hence publish and subscribe actions can take place within a transaction.

▶ SUMMARY

This chapter has attempted to cover some of the major issues that will be encountered when designing a distributed transaction processing system. The issues covered include:

- how client requests can be spread evenly across server objects to maximize resource usage;

- partitioning server interfaces to give finer grain control over load distribution;
- the advantages and disadvantages of deploying multi-threaded server processes, and a description of common multi-threaded server architectures;
- a discussion of when to utilize stateless as opposed to stateful server objects;
- the difficulties of caching database information in server objects, and recommendations of when caching should be used; and
- an explanation of publish–subscribe technologies and when they are appropriate.

These issues are rarely simple to resolve, and require experience and insight into the precise requirements of the application. The issues themselves are complex, even when considered in the abstract and divorced from any restrictions imposed by a selected implementation technology. Things however get even more difficult when logical application architectures must be refined and adapted to exploit the features and quirks of different distributed transaction processing products.

▶ FURTHER READING

There are a number of projects involved in detailed middleware technology evaluations. High-level reports are available from organizations like Ovum (**www.ovum.com**) and Cutter (**www.cutter.com**). Interesting and more technologically detailed comparisons can be found at **www.cmis.csiro.au/adsat** and **http://www.objectconsulting.com/report frame.html**.

A good coverage of the wider issues involved in building distributed systems is *Enterprise CORBA,* Slama *et al.,* Prentice Hall, 1999. While biased towards CORBA technology, the principles presented are general and applicable to most transaction processing systems.

Leading publish–subscribe vendors include TIBCO's Rendezvous product (**www.tibco.com**), Iona's OrbixTalk (**www.iona.com**), and IBM's MQ Series Publish–Subscribe (**www.ibm.com**).

An excellent general source of information on generic object and system architecture patterns, including the Publish-Subscribe approach, is *Pattern-Oriented Software Architecture*, Buschmann *et al.,* Wiley, 1996.

Chapter 4

The object transaction service

Introduction	68
Background: CORBA	68
OTS architecture and features	71
Programming the CORBA object transaction service	76
Recoverable resources	80
Summary	81
Further reading	82

▶ INTRODUCTION

This chapter will provide an overview of the salient features of the Object Management Group's (OMG) CORBA Object Transaction Service (OTS). It will demonstrate how transaction processing is handled in an object-oriented fashion in CORBA-based systems. The basic OTS client and server interfaces will be described from a programmer's perspective. This will include transaction demarcation, explicit and implicit transaction propagation, support for nested transactions, exception handling and resource objects. This material is an implementation-independent description of the OTS. It provides the necessary knowledge for the reader to continue with subsequent chapters and understand how Encina and OrbixOTM support the OTS. Simple examples of each OTS feature will facilitate this understanding.

There are many good books devoted to CORBA technology and its various implementations. For this reason, it is not the intention here to reproduce this material. The coverage of CORBA is deliberately brief, as this book is about transaction processing, not CORBA. If you want to be able to do more than bluff your way through a conversation with a CORBA nerd, the Further Reading section includes pointers to some of the best CORBA background material available. These are the sources in which to search for detailed CORBA information.

▶ BACKGROUND: CORBA

In 1989 the OMG was formed to define an Object Management Architecture (OMA) standard to support the development of object-oriented systems made up of independently developed off-the-shelf components. Part of the OMA reference model is the Object Request Broker (ORB) component, which has the primary role of transmitting requests and responses between distributed objects in a system. The Common ORB Architecture (CORBA) was initially adopted by the OMG in late 1991, and version 2.2 was released in February 1998.

Figure 4.1 shows the architecture of a CORBA ORB. The architecture consists of a number of components that are defined in terms of interfaces with associated semantics. The OMG does not produce a reference implementation of an ORB for vendors to utilize and to test compliance to the CORBA standard. In fact, vendors are free to adopt any underlying architecture that they wish, as long as the ORB interfaces and defined behaviors are preserved.

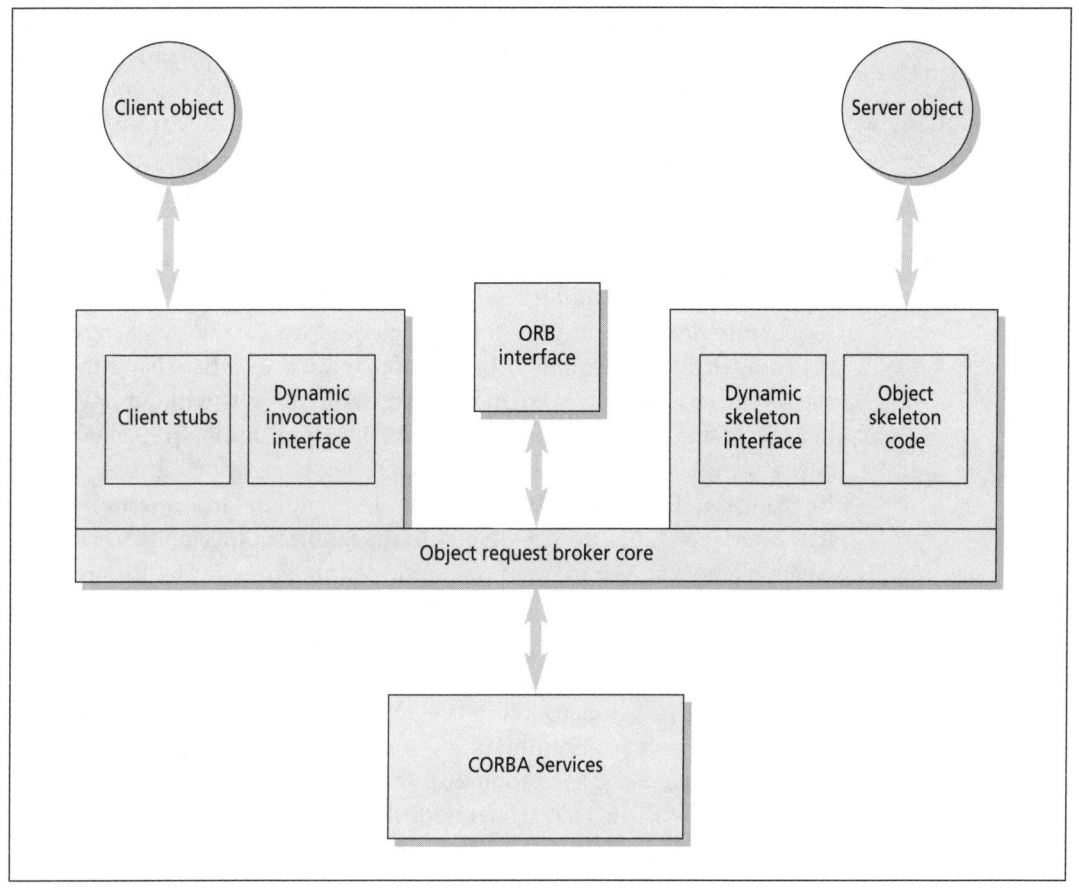

CORBA ORB architecture   **Figure 4.1**

The basic role, then, of an ORB is to provide an object-oriented abstraction for objects in a network to exchange messages. Server objects describe their interfaces using CORBA's Interface Definition Language (IDL). IDL descriptions for an object contain the names of the functions supported, along with the required parameters and returned values. An IDL compiler supplied with an ORB is used to process the IDL descriptions. The compiler produces client stub and server skeleton code in a target programming languages (C++ is the target in this book). The stub and skeleton code hide the complexities of distributed system communication between objects from the client and server applications, simplifying the programming effort required.

ORBs support a synchronous client–server model, in which clients can bind to server object methods either statically or dynamically. Static invocation requires the client to be compiled with the stub code generated by the IDL compiler for a given interface. The client application uses the stub code to create a client proxy object for the server object, and the proxy takes the responsibility of relaying the function call across the ORB to an actual server object. ORBs support static invocation using the aptly named Static Invocation Interface (SII). Static invocation is simple to implement and is the norm for most applications.

A more flexible but more complex method for calling server functions is provided by the Dynamic Invocation Interface (DII). Using the DII, clients can dynamically construct calls to server objects without having an IDL-generated client stub linked in with the application. To achieve this, clients must query a CORBA component known as the Interface Repository (IR). The IR is a database that contains information on the IDL interfaces supported by objects in the application. The IR has an API which clients can use to query the information stored in the IR, and construct correct member function calls using the DII. The DII then relies upon the ORB to deliver the function call to an actual server object.

Server objects remain oblivious as to whether a particular member function was called using the SII or DII. This obviously has advantages for server object programmers, who do not need to discern the exact mechanism the client used to invoke the function. Typically, server applications link with the IDL-generated object skeleton code for the server objects it supports. Server object method invocations are then called using the SII. The server-side equivalent of the DII is known as the Dynamic Skeleton Interface (DSI).

Use of the DSI is pretty rare, and is typically confined to facilitate the creation of gateways between CORBA and non-CORBA systems. The DSI allows a server application to register IDL interfaces for which it wishes the DSI to intercept all incoming function calls. The server informs the ORB of the name of a server function that should be called by the DSI when calls are received for the registered interface. This function has the responsibility of determining the identity of the object being called and the parameter types and values. The function can then perform the work required by the function, and construct any return values that the client expects. In a gateway, this would require the function to call the services of a non-CORBA system, wait for the results, and then return the results to the client. Clients would remain oblivious to the fact that a non-CORBA system had been called.

As different vendors' ORB's may co-exist in an organization, it is important that objects written for different ORBs should be able to communicate. To this end CORBA specifies a protocol known as the Internet Inter-ORB Protocol (IIOP). IIOP specifies message formats and low-level data representations for communications between ORBs. IIOP is probably most simply thought of as a CORBA-specific protocol layered on top of TCP/IP. Most, if not all, ORBs now provide IIOP support.

Figure 4.1 also shows the relationship between the ORB and the CORBAServices component of the OMA architecture. Each CORBAService adds some additional functionality to that provided by the base ORB. There are many CORBAServices specified by the OMG, and at the time of writing each ORB vendor typically supports only a relatively small number. In this book some of the CORBAServices supported in OrbixOTM will be covered. Specifically, these are the Naming Service, the Event Service, the Security Service, and the Object Transaction Service, the latter being the focus of the remainder of this chapter.

▶ OTS ARCHITECTURE AND FEATURES

As ORB applications grow in scale and provide mission-critical functionality, the need to reduce the effort of constructing reliable, high integrity systems becomes paramount. To this end, the CORBA OTS brings the transactional model so successfully utilized in traditional TP monitors to the CORBA environment. OTS-enabled CORBA applications acquire the ability to access and update multiple data sources and ensure they remain in a consistent state.

Figure 4.2 illustrates where the OTS fits in to the CORBA application architecture. As a CORBAService, it supplements the ORB's capability by providing transaction management for distributed objects. Objects, typically client objects, can begin a transaction, and then perform one or many operations on remote objects within the context of that transaction. When complete, the object can attempt to commit the transaction. The OTS will then drive the two-phase commit protocol and complete the transaction accordingly.

The OTS is designed to support interaction with XA-compliant resource managers and X/Open-compliant TP monitors. In many ways, the OTS can be thought of as an object-oriented implementation, using CORBA technology, of the X/Open reference model. For example, the OTS replaces the TX and XA procedural interfaces with CORBA IDL interfaces. It also supports the general transaction processing features, including:

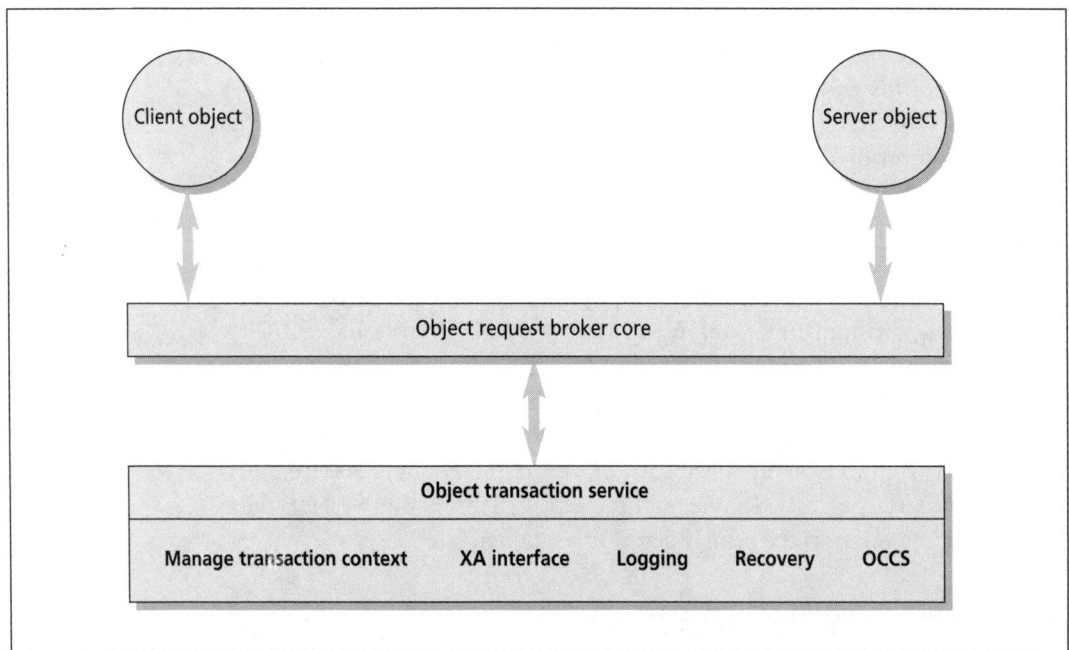

Figure 4.2   CORBA OTS architecture

- nested transactions (optionally);
- transaction suspension and resumption; and
- programmer-controlled transaction propagation.

In addition, the OTS design has been conceived to satisfy a number of specific requirements:

- portability, supported through specifying standard interfaces for interaction between the ORB and the OTS;
- support for both single and multi-threaded implementations at both the client and server;
- avoidance of OTS-specific extensions to CORBA IDL;
- ease of programming due to use of object-oriented technology; and
- achieving comparable performance with transactions services that implement the X/Open procedural model. In this context, performance is measured in terms of the number of network messages and disk accesses required, and the amount of data logged.

The OTS provides a number of interfaces in an IDL module known as `CosTransactions` for applications to use. These interfaces represent the set of abstractions that cooperate to support a transaction service.

The `Control` interface represents a top level or nested transaction. Applications use the `TransactionFactory` interface to return `Control` objects. These interfaces are shown in Figure 4.3.

```
interface TransactionFactory {
    Control create (in unsigned long time_out);
    Control recreate (in PropagationContext ctx);
};

interface Control {
    Terminator get_terminator()
        raises (Unavailable);
    Coordinator get_coordinator()
        raises (Unavailable);
};
```

Control and `TransactionFactory` interfaces **Figure 4.3**

`Control` objects provide the application access to `Coordinator` and `Terminator` objects. The interfaces for these objects are shown in Figure 4.4. Basically the `Terminator` interface has two services, one to commit a transaction, and one to rollback a transaction. These services are used by the transaction originator to mark the completion of a transaction. The `Coordinator` is more complex. It enables recoverable resources to register themselves as participants in a transaction, as well as the creation of subtransactions.

Recoverable servers actually register a `Resource` object with the `Coordinator`. The `Resource` object (*see* Figure 4.5) is responsible for responding to the two-phase commit protocol under the control of the transaction manager. It supports heuristic outcomes as explained in Chapter 2. It also supports an optimization to enable the transaction to terminate using a one-phase commit protocol. This is possible only when a single resource is registered in a transaction. The `Resource` interface is covered in more detail later in this chapter.

As all this seems somewhat complex, the OTS supports a simpler programming model for applications to utilize. The `Current` pseudo-object

```
interface Terminator {
    void commit (in boolean report_heuristics)
        raises(
        HeuristicMixed,
        HeuristicHazard
        );
    void rollback();
};

interface Coordinator {
    Status get_status();
    Status get_parent_status();
    Status get_top_level_status

    boolean is_same_transaction (in Coordinator tc);
    boolean is_related_transaction (in Coordinator tc);
    boolean is_ancestor_transaction (in Coordinator tc);
    boolean is_descendent_transaction (in Coordinator tc);
    boolean is_descendent_transaction (in Coordinator tc);
    boolean is_top_level_transaction ();

    unsigned long hash_transaction();
    unsigned long hash_top_level-tran();

    RecoveryCoordinator register_resource (in Resource r)
        raises(Inactive);

    void register_synchronization (in Synchronization sync)
        raises(Inactive);

    void register_subtran_aware (in SubtransactionAwareResource r)
        raises (Inactive, NotSubtransaction);

    void rollback_only()
        raises(Inactive);

    string get_transaction-name();

    Control create_subtransaction()
        raises(SubtransactionsUnavailable, Inactive);

    PropagationContext get_txcontext()
        raises(Unavailable);
};
```

Figure 4.4 `Terminator` and `Coordinator` interfaces

```
interface Resource {
    Vote prepare()
        raises(
        HeuristicMixed,
        HeoristicHazard
        );
    void rollback()
        raises(
        HeuristicCommit,
        HeuristicMixed
        HeuristicHazard
        );
    void commit()
        raises(
        NotPrepared,
        HeuristicRollback
        HeuristicMixed,
        HeuristicHazard
        );
    void commit_one_phase()
        raises(
        HeuristicHazard
        );
    void forget();
};
```

The Resource interface   **Figure 4.5**

provides these higher level services. A CORBA pseudo-object has an IDL interface, but does not have to adhere to the standard language mapping rules defined by the OMG. This essentially means that references to pseudo objects cannot be passed between objects. The Current interface is shown in Figure 4.6.

Current provides an application with most of the functions necessary to control a transaction. This includes transaction demarcation, suspension, resumption and status retrieval. When Current is used to start a transaction, the transaction context becomes associated with the calling thread identifier, which we'll call the transaction source. The transaction source then makes calls to one or more transactional objects. Each of these calls automatically passes the transaction context from the transaction source to the thread that handles the method execution for the transactional object. Upon transaction completion, the source uses the Current object to request that the transaction is committed (or rolled back) by the OTS.

```
interface Current {
    void begin()
    raises (SubtransactionUnavailable);
    void commit (in boolean report_heuristics)
        raises(
        NoTransaction,
        HeuristicMixed,
        HeuristicHazard
        );
    void rollback()
        raises (NoTransaction);
    void rollback_only()
        raises (NoTransaction);

    Status get_status();
    string get_transaction_name();
    void set_timeout (in unsigned long seconds);

    Control get_control();
    Control suspend();
    void resume (in Control which)
        raises (InvalidControl);
};
```

Figure 4.6   The `Current` interface

▶ PROGRAMMING THE CORBA OBJECT TRANSACTION SERVICE

To utilize the OTS, you must define transactional objects using the CORBA interface definition language (IDL). This is achieved by inheriting from the `CosTransactions::TransactionalObject` interface, as shown in Figure 4.7. This interface contains no operations: it merely acts as a flag to the OTS to indicate that the current transaction context should be automatically passed along with the method invocation. Any object that participates in transactions must be defined as transactional, or accept a transaction context as an operation parameter. With transactional objects, transaction propagation is said to be implicit as the OTS handles it with no programmer intervention needed. Passing the transaction context as a parameter is known as explicit transaction propagation, and requires complete programmer control.

```
//IDL example, must include OTS interfaces...
#include <ots/orbix/cos_ots.idl>

interface Part : CosTransactions::TransactionalObject {
    exception RejectOrder {
        string      Reason;
    };
    exception   DBNotAvailable  {};
    attribute   long  inStock;
    readonly attribute      string partName;
    void        Order ( in long amount) raises (RejectOrder);
    void        Query (out long amount) raises (DBNotAvailable);
}   ;
interface Store : CosTransactions::TransactionalObject {
    Part GetPart (in long part_id) raises (NoPart);
    void DeletePart (in Part p);
};
```

Defining transactional objects **Figure 4.7**

Note the OTS does not introduce any extensions to the CORBA IDL. In Figure 4.7 we define an interface called Part which supports a simple interface for stock item objects in a hypothetical stock control system. In such systems, transactional access is typically required for operations such as ordering a stock item. This requires updates to the quantity of the part in stock, creation of a customer order for the warehouse, creation of a customer invoice for the billing department, and may possibly trigger a reorder action for the part if its stock levels have fallen below the reorder level. Figure 4.7 also defines an interface Store that acts as a factory class to create Part objects for clients who supply the part key to the GetPart interface function.

Binding to transactional objects involves using standard ORB techniques, and is typically achieved using an Object Naming Service or some ORB-specific mechanism. In Orbix, the IDL compiler-generated _bind static member function can be used to create a client proxy object that is bound to a Store object at the server. This is shown in Figure 4.8.

Once the client has a reference to the factory object client proxy, it may create transactions and make use of the interface operations on the server object in these transactions. The OTS definition provides two transaction propagation methods, known as implicit and explicit models

```
int main (...)
{
    // Initialise the OTS
    Encina::Client::Initialise();
    Store_var    pStore;
    try    {
        // bind to the Store factory object
        pStore = Store::_bind (Server, host);
    }
    catch (CORBA::SystemExpection& ex) {
        cout << "Error Binding:" << &ex << endl;
        Encina::Client::Exit(1);
    }
    // rest of client code
    return 0
```

Figure 4.8   **Binding to objects**

respectively. In the examples, we cover only the implicit model, as it is preferred, and sufficient option in most cases.

The explicit model is more complex, but allows the programmer much more fine-grain control over management and propagation of the transactional context. Briefly, the explicit model requires the transaction context to be passed as an additional IDL parameter to a server object. Consequently, transactional objects that expect explicit transaction context propagation do not need to inherit from the CosTransactions::TransactionalObject interface. A new transaction context is obtained by issuing a request to a TransactionFactory, which returns a Control object. This can be used to manage the transaction completion and propagate the context to another object by passing the Control object as an explicit parameter. Control supports operations that return Coordinator and Terminator objects. Coordinator objects are used to enable transactional objects to participate in the transaction, and Terminator objects are used to commit or roll back the transaction. This architecture facilitates extremely flexible control over transaction propagation in systems that require careful management of transaction context.

An interesting implication of this discussion is as follows. The implicit model requires all the methods in an interface to be called within the scope of a transaction. Failure to do this causes an exception to be thrown. Using the explicit model, designers can decide which individual methods in an interface require transactional behavior and which do not.

These therefore become transactional methods, and only these need be called in a transaction.

As can be seen from Figure 4.9, creating and managing transactions using the implicit model is somewhat more straightforward. Using the `Current` class, the static `begin()` member function creates a transaction context and associates it with the calling thread. The transaction context is then passed automatically, along with the operation parameters, to each transactional object that is called within the scope of the transaction. The transaction scope terminates when the thread calls either the `commit()` or `rollback()` member functions of the `Current` object.

```
BOOL commit = TRUE;
try {
      CosTransactions::Current::begin();
      Part_var partObj = pStore->GetPart(id); // setting id not shown
      partObj.Order(55);
      CosTransactions::Current::commit();
}
catch (CORBA::TRANSACTION_ROLLBACK) {
      CosTransactions::Current::rollback();
      cout << "TransactionRollback exception:transaction aborted" << endl;
      commit = FALSE;
}
catch CORBA::UserException& uex) {
      CosTransactions::Current::rollback();
      commit = FALSE;
      cout << endl
           << "*** Transaction rollback due to"
           << "   " << uex << endl;
}
catch(...) {
      CosTransactions::Current::rollback();
      cout << 'Unknown exception - transaction aborted" << endl;
      commit = FALSE;
}
if (commit) cout << "Transaction committed. " << endl;
else cout << "Transaction committed. " << endl;
```

Transaction demarcation using the implicit model **Figure 4.9**

Within the scope of the transaction in Figure 4.9, two remote operation calls are made to transactional objects. The transaction context will be implicitly passed along with these calls, and the remote objects can then use their instances of the `Current` interface to manipulate the passed transaction context. If all operations complete successfully, the client will attempt to commit the transaction by calling `CosTransactions::Current::commit()`. If all transaction participants agree, the transaction will terminate successfully. If however any participant does not agree to commit, perhaps due to a communications failure, the OTS throws an exception and `CosTransactions::Current::rollback()` is called to undo all changes. Alternatively, if any operation called during a transaction throws a user-defined exception, this is caught by the client and the transaction is again rolled back.

One other important point is worth noting. Within the scope of a transaction, calls can be made to remote objects that are not transactional. In this case, no transaction context is passed to the called object and, in case of transaction failure, the object will not be required to rollback any changes it has made. If such behavior is needed, it must be programmed manually.

▶ RECOVERABLE RESOURCES

Most OTS systems interact via XA with XA-compliant resource managers such as relational databases or queuing systems. However, an application may wish to transactionally update databases such as OO databases or index-sequential file systems, which are not XA-compliant. To facilitate this, the OTS provides a set of interfaces that enable the implementation of recoverable objects that can participate fully in the two-phase commit protocol.

The major interface of interest is the `Resource` interface. Objects that support this interface must become participants in a transaction by becoming registered in the transaction context. This would typically occur in the method of a transactional object. The `Coordinator` object for the current transaction has a method `register_resource()`, which can be used for this purpose, taking a reference to a `Resource` object as a parameter.

The `Resource` interface supports four important methods that resource objects must implement. These are:

- `prepare`
- `rollback`
- `commit`
- `commit_one_phase`

Subsequently, during the transactions resolution, the OTS will call the resource's `prepare` method. The resource object must respond with a value of type `CosTransactions::Vote`. `VoteCommit` indicates that the object is prepared to commit its changes if and when required by the OTS. `VoteRollback` means the object cannot commit its updates, and the transaction must fail at all participants. `VoteReadOnly` means that the object has not updated any data during the transaction. In both the `VoteRollback` and `VoteReadOnly` cases, the resource object has completed its obligations for this transaction and can flush any state it has retained about the transaction.

During the second phase of a transaction's resolution, either the `rollback` or `commit` methods of the resource object will be called. When `rollback` is invoked, the resource object must undo any changes made to the data it manages during the transaction, and log that the transaction has rolled back. When `commit` is invoked, the object should make changes to the data it manages permanently, and log that the transaction has committed. In both cases, any state associated with the transaction can be deleted.

In circumstances where a transaction includes only one resource object, the OTS may, as an optimization, call the `commit_one_phase` operation. This is called without a corresponding prepare phase. Behavior is basically the same as for the commit method. The object simply returns the `TRANSACTION_ROLLEDBACK` exception if it cannot commit changes.

This is a fairly simple description of the required behavior of resource objects. The Further Reading section has pointers to more detailed descriptions of what must be implemented, including handling failures and recovery and resource locking using the Object Concurrency Control Service (OCCS).

▶ SUMMARY

The OTS extends the base ORB with the ability to manage transactions across distributed objects. The transaction service builds upon existing X/Open standards, providing an object-oriented architecture and a set of object interfaces that implementations must adhere to. The combination of an ORB or equivalent middleware technology with the OTS forms the core of products known as an Object Transaction Monitors (OTM). With that thought in mind, let's progress in the next chapters towards more detailed descriptions of the constituent components of OTM products, and examples of their use.

Finally, it should be noted that there's more to the OTS than has been covered in this chapter. Tasks like writing `Resource` objects are considerably more involved and typically rely on the Object Concurrency Control Service (OCCS), a counterpart CORBAService to the OTS. However, the material covered in this chapter will suffice for the vast majority of software engineers who ever develop code for OTM-based systems. For those who want or need to know more, the OTS description from **www.omg.org** is the definitive guide.

▶ FURTHER READING

A good place to start looking for information on all aspects of CORBA is the OMG's home page, **www.omg.org**. This has downloadable specifications of all the components of the OMA architecture, including the OTS.

Other good sources of CORBA information are the vendors' home pages, for example **www.iona.com** and **www.inprise.com**. Product documentation is also useful. For example, Iona's OTS documentation has a good example of how to create your own `Resource` object and how to use the OCCS.

In addition there are many worthy books on CORBA. Some I'd recommend (in no particular order) are:

The Corba Reference Guide: Understanding the Common Object Request Broker Architecture, Alan Pope, Addison-Wesley Longman, 1997.

CORBA Distributed Objects using Orbix, Sean Baker, ACM Press, Addison-Wesley Longman, 1997.

Essential CORBA System Integration Using Distributed Objects, Thomas J. Mowbray and Ron Zahavi, John Wiley & Sons and Object Management Group, 1995.

CORBA – Fundamentals and Programming, J. Siegel, John Wiley & Sons, 1996.

Corba Design Patterns, R. Malveau and T. J. Mowbray, John Wiley & Sons, 1997.

Chapter 5

Transaction processing monitors: Encina and the OrbixOTM

Introduction	*84*
Encina overview	*84*
OrbixOTM overview	*97*
Summary	*104*
Further reading	*105*

▶ INTRODUCTION

In this chapter, we'll briefly overview the two OO TP monitors that will be the focus of the remainder of this book. This is a transitional chapter, moving from the abstract concepts explained in the first four chapters to concrete realizations of these concepts in real products. Many of the concepts described in this chapter are explored fully in Chapters 7, 8 and 9 when full-blown example applications are developed.

Both Encina and Orbix have their heritage in world-class computer science schools. Encina grew from original research performed at Carnegie-Mellon University by Alfred Spector and his colleagues in the 1980s. They formed Transarc Corporation in 1989, and Encina was first released in 1991. Transarc's success with distributed software and file systems got them widely noticed, and in 1994 IBM acquired Transarc as a wholly owned independent subsidiary, and will fully absorb the company in 1999 when Transarc becomes integrated into the IBM structure. Transarc were instrumental in the definition of the OMG's Object Transaction Service, and were the first to fully implement the specification on Encina and Orbix. Recently Encina has been bundled with IBM's TxSeries and WebSphere product range, and the examples used in this book are based upon TxSeries 4.2.

Annrai O'Toole and colleagues are behind Orbix, which is based upon some of the pioneering work carried out at Trinity College, Dublin in the late 1980s. Much of the work was funded by the European Commission's ESPIRIT initiative. Iona Technologies was formed in 1991 and their core Orbix product was first released in 1993. Iona became listed on the NASDAQ stock exchange, and remains independent. The OrbixOTM product was first released in late 1997, and incorporated an implementation of the Object Transaction Service that Iona licensed from Transarc. The examples in the following chapters are based upon OrbixOTM v1.0c and Orbix 2.3c.

Let's move on to overview the architecture, functionality and programming models of both Encina and OrbixOTM. Bear in mind that this is an overview. Some details are deliberately glossed over or simplified, and there is no repetition of subjects that have been covered in earlier chapters (such as basic CORBA and OTS behavior). The Further Reading section at the end points interested readers to more detailed information.

▶ ENCINA OVERVIEW

Encina is a multi-platform TP monitor that exploits the Distributed Computing Environment (DCE) to provide scalable, high-performance systems with transactional integrity. Encina is supported on several flavors of UNIX and Windows NT, and supports XA to allow integration with resources managers. Encina has been used to build many successful systems worldwide, and has a large installed base. In this respect, Encina can be regarded as well-proven technology.

Architecture and functionality

Encina is constructed in a highly modular fashion. It comprises a number of distinct, layered components that build upon the core functionality for distributed systems provided by DCE. It's important to note that in Encina, DCE plays the role of a supporting infrastructure. DCE has existed as a product for most of the 1990s, and has a large and still growing deployed base. Still, few people would now design and implement a system based upon DCE, as it has complex procedural programming interfaces and is widely viewed as old technology.

In reality, DCE should be viewed as a set of low-level distributed operating system services, which have matured to the stage where they are fast and reliable. Products like Encina sensibly hide much of DCE's complexity from software engineers and system administrators. Therefore, while an understanding of the components of DCE is important in Encina systems, the main emphasis is on distributed transaction and object-based services. In fact, the high-level Encina services have no real dependency on DCE, and can be ported to run on top of alternative infrastructures. Alternatively, DCE is still being extended to incorporate alternative security services such as Public Key Infrastructures (PKI) and directory services such as the Lightweight Directory Access Protocol (LDAP). Figure 5.1 illustrates the overall Encina product architecture.

Firstly, let's examine DCE in more detail.

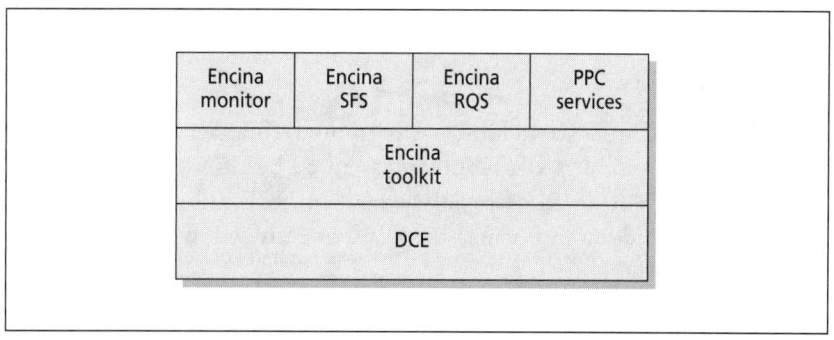

Basic Encina architecture   **Figure 5.1**

OSF's Distributed Computing Environment

The Open Software Foundation (OSF), now known as the Open Group after a merger with X/Open in 1996, is a vendor-neutral consortium of international software product vendors. In its original guise, the OSF was responsible for working with companies such as IBM and Hewlett-Packard to define a comprehensive set of fundamental services for distributed computing systems. The resulting Distributed Computing Environment (DCE) is now supported on all major versions of Unix, Windows and many other platforms including Tandem and IBM mainframes.

A major strength of DCE is its guarantee of interoperability in heterogeneous distributed systems. All DCE vendors license from the Open Group a reference implementation of the technology that they can then tailor to a given environment. The reference implementation helps to ensure that different vendor versions of DCE interoperate successfully.

DCE installations are organized into DCE cells. Administrators use the DCE administrative tools to assign users and servers to a named DCE cell. Each machine belongs to exactly one DCE cell. Security and other DCE services operate on a per cell basis. Hence typically users can log in to a cell and utilize server programs within that cell. It is possible for users and programs to communicate across cell boundaries, but this usually requires additional administrative effort if security is to be enforced.

To a software engineer, DCE comprises a number of programming interfaces that can be utilized to build distributed applications. The interfaces are somewhat low-level, reflecting DCE's true role as an operating system level set of services for distributed systems. The programming interfaces are grouped around a number of components that make up what is known as the Secure Core. These components, or services, are as follows:

- Remote Procedure Call (RPC);
- Cell Directory Service (CDS);
- Security Service; and
- Threads library.

The Secure Core also includes a Distributed Time Service (DTS). This enables operations in a distributed system to be timestamped using a common clock. Although a crucial element of DCE, the role of the DTS is pretty much hidden in Encina, and consequently will not be covered in any more detail here.

RPC

The RPC service provides a high-level abstraction over low-level network protocols to enable clients to communicate with servers across a network. It aims to make the process of calling a function offered by a server in a network as similar as possible to calling a function that exists in the same program or address space. The programmer uses DCE's Interface Definition Language (IDL) to describe the set of services a server provides. IDL is a C-like definition language for grouping function names into interfaces that a server supports. For each function, the types of the parameters are described, along with a directional attribute that indicates whether a parameter is an input, output or input/output value for the function. A slightly simplified IDL interface is shown in Figure 5.2.

```
interface Part {
      void   Order ([in} long amount);
      void   Query ([out] long amount);
   } ;
```

A DCE IDL interface   **Figure 5.2**

DCE provides an IDL compiler that processes interface definitions and produces the code necessary to call a function and exchange parameter values across the network. The code files produced are called client and server stubs, and must be linked into the client and server programs respectively. The client stubs pack the function call request and associated parameter values into a network packet and send it to the target server process. This is known as marshalling. The server stub receives the request, unpacks the details of the call and calls the actual function in the server process. This is called unmarshalling. When the function completes, the server stub marshalls the results and sends them to the client stub where they are unmarshalled and passed to the calling process. The calling part of this scheme can be seen in Figure 5.3, which shows the flow of control within an RPC.

Note that the RPC model supported in DCE is synchronous. The client waits until the function completes at the server and returns. To implement asynchronous RPCs in DCE, the programmer must use a separate thread on the client to handle the RPC call and return. This of course somewhat complicates matters, as the programmer is now responsible for synchronizing the threads at some stage in the future and handling the results. It is nevertheless effective.

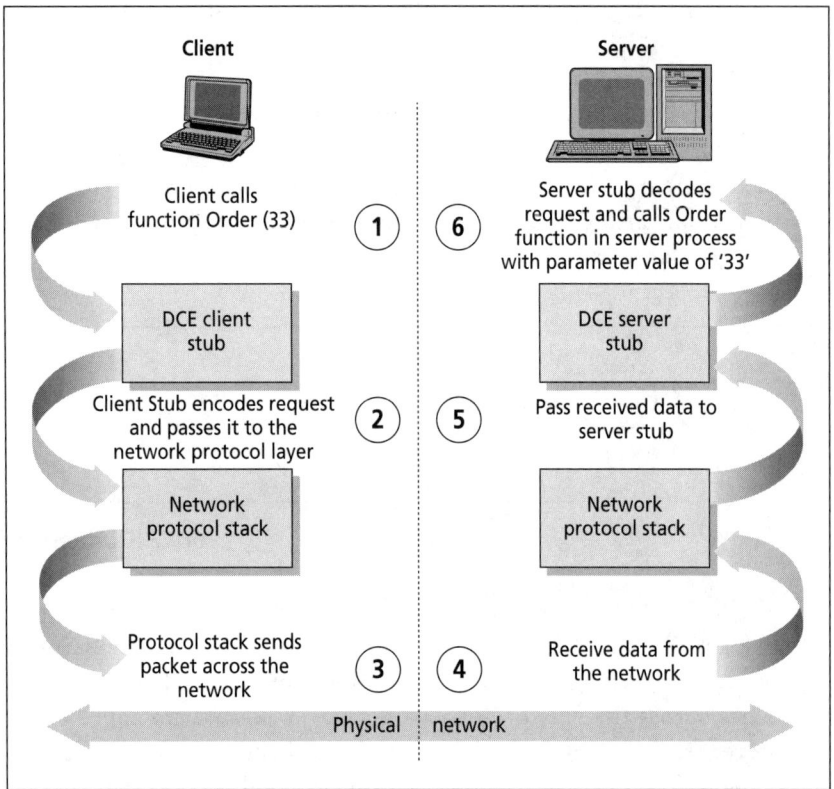

Figure 5.3   DCE RPC in action

Cell Directory Service

In order for a client to call a remote procedure, it must somehow locate a server process that supports the interface to which the remote procedure belongs. The relationship between a given client and server is known as a binding. Therefore clients must obtain a binding handle which fully identifies a server process before they call a remote procedure.

DCE supports this functionality through its Cell Directory Service (CDS). The CDS supports a hierarchical name space for a cell, which consists of directories and entries within directories. Server processes advertise their name, location and supported interfaces at a known location in the CDS by exporting partial binding information for clients to retrieve. The partial binding information comprises the network protocol that the client must use to communicate with the server (e.g. TCP/IP), and the network address of the server (e.g. the IP address).

Clients subsequently retrieve, or import, partial binding information from the CDS for a particular interface that they wish to use. As many servers may support a given interface, the client may have to choose between a number of candidate server processes. To obtain a complete binding handle, the client must also query the selected server machine to get the address at which the server listens for incoming RPCs. This is known as the server endpoint, and is stored locally on the server in the endpoint map. The endpoint information completes the information needed for the binding handle, and the client can now use this to directly call remote functions. The process of establishing a binding is depicted in Figure 5.4.

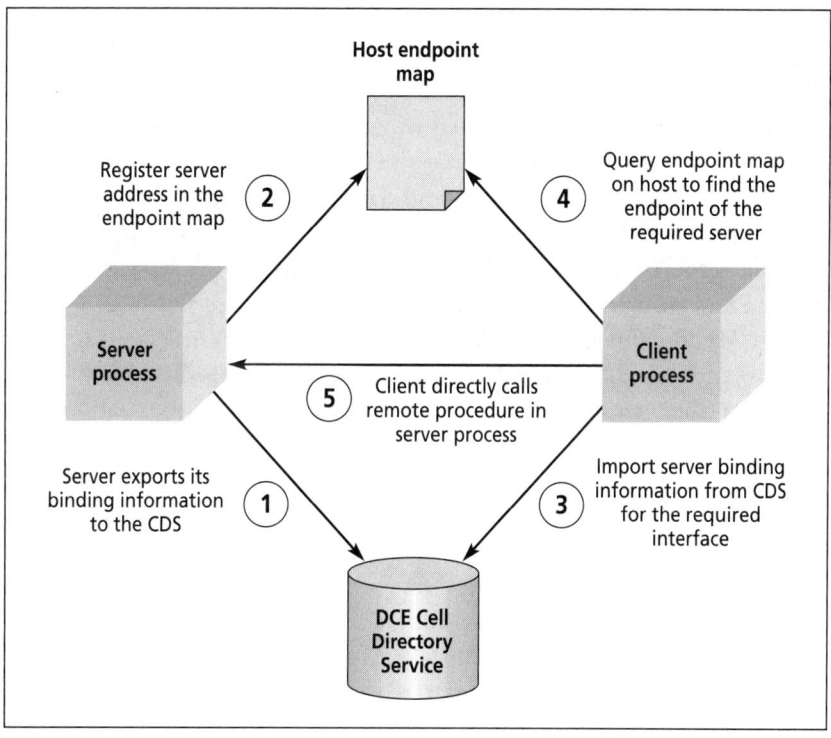

Binding in DCE   **Figure 5.4**

The CDS has many other features that won't be covered here. It is worth mentioning however that the CDS in a cell can be replicated or partitioned to help improve performance and reliability. For example, large cells spanning countries or continents can greatly benefit from CDS replication or partitioning. CDS queries can be directed to the local replica, saving wide area network traffic and improving response times.

Security Service

Distributed systems must provide a way of protecting resources from indiscriminate or undesirable use. For example, only certain users in an organization, such as administrators, may have access to certain functions, and users from outside the organization should be stopped from using all functions. In DCE the Security Service achieves this, with technology based on MIT's Kerberos version 5.0.

Users in a DCE cell are identified in a registry, along with passwords and other user profile information. Before any DCE servers can be utilized, the user must log in to DCE. The DCE Security Service checks that the user is a valid user for the cell and, if so, the user is said to be authenticated by DCE. Unauthenticated users are denied access to the cell, or their privileges are severely restricted.

DCE administrators can further assign specific permissions to resources, including administrative services, IDL server interfaces, individual functions within interfaces and data. Administrators create Access Control Lists (ACLs) for resources. The ACLs specify which users can access a resource, and what they can do. Permissions vary according to the type of resource being protected, but include actions such as *Create*, *Delete*, *Modify* and *Execute*. When a user attempts to access a resource, its ACL is checked. If the user has permissions to perform the requested operation, the operation is authorized and takes place. If the ACL forbids the operation, the user's request is unauthorized and the user receives an appropriate error message.

RPCs between clients and server also have an associated *protection level*. DCE provides seven gradually increasing levels of protection. For example, level 0 requires no authentication when a client calls an RPC. Level 3 requires client authentication at the beginning of each RPC. The highest level, level 6, requires client authentication for each RPC, verification that none of the data transferred to the server has been modified, and encryption of the RPC.

Protection levels are an application design decision, and should be based upon the level of security needed by an application. Of course, like all things in life and software, there's a price to pay for this additional security. Balancing security and performance is an essential skill for the distributed systems architect.

Threads library

DCE provides an implementation of the POSIX Pthreads library for use in applications. The Pthreads library provides a common set of calls across operating systems for creating, synchronizing and destroying threads in an application. The use of Pthreads instead of the platform's native thread routines should ensure that applications are portable across operating systems.

The Encina toolkit

In many ways, the Encina toolkit is the most interesting part of the Encina architecture. Built upon DCE, it comprises a number of libraries that form the core low-level services required in a TP monitor. Briefly, the most important of these are:

TRPC: TRPC implements transactional extensions to DCE's RPC. Encina has a Transactional IDL, which enables individual functions in an interface to be defined as transactional or non-transactional (*see* Figure 5.5). The Encina TIDL compiler processes TIDL interfaces producing equivalent DCE IDL interfaces that enable the transactional context to be passed as extra parameters on functions.

TRDCE: The Transarc/Encina DCE utilities library provides utilities for constructing client and server programs. Many of the TRDCE functions simply provide a simpler interface to underlying DCE APIs for common operations such as server registration and security.

LOCK: The Lock Service is a two-phase locking manager that permits synchronization of accesses to data. It ensures that simultaneous transactions behave as though their actions were serialised.

TRAN: The Distributed Transaction Service coordinates transactions for participants, making sure that transactions commit or abort, and participants are aware of the transaction outcome.

VOL: The Volume Service is a disk management library that provides a logical interface to actual physical storage, enabling volumes and files to span physical device boundaries.

LOG: The Log Service provides append-only functionality for logging transaction states to persistent storage.

REC: The Recovery Service uses the LOG and VOL libraries to provide clients with recoverable storage.

TM-XA: The Transaction Manager-XA Service implements the transaction manager side of the X/Open XA interface for interactions with XA-compliant resource managers.

ThreadTid: ThreadTid provides mechanisms for associating transaction contexts with individual threads.

```
interface Part {
       [transactional]   void Order ([in} long amount);
       [transactional]   void Query ([out] long amount);
}       ;
```

Figure 5.5   **An Encina TIDL interface**

When building Encina applications, most of the toolkit functionality is of no concern to the software engineer. The toolkit APIs can however be called directly in applications, and this is occasionally done, for example, to increase performance or override default Encina behavior.

Interestingly, the generalized, modular design of the toolkit can be used to build other TP monitors. The classic example of this is Distributed CICS. Distributed CICS offers the same API to applications as its mainframe counterpart, but utilizes parts of the Encina toolkit underneath the covers to implement TP monitor functionality.

The Encina monitor

Built upon the underlying functionality of the toolkit, the Encina monitor provides an administrative, run-time and application development environment for distributed TP applications.

Administratively, Encina provides command line and GUI-based tools for managing an Encina cell. A single Encina monitor cell exists within a single DCE cell (a DCE cell may have more than one Encina Monitor cell). A monitor cell basically comprises a single cell manager, one or more node managers and a set of application servers, as well as the necessary DCE infrastructure such as the CDS and Security Service

The cell manager is a process that manages the cell's repository. The repository contains configuration information about the nodes and applications servers that make up the cell. Administrative tools can query and update this repository. The cell manager is the first process that must be configured and executed when a monitor cell is brought on-line. It also periodically pings all the node managers in a cell, and if possible restarts them if they have failed for some reason.

Node managers run on each processor node that supports application servers in an Encina cell. Node managers are responsible for managing the application servers on a machine. This includes starting, stopping and automatically restarting servers, and managing the recoverable transaction log for all servers on the node.

Monitor Application Servers (MASs) are Encina applications that typically implement the middle tier in a three-tier system. Monitor clients call the functions provided in the MAS interfaces and the MASs satisfy the requests generally by accessing a resource manager on behalf of the client.

An Encina MAS comprises one or more Processing Agents (PAs). Each PA is essentially a replica of the MAS executable running on the same node. The number of PAs for a MAS is set administratively and can be modified while a MAS is active. PAs provide a simple method of running multiple instances of a server process on a node to provide parallel processing and fault tolerance. The node manager automatically restarts PAs that fail, and all other PAs for that MAS continue processing as normal while the restart takes place. In addition, the monitor provides load balancing of client requests across the PAs in a MAS, spreading client load and increasing overall system throughput. Figure 5.6 depicts the anatomy of a simple Encina monitor cell.

Developers use the monitor development environment and run-time to build and deploy MASs. The monitor API is available for application servers to utilize to initialize, configure, manage and terminate a MAS. The monitor API successfully hides away many of the underlying DCE functions (such as security and CDS access) from the application developer. This simplifies development and leads to highly integrated monitor functionality. Once deployed, the monitor run-time provides load balancing of client requests across servers, cell administration support and support for client–server bindings. The monitor run-time exists on each node in a cell, and also on clients, who link to a client monitor run-time library.

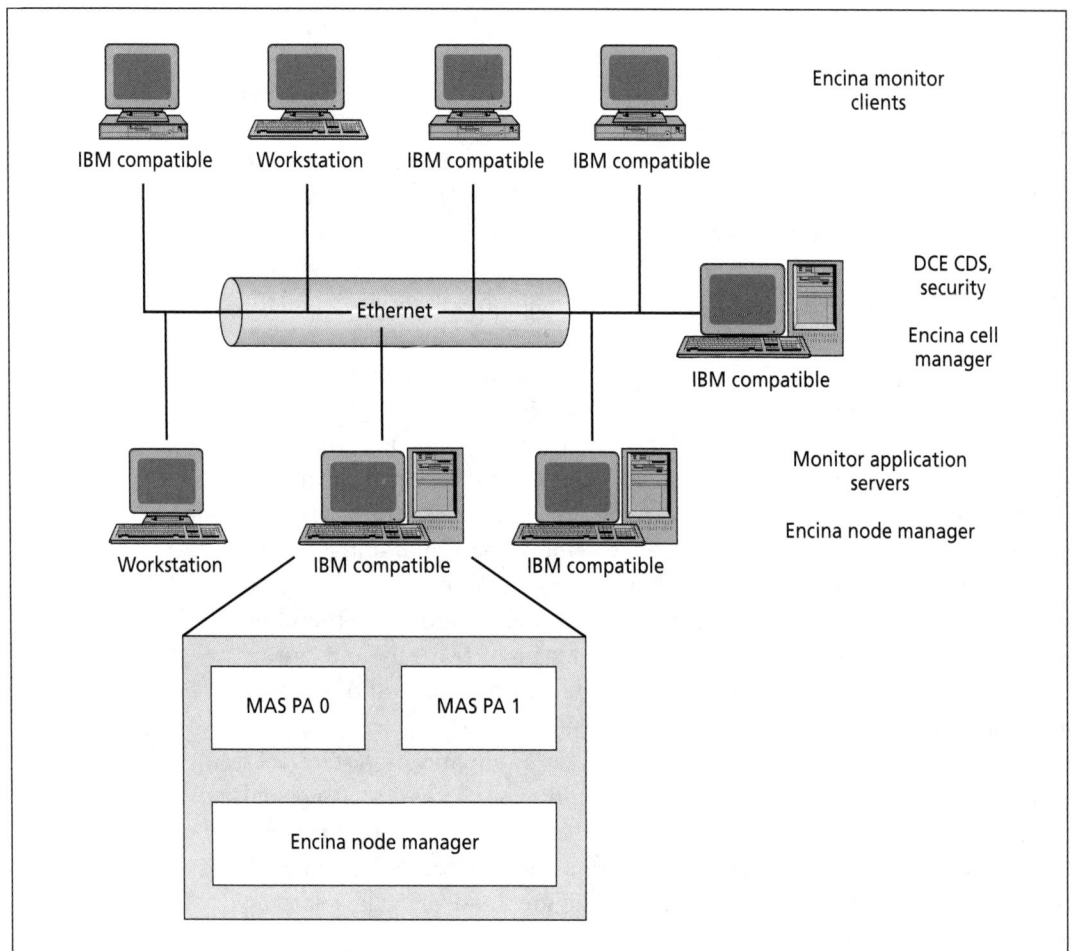

Figure 5.6   An example Encina cell

Encina RQS

As described in earlier chapters, the ability to parcel off portions of work in a transaction for delayed processing is important in TP systems. The Encina Recoverable Queuing Service (RQS) provides this capability to Encina applications. RQS allows transactions to write data to a recoverable queue. RQS guarantees that once a data item has been transactionally enqueued, it will remain there until it is subsequently dequeued from within another transaction. The data can later be retrieved and processed to complete the work for the transaction.

RQS has a reasonably rich set of features. Importantly, it allows items to be dequeued in FIFO order from a single queue, or in some priority order from a *queue set*. A queue set is a group of prioritized queues. Data can be added to a specific queue to assign it a priority. However, the dequeueing application treats the queue set as a whole, and is oblivious to the individual queue priorities. Queue sets can return data items in strict priority order, or use a weighting technique that ensures that low-priority queues do not suffer from starvation, with data items indefinitely held on the queue.

Encina SFS

Encina's Structured File System (SFS) provides an out-of-the-box transactional, recoverable file system for use in Encina applications. Although not widely used, it does provide a high-performance, low-cost alternative for systems that do not require the expense and overheads associated with a relational database. SFS is record-oriented, and uses indexes to support rapid record retrieval. In fact a compatibility library allows SFS files to be accessed as if they were standard ISAM (Indexed Sequential Access Method) files.

Access to SFS files requires an Encina cell to be running the SFS server. All data requests are submitted to the SFS server, which returns the results of the query to the application. SFS also has an administrative interface (sfsadmin) which allows administrators to create, delete and configure SFS volumes.

PPC Services

The Encina PPC (Peer-to-Peer Communications) Services provides mainframe access for distributed applications. It gives bidirectional transactional communications with systems that support SNA (Systems Network Architecture) LU (Logical unit) 6.2 communications. This means that Encina applications can transactionally access data on a mainframe, and mainframes can initiate requests to transactionally access data stored in an Encina system.

Programming models

Encina applications need to interact with the services Encina offers, namely the monitor, RQS, SFS and the PPC Services. Each of these services offers a procedural API that provides access to the underlying library functions. In addition, Encina applications can directly call the underlying Encina toolkit and DCE libraries if needed. This is usually only necessary when some exotic functionality is desired – the Encina Services APIs are designed to cover most common scenarios.

Application servers define their interfaces using TIDL, and the TIDL compiler generates the code needed for remote procedure calls, parameter passing and transporting the transaction context. Transactional programs initiate and complete transactions using two main programming interfaces, Transactional-C (Tran-C) and TX APIs.

Tran-C is actually a set of C macros and functions that provide a natural and extremely clear method for expressing transactional boundaries. However, as many Tran-C constructs are actually C macros, there are some restrictions in their use. The TX APIs provide general purpose functions for creating and controlling transactions, and adhere to the X/Open TX standard.

In addition to the procedural interfaces, the monitor, Transaction Service, RQS and SFS have C++ class interfaces. These are referred to as Encina++, RQS++ and SFS++ respectively. These class interfaces essentially are C++ wrappers around the procedural APIs, with some extensions to exploit object-orientation and C++ features. As we're concerned mainly with TP monitor programming, we'll concentrate on Encina++ and its transactional programming environment, and not touch on RQS++ and SFS++.

The core of Encina++ is an implementation of the OMG's Object Transaction Service (OTS). The OTS is accessed through a set of C++ classes which are almost completely compatible both across Encina running on DCE and applications running upon a CORBA-compliant object request broker. The OTS has mechanisms for creating and controlling distributed transactions, which can be used in Encina++ applications. In addition, Tran-C++, an object-oriented extension of Tran-C, provides macros and functions for transaction demarcation and completion. Either of these two interfaces can therefore be used in Encina++ clients and servers.

In Encina++, TIDL is still used to define server interfaces. A special flag supplied to the TIDL compiler causes the compiler to emit C++ class interfaces for each TIDL interface. The client and server Encina shadow stubs are also generated in C++. Clients now create proxy objects that bind to a server object of the correct type and call remote member functions as requested. Encina++ also provides specific management objects that hide away many of the details of interacting with the monitor.

Chapter 8 will show in-depth examples of the use of Encina++, so turn to those now if you can't wait.

▶ ORBIXOTM OVERVIEW

The OrbixOTM product is one of the first CORBA-based object transaction monitors to hit the market. The OTM packages a number of CORBA services along with the basic Orbix product to provide extensive facilities for building DTP applications. Orbix has impressive platform coverage including all major Unix platforms, NT and most recently MVS. Iona has also recognized the importance of interoperation with Microsoft's DCOM, and provides bridging technology as an additional product option.

Architecture and functionality

OrbixOTM brings together the following components to enable developers to build distributed TP applications:

Orbix: The basic ORB component.

OrbixOTS: An implementation of the OMG Object Transaction Service.

OrbixNames: An implementation of the OMG Naming Service.

OrbixSSL: An implementation of the Secure Sockets Layer (SSL) with Orbix to provide CORBA level 0 security.

OrbixManager: An application to manage Orbix applications.

OrbixEvents: An implementation of the OMG Event Service.

Basic ORB functionality has already been covered in the previous chapter. Hence the following section will describe how all the additional services and components integrate with the ORB to produce a more comprehensive and coherent product.

OrbixOTS

OrbixOTS brings distributed transactional capabilities to Orbix. It provides a complete implementation of the OMG OTS specification as described in the previous chapter, including subtransactions. The architecture of OrbixOTS not surprisingly reflects its Encina heritage. Each OTS client and server links with an OTS library that provides the ability to create, control and terminate distributed transactions. An XA component supports resource manager interactions using the X/Open XA interface, and logging and recovery services support transaction state recording and recovery after a process failure.

In addition, the OTS implements the OMG OCCS service. The transaction manager uses the OCCS to acquire and release locks on shared resources, and is designed to be tightly integrated with the OTS. Its primary use is in creating recoverable resource objects that can act as participants in transactions. The OCCS is not used when an application integrates with an XA-compliant resource manager, as these typically provide their own locking mechanisms.

OrbixNames

The CORBAServices Naming Service is intended to bring functionality similar to DCE's Cell Directory Service to CORBA systems. Like the CDS, it provides clients with a directory service that can be used to look up binding information for server objects. Using the Naming Service simplifies locating server objects in a network and introduces a mechanism for load-balancing client requests across candidate servers. OrbixNames implements the CORBAServices Naming Service specification, and adds some useful abilities to associate a single name with multiple server objects.

Following the OMG specification, OrbixNames implements a hierarchical name space known as a name context graph. Nodes in the graph represent either naming contexts, which behave like directories in a traditional file system, or actual objects. An example of this is shown in Figure 5.7, in which the leaf nodes represent actual objects. Federated name spaces are also permitted. This means that a single name space can be spread across more than one name server running on potentially different server machines. In a federated name space, naming contexts in one name server may point to naming contexts that exist in another name server. The name space partitioning is transparent to clients, who remain unaware that a name look-up may actually involve the participation of multiple name servers.

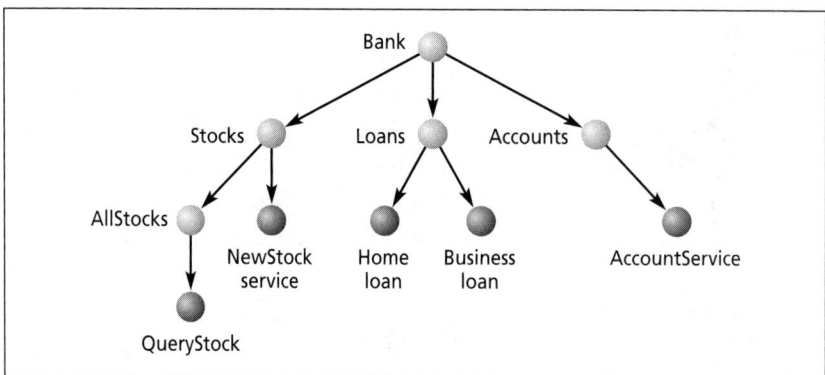

Figure 5.7   An example OrbixNames name space

The process of locating server objects is as follows. When server objects are created, they use OrbixNames to bind their object reference to an entry in the name space. Clients may subsequently specify a naming context and object name in the name space that they wish to bind to. Assuming this entry exists in the name space, an object reference is returned to the client. Clients now directly use the object reference to access the server.

To support load-balancing, OrbixNames extends the basic CORBAServices Naming Service to include the concept of object groups. Object groups facilitate a mapping from one name entry in the name space to one or more target server objects. Creating an object group requires the specification of a member selection policy for the group. Currently object groups can be created to return object references for their members in a random or round robin fashion. A client simply specifies the name of the object group, and OrbixNames returns an object reference for one member of the group using the specified policy.

OrbixSSL

The Secure Socket Layer (SSL) provides applications running across the TCP/IP protocol with data security. SSL sits between the application and the standard IP protocol stack, providing authentication, privacy and data integrity.

Authentication means applications can verify the identities of other applications with which they communicate. SSL actually uses public key cryptography, giving each application both a public and private key. The two basic rules are:

1. Data encrypted using the application's public key can only be decrypted using the private key.

2. Data encrypted using the application's private key can only be decrypted using the public key.

Applications sending data therefore encode it with their private key, which only they know. This encoding is done to facilitate authentication. Receiving applications can decode the data using the application's public key, thus ensuring (authenticating) the identity of the sending program. In order for this scheme to work correctly, public keys are exchanged as part of an X.509 certificate, whose aim is to validate that the public key does in fact belong to the application. X.509 is a standard format for certificates that includes:

- the name of the application identified by the certificate;
- the public key for the application; and
- the name of the Certification Authority (CA) that created the certificated.

The CA is a trusted authority that digitally signs the certificate. The CA's signature verifies that the application name and public key are a valid pairing. Essentially the CA's signature is a message encoded using the CA's private key. The CA's public key is made available to applications, which can use it to decode the CA's signature to check the signature is valid. OrbixSSL provides utilities for creating a CA to use in a system and to sign certificates.

SSL security is enhanced further to provide an additional level of encryption. Client applications can select an encryption algorithm that is subsequently used for all communications. Typically the encryption algorithm used is the Data Encryption Standard (DES).

Finally SSL data integrity allows applications to detect if encrypted data has been modified in transit. Using the message contents, the SSL layer calculates a message authentication code (MAC) generally known as a checksum, and includes this in an encrypted form in the message. When the message is received, the MAC is decoded and the calculation repeated on the message contents. If the result doesn't match the MAC, then the message has been modified in transit, and can be discarded.

The exact details of the operation and protocols that the SSL uses are hidden from Orbix developers. A number of routines are available for incorporating OrbixSSL into an application and, once this is set up, the SSL usage is transparent. Figure 5.8 depicts a simple overview of where the SSL fits into an application.

OrbixManager

Run-time management and monitoring of distributed applications is a difficult and often overlooked task. Early CORBA vendor implementations pretty much ignored system management. This required application designers to build management infrastructure and functionality in to their deployments. Not surprisingly, this was expensive, time-consuming and hard to get right.

OrbixManager is an attempt to provide administrators with graphical tools to manage distributed OrbixOTM applications. Administrators must define management domains that comprise a group of machines that run managed applications. A managed application is an Orbix client

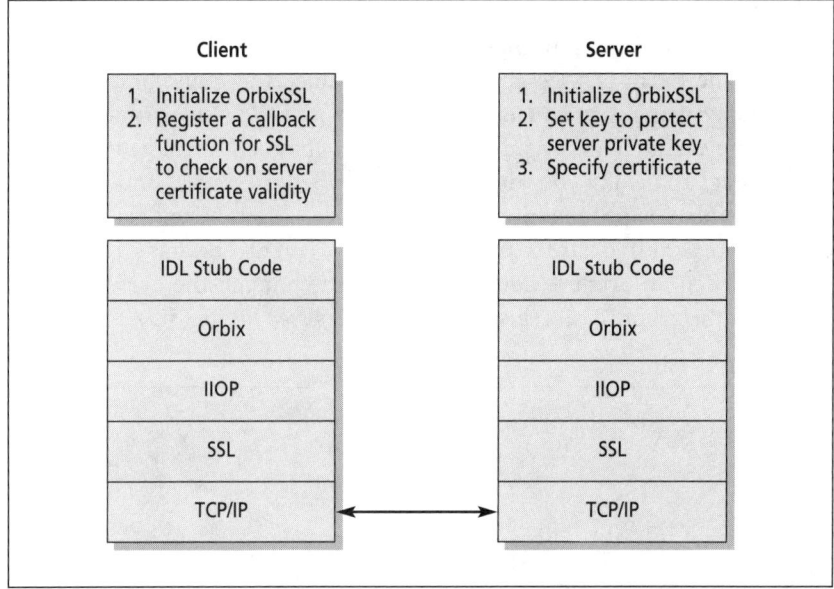

Secure socket layer overview **Figure 5.8**

or server that can communicate with OrbixManager. This requires some initialization code and linking with a specific OrbixManager library. The Orbix management service can then communicate with managed hosts and gather information for monitoring and administration. OrbixNames plays an integral part in this scheme, as managed applications use the name service to advertise their binding information for the management service. Once a management domain is defined, OrbixManager can be used for a number of specific tasks, such as:

- monitoring the health of applications;
- shutting down applications;
- viewing notifications of applications failures and CORBA exceptions;
- viewing the workload associated with applications;
- configuring an application's environment and setting application-specific properties; and
- monitoring an application's client–server connections.

We'll see examples using OrbixManager in later chapters. These will illustrate the concepts and functions described here.

OrbixEvents

OrbixEvents is Iona's implementation of the CORBAServices Event Service. The Event Service allows CORBA objects to communicate asynchronously using a producer–consumer model. Producer objects send interesting events to an event channel. Event channels are essentially message queues that may contain typed or untyped messages, and that take responsibility for propagating events to other objects. Consumer objects can register their desire with one or more event channels to receive events. When an event is added to the event channel, the event channel forwards the event to all registered consumers (*see* Figure 5.9).

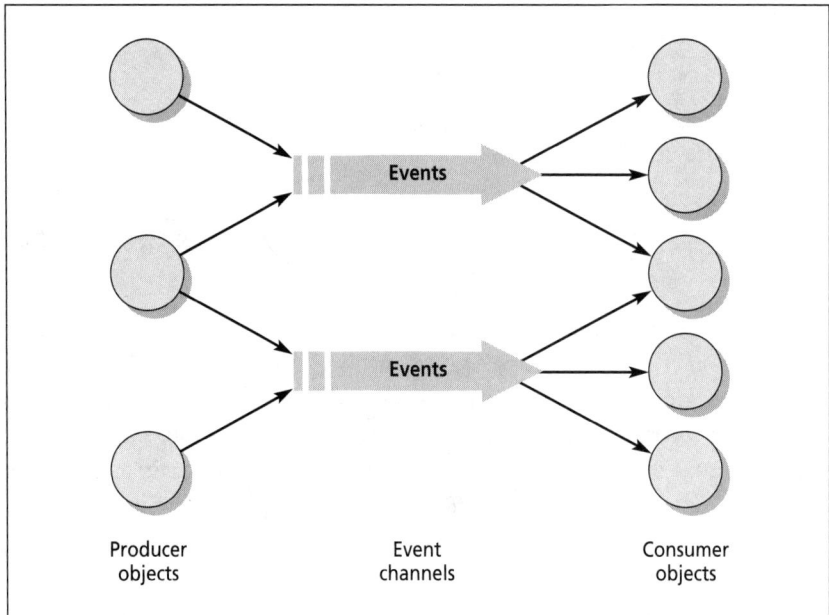

Figure 5.9 The CORBA event service

In this manner, the Event Service facilitates one-to-many communications between highly decoupled objects in a flexible and dynamic manner. Objects can decide when they wish to generate and receive events at run-time. Two-way communications can be provided by utilizing two event channels.

In other systems, this architecture is known as *publish–subscribe*. However, as the use of OrbixEvents is beyond the scope of this book, see the Further Reading section for more detailed information.

```
module CosNaming {

    // typedefs/etc not shown

    interface NamingContext {

        // exception definitions removed

        void bind (in Name n, in Object obj)
              raises (NotFound, CannotProceed, InvalidName, AlreadyBound);

        void rebind (in Name n, in Object obj)
              raises (NotFound, CannotProceed, InvalidName);

        void bind_context (in Name n, in NamningContext nc)
              raises (NotFound, CannotProceed, InvalidName, AlreadyBound);

        void rebind_context (in Name n, in NamingContext nc)
              raises (NotFound, CannotProceed, InvalidName);

        Object resolve (in Name n)
              raises (NotFound, CannotProceed, InvalidName);

        void unbind (in Name n)
              raises (NotFound, CannotProceed, InvalidName);

        NamingContext new_context ();

        NamingContext bind_new_context (in Name n)
              raises (NotFound, CannotProceed, InvalidName, AlreadyBound);

        void destroy () raises (NotEmpty);

        void list  (in unsigned long how_many,
                    out BindingList bl, out BindingIterator bi);

        Object resolve_object_group (in Name n)
              raises (NotFound, CannotProcees, InvalidName);

        Object OBfactory();
    };

    interface BindingIterator {

        boolean next_one (out Binding b);

        boolean next_n (in unsigned long how_many, out BindingList bl);

        void destroy ();
    };
};
```

CORBA IDL for the name service **Figure 5.10**

Programming models

As is the norm for CORBA systems, each of the OrbixOTM components defines their own CORBA IDL interfaces. The exception to this is OrbixSSL, which defines its own class-based API. Consequently an application wishing to utilize the functions of a component must use the functions defined in the IDL or, for security, the OrbixSSL API.

As an example, OrbixNames defines an IDL module and interfaces to enable objects to use the name service. A portion of this is shown in Figure 5.10. In order for an application to use OrbixNames, this interface definition must be compiled using the Orbix IDL compiler for the target programming language (in this book, C++). The resulting library stubs are then compiled and linked with the application.

Orbix SSL defines a number of classes for use in applications, the most important being `IT_SSL`. Applications use a global object of this type known as `OrbixSSL`. As OrbixSSL code tends to be common across many applications with the same security needs, it is an excellent candidate for extracting into shared library functions for applications to utilize. This avoids cluttering the application code with SSL calls.

▶ SUMMARY

This chapter has covered the major architectural elements of Encina and OrbixOTM. It should be no surprise that, at an architectural level, there is a fair degree of commonality. Enterprise-scale mission-critical systems require components that deliver scalability, reliability, manageability and security. These features are all supported in the two products to some degree. The two products have naming services and security facilities, both support management and monitoring of distributed applications, and both support transaction processing and database interactions.

It is only when one digs deeper that the real differences emerge. Subtle differences begin to emerge in areas such as performance, application design, amount of code required and detailed functionality of components. Sometimes these are highly significant, possibly to the extent that applications can succeed or fail based on the precise workings of some architectural component. That's what makes middleware such a difficult thing to evaluate for any given application environment.

The remainder of this book demonstrates these products in use, and sheds some light on some of these major product differentiators. Only by actually developing software and exercising it thoroughly do problems and pitfalls begin to emerge.

▶ FURTHER READING

Websites are generally excellent places to get product information. For example, Transarc publishes all its product documentation on its WWW site **www.transarc.com**, along with a number of case studies and technical support information. Iona don't yet publish all their documentation, but nevertheless their site is a wealth of information: see **www.iona.com**. DCE information can be sourced from the Open Group's WWW site, **www.opengroup.com**.

Not surprisingly, both sets of product documentation are the places to look, at least initially for in-depth product details. Transarc and Iona also run annual user conferences known as Decorum and IonaWorld respectively. These contain a wealth of information, from detailed descriptions of the products' inner workings, to user accounts and experiences. Many, if not all, of the articles at these conferences are also available through the company's WWW sites.

Detailed information on the SSL for security enthusiasts can be found at Netscape's WWW site, **www.netscape.com**. The latest specification available for the SSL is version 3.0.

Chapter 6

Case study

Introduction	*108*
The Stock-OnLine system	*108*
Database design	*115*
Summary	*117*
Further reading	*117*

▶ INTRODUCTION

In this chapter we'll introduce an example problem which will be the focus for the remainder of this book. By focusing on a particular sample application, and showing how it can be built using Encina++ and OrbixOTM, many important issues of design, implementation and management will be explored. This chapter will cover a statement of requirements and an initial design.

▶ THE STOCK-ONLINE SYSTEM

Buying and selling stock on the Internet is becoming a common service. The hypothetical Stock-OnLine system specification below covers the basic services that are required by customers to establish accounts and perform on-line transactions. These basic services will be sufficient to demonstrate a range of design and implementation techniques. Obviously there are many other services that would be (and are!) provided by a real stockbroking service, but in this context, they would add little value for the reader.

Stock-OnLine requirements

Stock-OnLine is an on-line stockbroking system. It enables subscribers to buy and sell stock for a small transaction fee, enquire about the up-to-date prices of particular stocks, and get a holding statement detailing the stocks they currently own. From a subscriber's perspective, the following services are offered:

Create Account: A person wishing to enroll with Stock-OnLine can create a subscriber account for themselves with the service provider.

Update Account: A subscriber can modify various fields in their account details.

Query Stock Value: A subscriber can query the current price for a given stock.

Buy Stock: A subscriber can place an order to buy a given number of a specified stock. If successful, a purchase note record is created for later processing.

Sell Stock: A subscriber can place a request to sell a specified number of any stock that they have purchased through Stock-OnLine. If successful, a sale note record is created for later processing.

Get Holding Statement: A subscriber can request a statement of all the stock they have purchased through Stock-OnLine and still own.

In addition, the Stock-OnLine service receives constant updates from a live data feed that sends messages containing the latest values of individual stocks as their prices fluctuate. To allow the Stock-Online database to be updated with these values, another service is supported:

Update Stock Value: A dedicated client program reads the live data feed messages and updates the stock's value in the Stock-OnLine service database.

Figure 6.1 shows a use-case diagram for the system. It depicts the four main actors in the system, and each service as an individual use-case. The actors are:

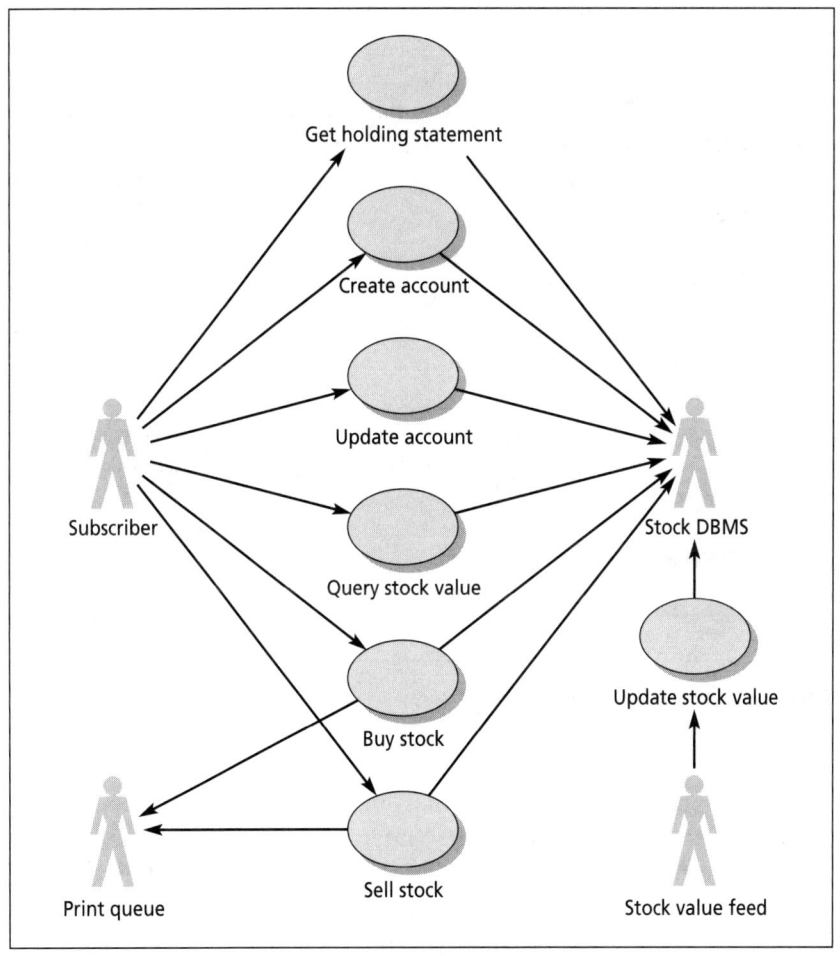

System use-case diagram for Stock-OnLine   **Figure 6.1**

Subscriber: Someone who uses the system to trade stocks.

StockDBMS: The persistent data store that holds subscriber, transaction and stock information.

PrintQueue: A queue that stores requests for sending sale and purchase notes associated with subscriber transactions.

StockValueFeed: A program that updates the StockDBMS based on information it receives from the live data feed on current stock prices.

Stock-OnLine design issues

A high-level architecture for the Stock-OnLine system, expressed in UML packages, is shown in Figure 6.2. The two client packages, StockValueFeedClient and SubscriberClient, encapsulate the objects that drive the transactions in the system. The Services package represents the objects that the clients will use to initiate and fulfill their requests. The StockDBMSAccess package encapsulates the classes required to store and retrieve the objects that need to be made persistent in the StockDBMS.

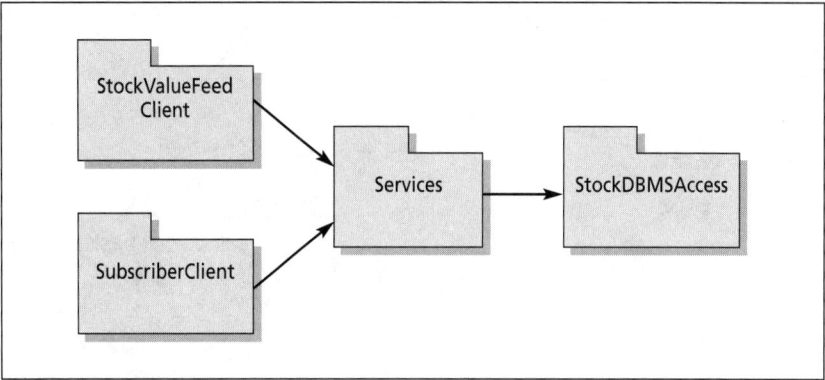

Figure 6.2 Packages for the Stock-OnLine system

For the purposes of this case study, the internal object architecture of the two client packages is not very interesting. The client implementations in the following chapters will only demonstrate the functionality needed to communicate with the appropriate server objects. We won't get into the highly interesting, but separate, issues of building useful interfaces for the clients. The examples will simply present a text-based interface so that the discussions can focus on the core middleware issues. In reality, the SubscriberClient package would no doubt comprise classes that provide the desired GUI look-and-feel as well as classes associated with the middleware technology. Likewise, the StockValueFeedClient package would contain classes that encapsulate access to the live data feed, along with some GUI classes for monitoring and management purposes, and classes to communicate with the middleware.

The Services and StockDBMSAccess packages are, from the distributed system architect's perspective, where the real action is. Let's start by looking at a simple class design for the StockDBMSAccess package, illustrated in Figure 6.3.

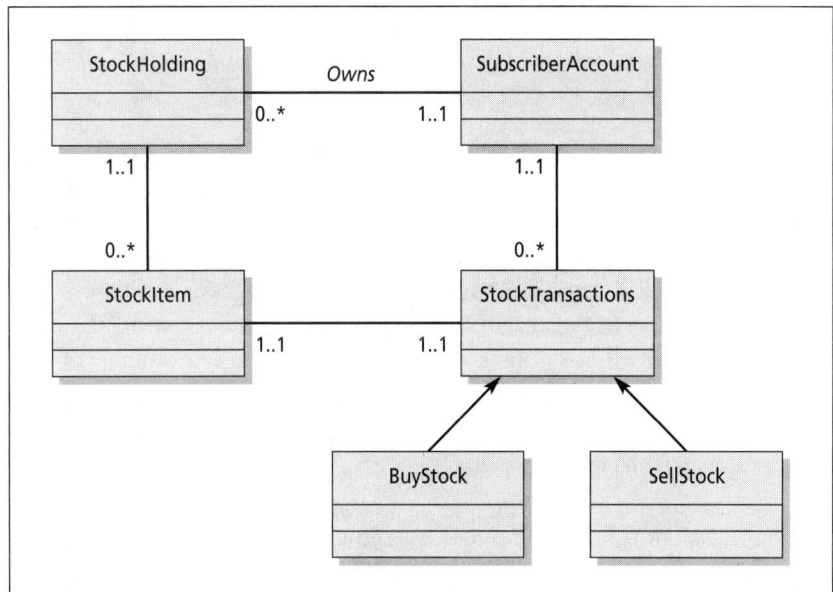

Classes for the StockDMBSAccess package Figure 6.3

The classes in this package represent the business objects, and come directly from the problem requirements. A brief explanation of the purpose of each class is below:

SubscriberAccount: This class holds all the information about a Stock-OnLine subscriber, such as name, address, credit limit and so on. There will be one object of this class for every subscriber.

StockHolding: When a subscriber purchases a stock, a StockHolding object will be created. It includes the type of stock, amount, purchase price and date, and stock reference number. There is a StockHolding object for every purchase that a subscriber makes using the system.

StockItem: For every stock that the Stock-OnLine system deals in, there is a single StockItem object. The StockItem class holds information about each stock including its stock code, current price, highest and lowest prices, and number of buy and sell transactions.

StockTransaction: Each time a subscriber wishes to buy new stock, or sell some of their stock, a StockTransaction object will be created. StockTransaction is an abstract class that holds all the information common to a sale or purchase business transaction. The two concrete sub-classes, BuyStock and SellStock, augment their parent class's attributes and behavior by providing the necessary functionality to carry out an actual transaction.

Additionally, each of the classes in the StockDBMSAccess package has the responsibility of storing and retrieving its attributes from a persistent storage medium. In the implementation, the persistent storage will be provided by a relational database system. Consequently, the classes will need to execute the SQL statements necessary to access the required database tables, and construct complete objects from the data. Hiding all the database access within a set of logically coherent classes in a package provides a level of abstraction that ensures the rest of the application is insulated from database technology changes and minor database structure changes.

If the classes in the *StockDBMSAccess* package encapsulate all the database access that the application requires, it would be possible to expose the class interfaces in IDL (CORBA or TIDL) and allow clients to call the functions directly. This is undoubtedly a strategy that many systems will use. It would require each client to begin a transaction, get object references to the business objects on a middle tier server, call the functions to carry out the transaction, and then attempt to commit the work. Logically this is a clean and attractive solution, well designed along object-oriented principles.

However, there is a real problem with this approach. It arises from ignoring address space boundaries in the design. A general design rule is to minimize calls to remote objects in a distributed system. This is because accessing remote functions is an order of magnitude slower than accessing functions in the same process address space. This is especially true when the remote object lives on a different host, as this involves sending data across the network. Ignoring the effects of remote accesses is likely to have some unfortunate and unexpected consequences on the performance of the system, especially as the load on the system increases.

This is a common design mistake made when designing distributed object-oriented systems. It is a classic case of pragmatics asserting themselves in the face of a clean, logically coherent design. I have seen many system designers frantically redesigning their system to eliminate unnecessary remote function calls in the face of unacceptable system performance. The solution is to place a service layer between the client and the business objects. Figure 6.4 shows the internal structure of the *Services* package and the relationships with the business objects in the *StockDBMSAccess*.

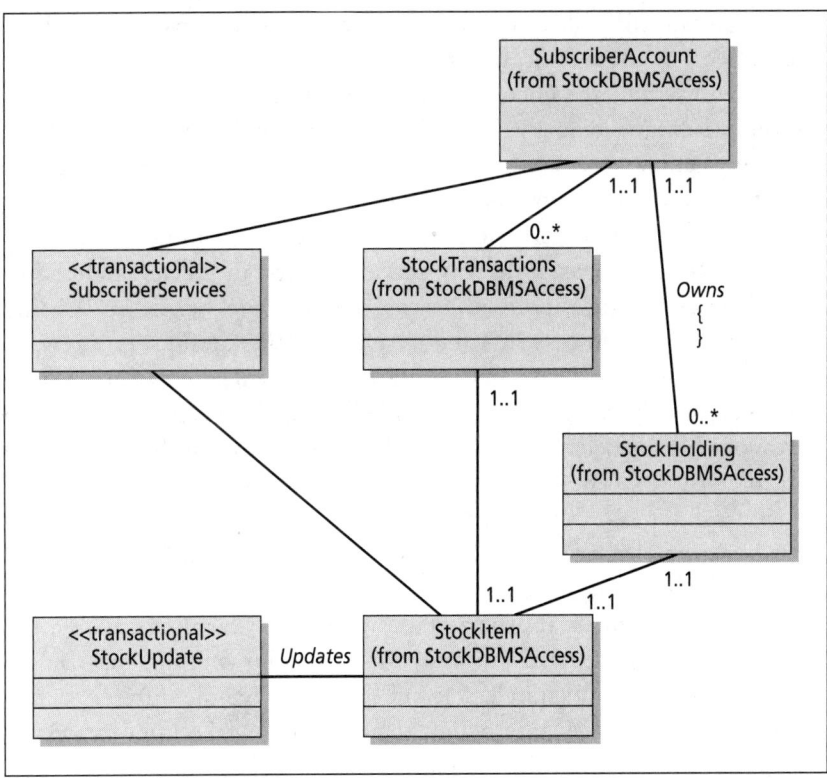

Classes for the Services and StockDBMSAccess package **Figure 6.4**

The two classes in the *Services* package are:

SubscriberServices: This class supports the transactions that subscribers to the system can perform. These include setting up an account, buying and selling stock, and getting a statement. *SubscriberServices* objects will accept requests from any subscriber client. This allows client requests to be load-balanced across SubscriberServices objects, and doesn't tie up individual objects for a particular subscriber for a long period of time.

StockUpdate: This class accepts requests from *StockValueFeedClients*. Again, any client can connect to any StockUpdate object to facilitate load-balancing across server objects.

The major implication of this design is that the classes in the *Services* package are stateless. They do not remember any client-related data between client invocations, as the server objects cannot know which client they are required to service next. The downside of this design is that it makes it difficult to cache data on a server for a particular client. This is because there is no guarantee that an object in the same server process will service the client's next request. Caching client-related data can reduce database accesses and hence improve overall performance. Like any caching strategy, however, it has complications, such as cache consistency and managing cache storage.

The advantages of stateless server objects are numerous. Load-balancing becomes easier, as any server object can service any client. Object life cycles are simplified. Server objects merely exist for the lifetime of the server process that they live in. When stateful server objects are created specifically to service a particular client, the server must be concerned with how long the server object exists. While the client should be responsible for deleting the server object when it is finished, there's no guarantee of this. The client may fail before it finishes all its work, or may not call the object's delete method. This means servers must be concerned with managing many objects on the server, and somehow ensure that objects the clients forget about are garbage collected.

In reality, the most appropriate design for a system depends on the application requirements. Some systems successfully mix the approaches, employing stateful and stateless server objects to handle different forms of user and sub-system interaction. Understanding the implications of each approach is what really matters.

DATABASE DESIGN

In a real implementation of an on-line stockbroking system, the database would need to store many details in order to track customers, their transactions, payments and so on. In the example that follows we'll use a simple database design containing the minimum tables and fields to allow the system to operate sensibly. This will avoid cluttering the example code with database-related code and API calls.

The examples will use Microsoft's SQL Server 6.5 as a resource manager to store the Stock-OnLine persistent data. There are four tables, which correspond roughly to the four main objects in the StockDBMSAccess package.

The SubAccount table holds basic information on a subscriber to the system. The SQL statement to create the table is as follows:

```
CREATE TABLE SubAccount (
   sub_accno int NOT NULL ,
   sub_name varchar (30) NOT NULL ,
   sub_address varchar (60) NOT NULL ,
   sub_credit int NULL
)
```

The primary key for `SubAccount` is the subscriber's account number, `sub_accno`. For simplicity, the name and address fields are not broken down into their constituent parts (e.g. street, city, name). The `sub_credit` field holds the amount of credit a subscriber has with the Stock-OnLine system. This field is credited and debited when the subscriber sells and buys stock respectively.

When a new account is created, the system needs to allocate a new, unique account number. One solution for this problem is to have a database table that contains a record holding the next account number to be used.[1] This value is read and used as the key for new accounts, and is then incremented and updated in the database as part of the transaction. The SQL statement to create the table is:

```
CREATE TABLE KeyTable (
   recID int NOT NULL ,
   nextVal int NOT NULL ,
)
```

The `StockHolding` table contains information on the amount of a given stock that a subscriber holds. The composite primary key is {`sub_accno, stock_id`}. The SQL statement to create the table is:

[1] Most databases also have a facility for providing this functionality directly, usually called something like an auto-increment field. While this would work in the Stock-OnLine example, the use of a separate table makes the transactions more heavyweight, which is useful when we look at their performance in Chapter 9.

```
CREATE TABLE StockHolding (
   sub_accno int NOT NULL ,
   stock_id int NOT NULL ,
   amount int NOT NULL
)
```

Information about each stock that a subscriber can trade through Stock-OnLine is held in the `StockItem` table. The primary key is `stock_id`, and the other fields represent the stock's trading code, company name, current value and recent high and low values. Updates to this table are triggered from the `StockValueFeedClient`. The SQL statement to create the table is as follows:

```
CREATE TABLE StockItem (
   stock_id int NOT NULL ,
   name varchar (30) NOT NULL ,
   code char (4) NOT NULL ,
   current_val float NOT NULL ,
   high_val float NULL ,
   low_val float NULL
)
```

Finally, there is the `StockTransaction` table, which contains information on each transaction that a subscriber performs. The primary key is `trans_id`, which is generated in a similar manner to new accounts through the use of a record in `KeyTable`. The `trans_type` is a code that represents a buy or a sell transaction. Other fields record the subscriber who performed the transaction, the stock item sold or purchased, the amount of stock involved, and the price and the date of the transaction. The SQL statement for this table is:

```
CREATE TABLE StockTransaction (
   trans_id int NOT NULL ,
   tran_type varchar (3) NOT NULL ,
   sub_accno int NOT NULL ,
   stock_id int NULL ,
   amount int NULL ,
   price float NULL ,
   date varchar (8) NULL
)
```

▶ SUMMARY

The Stock-OnLine system is a simple but representative example of many of the problems experienced in real distributed transaction systems. The outline design presented here is one of many possible alternatives. Designs for applications need to take into account the (usually conflicting) requirements for the solution, and steer a path that attempts to resolve the many forces involved. This isn't an easy task.

▶ FURTHER READING

Readers unfamiliar with the UML notation will find many excellent guides, such as:

Unified Modelling Language User Guide, Booch *et al.*, Addison-Wesley Longman, 1999.

Rational's WWW site is an excellent place to download information on the UML: see **www.rational.com**. Also, using the UML with Rational Rose is covered in:

Visual Modeling with Rational Rose and UML, Terry Quatrani, Addison-Wesley Longman, 1998.

Chapter 7

Building the case study with OrbixOTM

Overview	120
The Stock-OnLine CORBA interfaces	120
The subscriber client	123
The StockFeed client	141
The StockDBMSAccess server	142
Implementing the server object	150
Communicating with MS SQL Server	157
Summary	162

▶ OVERVIEW

This chapter will demonstrate how the Stock-OnLine case study can be constructed using OrbixOTM. We'll start by looking at the CORBA IDL needed to support the server interfaces, then the chapter will focus on the implementation of the client and server processes, interacting with the database and exploiting the OTM environment. The chapter includes code examples for the key parts of the system. Complete code listings, including the SQL Server database access functions, are downloadable from this book's WWW site, www.awl.com/cseng.

▶ THE STOCK-ONLINE CORBA INTERFACES

The Stock-OnLine UML design uses the objects in the Services package to implement the business logic of the system. Consequently, these objects must offer IDL interfaces to enable them to be accessed by client processes. In addition, these two objects have the *transactional* stereotype, indicating that clients must call their methods in the context of a transaction. With these points in mind, let's look at the IDL interface in detail.

First, note the whole interface is enclosed in an IDL module, namely:

```
module Stock {
   // interfaces are in here
}
```

IDL modules are analogous to C++ name spaces, and in fact map to name spaces in the generated C++ code. Their purpose is to qualify the name of individual IDL types and interfaces to help ensure the names do not clash with those defined in other IDL interfaces.[1] Use of modules is not mandatory, but it makes a lot of sense in object-oriented, distributed systems, as it reduces the chances of unexpected name clashes during the development and ongoing maintenance of the software.

Within the `Stock` module, there are two distinct parts. These are the data type definitions used in the interfaces, and the definition of the server object interfaces themselves. The data type definitions include useful constants and types, along with exceptions. These are shown below:

```
// exception definition for the interfaces
exception DBError { string reason; };

// Consts/Typedefs for zero terminated strings
const short subscriberName = 30 + 1;
typedef string<subscriberName> TSubscriberName;
const short subscriberAddr = 60 + 1;
```

[1] This is often spoken of as reducing the pollution of the global name space.

```
typedef string<subscriberAddr> TSubscriberAddr;
const short stockCode = 4 + 1;
typedef string<stockCode> TStockCode;

const short MAX_ENTRIES =20 ;
// structures
struct TSubscriber {
        TSubscriberNamesName   ;
        TSubscriberAddrsAddr   ;
        unsigned long   sCredit          ;
};

struct TStockHolding {
        unsigned long stock_id      ;
        unsigned long amount  ;
};

// Sequence Typedefs to handle return of Stock Holdings (0-20 possible)
typedef sequence<TStockHolding, MAX_ENTRIES> TStockHoldingSeq ;
```

The `DBError` exception can be thrown by any server function that accesses the database. It indicates that some failure has occurred between the database and the server object. This may be a network failure, a problem at the database such as a deadlock, or some XA-related error. The `reason` string allows the database access code to communicate a meaningful message back to the client to explain the cause of the error.

The structures `TSubscriber` and `TStockHolding` are used to pass subscriber and stock holding information respectively between client and server objects. CORBA 2.0 does not support passing objects by value, therefore objects must be mapped to IDL structures before they are passed as parameters between objects.

The `TStockHoldingSeq` sequence is used to return a collection of up to 20 `TStockHolding` structures to the client in response to a server object request. IDL sequences behave like one-dimensional arrays, and may be bounded or unbounded. `TStockHoldingSeq` is bounded to a maximum size of 20, but can be of variable size as determined at run-time. Unbounded sequences have no maximum size and are convenient in many applications. They do however pay a performance penalty for this convenience.

The `Stock` module contains two interfaces: these are defined below. Both are transactional, as they inherit from the OTS interface `CosTransactions::TransactionalObject`. This requires the callers of functions in these interfaces to start a transaction before the function is invoked.

```idl
interface SubscriberServices : CosTransactions::TransactionalObject {

    void CreateAccount ( in TSubscriber subscriberInfo,
                         out unsigned long subAccNo )
                    raises (DBError);

    void UpdateAccount (  in unsigned long subAccNo,
                          in unsigned long sCredit )
                    raises (DBError);

    void QueryStockValueByID ( in unsigned long stockID,
                          out float currentVal,
                          out float highVal,
                          out float lowVal )
                    raises (DBError);

    void QueryStockValueByCode (  in TStockCode stockCode,
                          out float currentVal,
                          out float highVal,
                          out float lowVal )
                    raises (DBError);

    void BuyStock( in unsigned long subAccNo,
                          in unsigned long stockID,
                          in unsigned long amount )
                    raises (DBError);

    void SellStock(in unsigned long subAccNo,
                          in unsigned long stockID,
                          in unsigned long amount )
                    raises (DBError);

    void GetHoldingStatement (    in unsigned long subAccNo,
                              in unsigned long startStID,
                              out TStockHoldingSeq stockList )
                    raises (DBError);
} ; //end SubscriberServices

interface StockUpdate : CosTransactions::TransactionalObject{

    void UpdateStockValue (    in unsigned long stockID,
                           in float newVal    )
                    raises (DBError);

} ; // end StockUpdate
```

The `SubscriberServices` interface has seven functions that enable subscribers to create and update accounts, get statements, query stock prices, and buy and sell stock. All the functions are stateless, meaning that any object that supports this interface can service any subscriber client. This promotes scalability and reliability. An implication however is that certain IDL functions require additional parameters to carry state information for the server. Examples of this are the subscriber account number, `subAccNo`, which is the first parameter for `SellStock`, `BuyStock` and `GetHoldingStatement`. If server objects maintained client state, this parameter would not be necessary.

The `StockUpdate` interface has a single function. The StockValueFeed client uses this to provide regular updates to the stock item values in the StockItem table. Again, this function is stateless, enabling multiple server objects to support this interface, with the load from multiple clients spread amongst the different server objects.

A further point to note is that all the functions in both interfaces return `void`. This of course does not give the client a way to determine the outcome of the call through a status return value. So how does the client determine the success or otherwise of the call? It's possible because the client starts the transaction before calling the server object function. For the call to succeed, the transaction must commit. If it fails for any reason, the client will be informed during the transaction resolution, when an appropriate exception will be thrown for the client to catch and process. Hence, transactional services do not need special return codes in this example. This will become clear when we examine the client code in more detail in the following sections.

▶ THE SUBSCRIBER CLIENT

The functionality of the subscriber client is to:

1. Initialize OrbixOTM on the client.

2. Bind to the OrbixNames name server and find a server object to utilize.

3. Accept requests from the subscriber and communicate with the server object to fulfill the requests.

Let's look at each of these in turn.

Initializing the client

The standard `main` function is where the client initializes the OTM. Note that, as shown in the code below, we're passing an argument to the subscriber client from the command line. The value of this argument, `argv [1]`, is the host name of the OrbixNames server. The client will use this to get a binding to a server object. An alternative method of passing the name server host to the client would be to set environment variables, or registry entries on Windows.

```
#include <OrbixOTS.hh>

int main(int argc, char* argv[])
{
  // check the number of parameters for the name server host name...
  // exit if its not there!
  if (argc != 2) {
    cerr << "usage: " << argv[0] << " <Name Server>" << endl;
    cerr << endl;
    exit(1);
  }

  OrbixOTS::Client_var ots; // Reference for OrbixOTS (client).
  // Initialise OrbixOTS (client side).
  ots = OrbixOTS::Client::IT_create();
  ots->init();

  // pass name server host name in argv[1]
  doSubClient(argv[1]) ;

  // OrbixOTS::Client::exit()ensures that any
  // outstanding transactions are cleaned up.
  ots->exit(0);

  return 0;
}
```

Client initialization simply requires the creation of an `OrbixOTS::Client` object. This is a pseudo object, and hence a reference to the object is initialized by calling the function `OrbixOTS::Client::IT_create()`. Client initialization is completed by calling the `init()` member function, which is responsible for creating the client-side OTS objects and services.

Once the OTS is started, the client calls the function `doSubClient()`, shown below, which implements the client-specific behavior. Note that when `doSubClient()` returns, the client terminates by calling `ots->exit(0)`. This ensures that all incomplete transactions are either committed or rolled back before the client terminates, and ensures all the OTS services are shut down in an orderly manner. The argument to `exit` takes one function which, in the traditional manner, is an integer value that is returned to the calling environment.

Finding server objects with OrbixNames

While there are a number of ways for clients to find, or bind to, server objects, the use of a naming service is by far the most appropriate for high performance TP systems. In the subscriber client, OrbixNames is used as the name server. As we'll see later, the servers publish information about their objects in OrbixNames, and clients retrieve object references to the server objects as and when required.

The Stock-OnLine system exploits the object groups feature of OrbixNames. Server objects bind their object reference to a well-known element in the OrbixNames name space. Many server object references can therefore be associated with a single name which is known by clients. The name space is arranged hierarchically, and within the root name context, the object group is known as StockRandom within the StockSubClient name context. This is illustrated by the screendump of the OrbixNames administration tool, as shown in Figure 7.1.

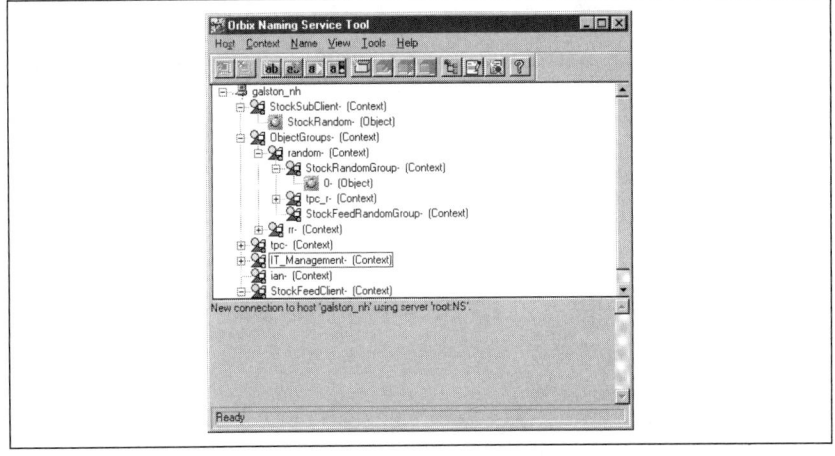

OrbixNames name space for the *StockRandom* object group **Figure 7.1**

The object group uses a random selection policy to hand out the object references in the group to clients. This gives a rudimentary form of load-balancing, by ensuring that server object references are distributed randomly amongst clients.

The subscriber client utilizes a simple class to abstract out some of the details of interacting with OrbixNames. The `nameServerClient` class, shown below, provides a service to initialize the name server, create the name for the object group, and to retrieve a `Stock::SubscriberServices` object reference from the object group.

```cpp
#include <NamingService.hh> // OrbixNames header
#include <stock.hh>         // Stock::SubscriberServices IDL header
class nameServerClient {
private:
    CosNaming::NamingContext_var rootCtx; // NS binding handle...
    char *                       nsHost; // OrbixNames host
public:
    nameServerClient( const char * ns) {

        if ( ns != NULL ) {
            nsHost = new char [ (strlen (ns)) +1 ] ;
            strcpy (nsHost, ns) ;
        } else {
            TRACE("nameServerClient::nameServerClient: OrbixNames
                server name not set") ;
            nsHost = NULL ;
        }
    }
    virtual nameServerClient::~nameServerClient() {
        if (nsHost != NULL )
            delete nsHost;
    }
    virtual ~nameServerClient() ;
    bool init() ;
    void new2LevelName ( CosNaming::Name_var& tmpName,
                         char * n1,
                         char * n2 );
    bool BindObject (    Stock::SubscriberServices_var& subObj,
                         CosNaming::Name_var tmpName) ;
};
```

The constructor and destructor (embedded in the class definition for presentation purposes) are simply responsible for allocating space for the OrbixNames host name, which is passed to the constructor. This is used in the `init()` function:

```
bool nameServerClient::init()
{
        if ( nsHost == NULL ) {
                TRACE("nameServerClient::nameServerClient: OrbixNames
                server name not set") ;
                return false;
        }
        // try to bind to the OrbixNames server
        try {
                TRACE("Binding to OrbixNames server") ;
                rootCtx = CosNaming::NamingContext::_bind("root:NS",
                                                            nsHost);
        } catch (CORBA::SystemException &sysEx) {
                cerr << "Unexpected system exception on Name Service
                        Access" << endl;
                cerr << &sysEx;
                return false;
        } catch(...) {
                cerr << "Unexpected/Unknown exception on Name Service
                        Access" << endl;
                return false;
        }
        return true;
}
```

After ensuring the OrbixNames host name is set, `init()` attempts to bind to the name server. For simplicity, the code uses the Orbix-specific `_bind()` mechanism to get an object reference to the OrbixNames root context. Two other methods are possible.[2] One, using the CORBA Initialization Service, provides a CORBA-compliant method for finding the initial name context. Another stores the IOR for the root naming context in a file, which is read at start-up and converted to an object reference using `CORBA::Orbix.string_to_object()`.

Once a reference for the root naming context is successfully obtained, the client can construct a name object for the object group. `nameServiceClient` provides a dedicated member function for this purpose, `new2LevelName()`:

[2] These are explained in more detail in the OrbixNames manual on page 18.

```
void nameServerClient::new2LevelName (CosNaming::Name_var& tmpName,
                                      char * n1,
                                      char * n2 )
{
    tmpName->length(2);
    tmpName[(CORBA::ULong)0].id = CORBA::string_dupl(n1);
    tmpName[(CORBA::ULong)0].kind = CORBA::string_dupl("");

    tmpName[(CORBA::ULong)1].id = CORBA::string_dupl(n2);
    tmpName[(CORBA::ULong)1].kind = CORBA::string_dupl("");
}
```

This function sets the components of a two-level `CosNaming::Name` object to equal the two string arguments passed to the function. `CosNaming::Name` objects are defined as a an unbounded sequence of `NameComponent` structures. The `CosNaming` IDL module defines this as:

```
module CosNaming {
    typedef string IString ;
    struct nameComponent {
        IString id;
        IString kind ;
    }
    typedef sequence<NameComponent> Name ;
    // lots of other things missing
}
```

The `id` member is the actual name entry in OrbixNames. The `kind` member is application-specific, allowing an arbitrary string to be associated with a name in the name space. This is not used in the above example.

Finally, once the name is initialized successfully, the client can attempt to bind to the object group specified by the name. This is performed by the `BindObject()` member function:

```
bool
nameServerClient::BindObject (  Stock::SubscriberServices_var& subObj,
                                CosNaming::Name_var tmpName )
{
    bool success = false;
    int retries = 5 ;

    while ( (!success) && (retries > 0) )
    {
```

```cpp
        try {
            //resolve name
            CORBA::Object_var objvar = rootCtx->resolve (
                                        tmpName) ;
          if (subObj =
                Stock::SubscriberServices::_narrow(objvar) ){
                TRACE ("Bind Via Name Service Successful");
                success = true;
          } else {
                TRACE ("Bind Via Name Service Failed - narrow
                        operation error");
                success = false ;
                retries--;
          }
        }catch (CosNaming::NamingContext::NotFound &ab){
            cerr <<"Could not resolve " <<
                    tmpName[(CORBA::ULong)0].id <<
                    tmpName[(CORBA::ULong)1].id << endl;
            success = false ;
            retries--;
        }
        catch (CosNaming::NamingContext::InvalidName &iv){
            cerr << "Invalid name on
                    CosNaming::NamingContext::bind" << endl;
          success = false ;
          retries--;
        }
        catch (CORBA::SystemException &sysEx) {
            cerr << "Unexpected system exception on Name Service
                    Access" << endl;
            cerr << &sysEx;
            success = false ;
            retries--;
        } catch(...) {
            cerr << "Unexpected/Unknown exception on Name
                Service Access" << endl;
            success = false ;
            retries--;
        }
    } // end while

    return success ;

}
```

BindObject() attempts to return a valid Stock:
:SubscriberServices_var reference by using the supplied name in
the OrbixNames resolve() operation. resolve() returns an object
reference for the object bound to the name supplied as a parameter. In
the case of an random object group, an object reference for a randomly
selected object in the group is returned. It is important that the client
code is oblivious to this difference. Also note that resolve() returns a
CORBA::Object_var. This must be narrowed explicitly, in this case
using Stock::SubscriberServices::_narrow() to obtain an
object reference of the correct type.

Since obtaining an object reference from OrbixNames is such a critical part of the client's operation, BindObject() will retry the
resolve() operation up to five times before passing an error back to
the calling client. This should help to ensure any transient network errors
do not become the concern of the mainline client code.

The client code which uses the nameServerClient object resides in
the doSubClient() function, which is called from main(). The first
part of this function is shown below:

```
void doSubClient (char * nsHost)
{
    TRACE ("doSubClient Entry");
    int i;
    // Get a Reference to the OTS Current object
    CosTransactions::Current_var current;
    current = CosTransactions::Current::IT_create();

    // Set timeout value for new transactions to be 20 seconds.
    current->set_timeout(20);

    // bind to OrbixNames..create and init the client object
    nameServerClient nsClient(nsHost);
    Stock::SubscriberServices_var subObj;
    CosNaming::Name_var tmpName = new CosNaming::Name(2);
    if ( nsClient.init() ) {
        // construct the name of the object group to bind to
        nsClient.new2LevelName ( tmpName, "StockSubClient",
                                          "StockRandom");
        // get an initial object binding
        if ( nsClient.BindObject( subObj, tmpName ) == false ) {
            TRACE ("doSubClient: Can"t bind to object group") ;
```

```
            exit (1);
        }
    } else {
        TRACE ("doSubClient: nameServerClient::Init() failed") ;
        exit (1);
    }
    // more to come….
}
```

doSubClient() first gets a reference to the CosTransactions::Current object, which represents the transactional context for the client. The client will use this object to create and control the outcome of transactions. As it is a pseudo-object, it is initialized using its IT_create() function. An important part of the initialization is to set the time-out period for transactions, using the set_timeout(int) member function. The integer parameter represents the time a client will wait for a transaction to complete before the client explicitly aborts the transaction. In this example, we've set it to 20 seconds.

Next, doSubClient() creates a nameServerClient object, nsClient, and a Stock::SubscriberServices_var[3] object that will be initialized by an object reference obtained from Orbix Names. The services of nsClient are then used to bind to OrbixNames, create the Name for the object group, and finally obtain a server object reference, subObj. This completes the initialization of the client.

Performing transactions

doSubClient() uses a helper class, subCommand, to encapsulate all transaction-specific user interactions and accesses to the server objects. As illustrated below, subcommand has a member function for each user transaction, as well as a method to display a menu to enable users to select program options.

[3] Orbix object references with _var after their type name behave syntactically like ordinary object pointers, but Orbix will ensure that the object associated with the _var is automatically destroyed when it goes out of scope. In this sense, they behave like smart pointers, relieving the programmer of some of the burden of memory management.

```
#include <stock.hh>

class subCommand {
public:
    void CreateAccount ( Stock::SubscriberServices_var subObject) ;
    void UpdateAccount ( Stock::SubscriberServices_var subObject) ;
    void QueryStockValueByID (    Stock::SubscriberServices_var
                           subObject ) ;
```

```cpp
    void QueryStockValueByCode (   Stock::SubscriberServices_var
                                     subObject) ;

    void BuyStock(Stock::SubscriberServices_var      subObject ) ;

    void SellStock(Stock::SubscriberServices_var     subObject ) ;

    void GetHoldingStatement (Stock::SubscriberServices_var
                                     subObject ) ;

    subCommand (CosTransactions::Current_var tran,
                unsigned long accNo ) ;

    void getMenuSelection (char & choice ) ;
private:
    CosTransactions::Current_var   m_tran ;
    unsigned long subAccNo ;
} ;
```

The constructor for `subCommand` takes the client's transactional context and the subscriber's account number as parameters. The individual member functions of the `subCommand` class start and end transactions, using the private data member `m_tran`, which is initialized in the constructor. The account number is entered by the subscriber and stored in the class for subsequent use when calling server functions.

Note also that the `subCommand` member functions that drive transactions are passed the reference to the transactional server object (i.e. `Stock::SubscriberServices_var`) they must use in the transaction. `subCommand` is deliberately oblivious of the `nameServerClient` class, simplifying its design. Of course, there's no reason why `subCommand` should expect to always receive a reference to the same server object! In fact, the actual server object reference passed is determined by the subscriber client's load balancing policy. As we'll see, this is decided by the calling code of the `subCommand` object, namely `doSubClient()`.

The remainder of the `doSubClient()` function is included below. First, it prompts the subscriber for their account number and creates a `subCommand` object. It then enters a loop that interacts with the user to get a transaction selection (i.e. `cmd.getMenuSelection()`), and calls the associated `subCommand` member function for the selected transaction.

```cpp
void doSubClient (char * nsHost)
//This is the continuation of doSubClient. The previous section (shown
//above) depicted initialization of transaction/server object.
//next…read on!
    // create the command object to interact with user..
    unsigned long accNo ;
    cout << "Enter Account No (or zero for a new account):" << endl ;
    cin >> accNo;
    subCommand cmd ( current, accNo) ;

    bool finished = 0;
    while (! finished) {

        // Output menu.
        char choice ;
        cmd.getMenuSelection (choice) ;

        if (cin.eof()) {
         finished = true;
         continue;
        }
        cout << endl;

        switch (tolower(choice)) {
            case 'c':
              cmd.CreateAccount ( subObj ) ;
              break;
            case 'u':
              cmd.UpdateAccount ( subObj ) ;
              break;
            case 'i':
              if ( !nsClient.BindObject( subObj, tmpName )) {
                  TRACE ("doSubClient: Bind to object group
                          failed, using old object reference") ;
              }
              cmd.QueryStockValueByID ( subObj ) ;
              break;
            case 'q':
              if ( !nsClient.BindObject( subObj, tmpName )) {
                  TRACE ("doSubClient: Bind to object group
                          failed, using old object reference") ;
```

```
                    }
                    cmd.QueryStockValueByCode ( subObj ) ;
                    break;
                case 'b':
                    cmd.BuyStock ( subObj ) ;
                    break;
                case 's':
                    cmd.SellStock ( subObj ) ;
                    break;
                case 'g':
                    cmd.GetHoldingStatement ( subObj ) ;
                    break;
                case 'e':
                    finished = true;
                    break;
                default :
                        break ;
            } // end switch
        }   // end while
        TRACE ("doSubClient Exit" ) ;
}
```

Rudimentary load-balancing is initiated when the user selects a `Query` option (either by stock ID or code). When this occurs, the client attempts to get a new binding from OrbixNames. As the client resolves to a random object group, it is highly likely that it will get an object reference to a different server object. As all clients will periodically get new, randomly selected object references, this scheme provides a dynamic distribution of client load across server objects.

Of course, much more complex load-balancing schemes can be constructed using the naming service. As always with distributed applications, these should be carefully designed to meet the application's needs. A reasonable trade-off between complexity and performance would be to initialize a small cache of server object references from the name server at client start-up. The client can then switch between the cache entries to execute transactions. This scheme incurs a start-up overhead that is proportional to the number of entries in the cache. However, once the cache is initialized, no additional overheads are incurred when executing transactions.

The member functions of `subCommand` are where the calls to the server objects take place. As many of these have similar behavior, not all are shown here. The `subCommand::CreateAccount` member serves as an example to demonstrate this commonality. Its basic structure, which is followed by all `subcommand` member functions, is as follows:

1. Declare the IDL data items needed to communicate with the server.

2. Get the necessary information from the user and initialize the IDL data items.

3. Start the transaction.

4. Make the appropriate call to the server object.

5. Attempt to commit the transaction, handling any exceptions that are thrown.

In `CreateAccount`, a `Stock::TSubscriber` structure must be initialized and passed to the server object. Two of the members of this structure are character strings, `sName` and `sAddr`. These map to `String_mgr` types in the C++ generated by the IDL compiler, as shown below:

```
struct IT_DECLSPEC_stock TSubscriber {
    CORBA::String_mgr sName;
    CORBA::String_mgr sAddr;
    CORBA::ULong sCredit;
    // Generated member functions omitted
  };
```

`String_mgr` objects behave very like `String_var` objects. They wrap a pointer to a character string and provide automatic reclamation of the memory associated with the string when they go out of scope. The difference is that the `String_mgr` default constructor initializes the managed pointer to the empty string, not a NULL pointer as in `String_var`. The reason for this is that it is illegal to pass a NULL pointer across an IDL interface. As `String_mgr` objects initialize their managed pointer to a valid (albeit empty) string, they can be passed to IDL objects as parameters without explicit initialization.

In `CreateAccount`, we need to set `sName` and `sAddr` to data entered by the user. Hence the two members are explicitly initialized with dynamically allocated strings large enough to hold the user's details. These are then set during the interactions with the user. And as

String_mgr objects manage their associated data, there is no need to explicitly free this memory later in the function.

```cpp
void subCommand::CreateAccount (Stock::SubscriberServices_var
                                subObject )
{
    Stock::TSubscriber subInfo ;
    subInfo.sName = CORBA::string_alloc(Stock::subscriberName ) ;
    subInfo.sAddr = CORBA::string_alloc(Stock::subscriberAddr ) ;

    // get account details from the user
    cout << "Create Accout" << endl ;
    cout << "Enter Account Name (max 30 chars): " ;
    cin.ignore(256, '\n');
    cin.getline(subInfo.sName, Stock::subscriberName);
    cout << "Enter Address (max 60 chars): " ;
    cin.getline(subInfo.sAddr, Stock::subscriberAddr);
    cout << "Enter Requested Credit Limit: " ;
    cin >> subInfo.sCredit ;

    try {
        m_tran->begin() ;          // start transaction
        subObject->CreateAccount (subInfo, subAccNo ) ;
        m_tran->commit(TRUE);
    } catch (CORBA::TRANSACTION_ROLLEDBACK) {
        cerr << " OTS rolledback transaction rolledback!" << endl;
        subAccNo = 0;
    } catch (const Stock::DBError ex) {
        cerr << " (Database error occured)" << endl;
        cerr << " " << ex.reason << endl;
        // Rollback the transaction.
        m_tran->rollback();
        subAccNo = 0;
    } catch (CORBA::SystemException &ex) {
        cerr << " (system exception - transaction failed)" << endl;
        cerr << " " << ex << endl;
        // Rollback the transaction.
        m_tran->rollback();
        subAccNo = 0;
```

```
        } catch (CORBA::UserException &ex) {
            cerr << "(user exception - transaction failed)" << endl;
            cerr << " " << ex << endl;
            // Rollback the transaction.
            m_tran->rollback();
            subAccNo = 0;
        } catch (...) {
            cerr << "(unknown exception - transaction failed)" << endl;
            // Rollback the transaction.
            m_tran->rollback();
            subAccNo = 0;
    }
        cout << "Create Account Succeeded: Account Number is: " <<
                     subAccNo << endl ;
} //end CreateAccount
```

Once `CreateAccount` has the user's name, address and requested credit limit, it attempts to perform the transaction. The local `m_tran` object is used to create the transactional context, and a call to the server object's `CreateAccount` service is made. As with any remote function invocation, this should take place within a `try-catch` block so that exceptions can be caught. In transactional systems, the client must be able to catch exceptions thrown by the transaction manager, as well as normal application and ORB exceptions.

Specifically, the transaction manager can throw a `CORBA::TRANS-ACTION_ROLLEDBACK` exception. This typically occurs when the transaction originator requests a commit, and one of the participants has marked the transaction for rollback. In addition, server applications will usually define at least one exception that is thrown when resource manager access problems occur. This might be because the connection to the database has been lost, or perhaps a SQL deadlock has occurred due to locking problems. In Stock-OnLine, this role is played by the `Stock::DBError` exception. The server can set an associated error string that is passed along with a `DBError` exception to identify the cause of the problem to the client.

Assuming no system or application exceptions are raised during the call to the server object, the client attempts to commit the transaction. This signals the transaction manager to drive the two-phase commit protocol and complete the transaction. Note that should any other exceptions be raised during this whole process, the client catches them and explicitly rolls back the transaction, ensuring the transaction completes. The returned subscriber's account number, `subAccNo`, is also reset to zero to ensure consistency because, if the transaction has failed after the server object call returns, no database record will have been created for the new subscriber.

Nearly all the remaining `subCommand` class member functions follow a similar pattern of behavior to `CreateAccount`. Consequently, these won't be discussed here, and the reader is referred to the example code on the website. The exception is `GetHoldingStatement()`, which is somewhat more interesting and, for this reason, is described below to conclude the presentation of the subscriber client.

`GetHoldingStatement()` is an example of what is commonly known as a *scrolling* transaction. The term scrolling is used here to describe a transaction that can return a potentially long list of data items, in this case a sequence of objects. If a subscriber has 200 different stock holdings, this transaction could potentially return 200 `TStockHolding` objects, one for each stock holding. As 200 items is more than could be displayed on a screen for the user at any one time, there are two main design options for such transactions, namely:

1. Return all selected items for the transaction in one hit, regardless of whether the user wants all the results.

2. Use a transaction to get one page of results at a time, allowing the user to get more pages of results on demand by submitting new transaction requests.

As always, both approaches have their advantages and disadvantages. The first requires only a single remote server and database access. It however may read and return considerably more data than the user actually needs. This is especially true if the transaction can potentially return a large result set, perhaps thousands of records. This means the transaction may take a long time to display the first page, but subsequent pages will be fast as the data already resides at the client. The second is efficient in terms of returning a predictable amount of data (and response time) for each transaction. It does however require one remote server and database access for each page requested by the user. If it takes 15 pages to find what the user wants, this can be expensive as it takes 15 transactions and database accesses.

Each solution is usually applicable to different types of applications, and should be adopted where appropriate. In addition, if state is maintained at the server objects, it's possible to combine the two approaches. The first transaction requests the server object to select all results from the database, but only return the first page. The server object caches the remaining results, and returns these one page at a time to the client as and when requested. This solution reduces the number of database accesses to one, and speeds up subsequent page retrieval as the results are in memory at the server. It also ensures that network traffic is minimized as only results that the user requests are sent to the client. Like most stateful server approaches, this solution is also more complex. Who tells the server to flush the cache? We can't rely on the client as it may crash, or the user may go for a cup of coffee and not return for an hour. Potential solutions are numerous, and left as an exercise to the reader!

In Stock-OnLine, as we have stateless servers, we'll adopt the 'one page at a time' solution. This would be justified in a real application if the number of results returned was typically small, seldom extending over a page. The subCommand::GetHoldingStatement() function demonstrates the implemention. It enters a loop and submits a transaction in each loop iteration. The loop terminates when the user selects the 'no' option.

Each transaction returns up to Stock::MAX_ENTRIES in a sequence of TStockHolding objects. The client iterates through the sequence, displaying the results for the user. The transaction inputs are the user's account number and a stock ID, startStID. The purpose of startStID is to inform the server object where to start its query in the database table. Initially startStID is set to zero. This tells the server to return the first page of results with stock ID greater than 0. After the transaction commits, if a full page has been returned, the clients sets startStID to the value of the stock ID in the last returned TStockHolding object. Assuming the user wishes to get another page of results, the new value of startStID is passed to the server, which starts retrieving results with values greater than startStID.

```
void subCommand::GetHoldingStatement (Stock::SubscriberServices_var
                                                    subObject )
{
        char choice = 'y';
        unsigned long startStID = 0;
        int i;
```

```cpp
            cout << "STATEMENT LISTING" << endl;
    while ( tolower(choice) == 'y' ) {
    Stock::TStockHoldingSeq * list = NULL ;
    try {
            m_tran->begin() ;
            subObject->GetHoldingStatement (subAccNo, startStID,
                                                            list ) ;
            m_tran->commit(TRUE);
            cout << "Stock ID \t " << "Amount" << endl ;
            cout << "---------------------------" << endl ;

            for (i = 0 ; i < list->length() ; i++ ) {
                    cout << (*list)[i].stock_id << "\t\t" <<
                            (*list) [i].amount << endl ;
            }
            if (list->length() == Stock::MAX_ENTRIES ) {
                    // remember last key returned
                    startStID = (*list) [i].stock_id ;
                    cout << "Next Page? ((y/n)" << endl ;
                    cin >> choice ;
            } else {
                    choice = 'n';
            }

            if ( list != NULL ) delete list ;

      } catch (CORBA::TRANSACTION_ROLLEDBACK) {
            cerr << " OTS rollbacked (transaction rolledback)!"
                    << endl;
            choice = 'n';
      } catch (const Stock::DBError ex) {
            cerr << " (database error)" << endl;
            cerr << " " << ex.reason << endl;
            // Rollback the transaction.
            m_tran->rollback();
            choice = 'n';
      } catch (CORBA::SystemException &ex) {
            cerr << " (system exception)" << endl;
            cerr << " " << ex << endl;
            // Rollback the transaction.
            m_tran->rollback();
```

```
                choice = 'n';
        } catch (CORBA::UserException &ex) {
            cerr << "(user exception)" << endl;
            cerr << " " << ex << endl;
            // Rollback the transaction.
            m_tran->rollback();
            choice = 'n';
        catch (...) {
            cerr << " (unknown exception)" << endl;
            // Rollback the transaction.
            m_tran->rollback();
            choice = 'n';
        }
    }// end while
} // end GetHoldingStatement
```

This is obviously a simple client implementation. The major simplification is that it does not support scrolling back in the list to a previous page of results. A serious implementation would support this, most likely by caching results in the client. Also note that the exception handling code for `subCommand::GetHoldingStatement()` is slightly more complex. It requires exceptions to rollback the transaction and set the loop exit condition, returning the user to the main menu.

▶ THE STOCKFEED CLIENT

It probably comes as no surprise that the StockFeed client has a very similar structure to the subscriber client. The simple `StockUpdate` interface in the `Stock` module, namely:

```
interface StockUpdate : CosTransactions::TransactionalObject{

    void UpdateStockValue   ( in unsigned long stockID,
                              in float newVal        )
                              raises (DBError);
} ; // end StockUpdate
```

supports the functionality the StockFeed client needs. StockFeed repeatedly receives updates on new stock prices, binds to server objects, creates a transaction and submits the update to the server. The client simulates the periodic arrival of new stock values, and makes calls to server objects. As there's very little new in StockFeed to discuss, let's move on to the server.

▶ *THE STOCKDBMSACCESS SERVER*

The StockDBMSAccess server supports the IDL interfaces defined in the `Stock` module. During its initialization, it establishes the connection with the stock database, initializes its transaction log files, and creates the server objects to respond to client requests. First, let's look at the initialization code before delving into the processing of client transactions.

Server initialization

The server start-up code makes up the `main()` function. Let's break down `main()` to examine what it does.

First, the server processes its command line and initializes the OTS. The code for this is as follows:

```
const int MAXSERVERS = 50 ; // limit of server replicas on one host
int main(int argc, char **argv)
{
   char serverName[50] ;

   if ( (!argv[1]) || ( atoi(argv[1]) > MAXSERVERS ) || (argc < 3)){
        cerr << "Usage : server <N> <Name Server Host>" << endl ;
        cerr << "Where <N> is the unique server instance on
                   this host" << endl ;
        cerr <<     " <Name Server Host> is host name for
                   Orbix Names" << endl ;
        exit (1) ;
   }

   OrbixOTS::Server_var ots = OrbixOTS::Server::IT_create();

   // Set the server name, log device, restart file and mirror
   // restart file attributes of the OrbixOTS server object.

   sprintf (serverName, "STOCK_%s", argv[1] );
   char logName[50], resName[50], mirrorName[50] ;
   sprintf (logName, "ots%s.log", argv[1] );
   sprintf (resName, "ots%s.r1", argv[1] );
   sprintf (mirrorName, "ots%s.r2", argv[1] );

   ots->serverName(serverName);
   ots->logDevice(logName);
   ots->restartFile(resName);
```

```
ots->mirrorRestartFile(mirrorName);

OrbixManagement om;
om.set_property ( " APPLICATION ", serverName) ;
// more code in this function - see below…
```

The server command line contains two arguments. These represent the unique server identifier, which is an integer between zero and `MAXSERVERS`,[4] and the host name of the OrbixNames server. In Orbix, each server running on a host must have a unique name so that it can be registered with the Orbix daemon. In order to execute the same Orbix server process multiple times on the same host, there must be some way of each server process having a unique name, despite sharing the same executable code. This is achieved by taking the unique integer from the command line and appending it to a string of `"STOCK_"`, giving each server its own name such as `STOCK_0`, `STOCK_1`, and so on. This string is then passed to Orbix to identify the running process to the Orbix daemon. Administratively, the Orbix `putit` command must be used to register the server on each host, i.e.

[4] *A better and more flexible solution would be to use an environment variable instead of a constant. A constant is used here for simplicity and brevity.*

```
putit STOCK_0 -persistent
putit STOCK_1 -persistent
```

Note the use of the `-persistent` option to register the processes with the Orbix daemon. This tells the daemon that the server process will be started manually, and should not be activated automatically when a call to the server's object is detected. Although automatic activation of server processes is common in CORBA systems, it is not a good idea in a high performance transaction processing system. This is because of the overhead of starting up a server, including initializing its transaction log and connecting to resource managers. The initialization can often take several seconds, which is far too long for most applications. Consequently, servers are started manually, usually in a script, and do not time-out and terminate after periods of inactivity.

Next the server creates a pseudo-object of type `OrbixOTS::Server`. This object encapsulates many of the services needed for a CORBA OTS process, and there must be one such object in each OTS server process. Typically, from the programmer's perspective, the OTS server object is used to set the server's name for Orbix, and specify the name and location of the server's transaction log file and its restart files. This usage is shown in the above code. The unique server name, constructed from the command line argument, is passed to the `serverName()` member function. In a similar fashion, a unique transaction log and restart file names are constructed, and these are passed to the `logDevice()`, `restartFile()` and `mirrorRestartFile()` member functions respectively.

OrbixOTM provides a management tool, OrbixManager, which can be used to monitor server applications. To become a *managed* server, an application must simply create an object of type `OrbixManagement`. Optionally, the server application can set named properties that can be viewed through OrbixManager. In Stock-OnLine, the system administrator sets the APPLICATION property to the server's unique name for easy identification.

Configuring OrbixManager requires the deployment of a management service daemon, *orbixms*. This daemon manages the Orbix processes running on a set of machines that comprise a management domain. OrbixNames is used by the management service to store information on the location of the managed applications in a domain. Hence OrbixManager requires the use and configuration of OrbixNames, or some compatible CORBA naming service implementation.

OrbixManager contains a useful list of features available through its GUI. These include:

- displaying all the hosts and servers in a domain;
- displaying which servers are alive, and which have failed unexpectedly;
- showing which clients are connected to a server; and
- displaying counts of the request load at a server, throughput, and CPU time used.

While a useful tool, OrbixManagers provide no mechanisms for resolving in-doubt transactions, and automatically restarting and recovering failed servers. These have to be carried out using scripts and tools such as `otsadmin`, which has an extensive range of commands for managing server activity.

Continuing with the server's `main()` function, it must next initialize a connection to the resource manager to be used. In Stock-Online, this will be Microsoft's SQL Server. The server uses the function `db_init()` to establish the database connection. The precise operation of this function is explained in detail in the later section on accessing SQL Server. At this stage, it is sufficient to assume that if successful, `db_init()` will establish a useable database connection.

```
// Continuation of server main() function..
// Initialise the database connection
char* status = db_init();
if (status != DB_SUCCESS) {
    cerr << "Error initialising SQL Server database" << endl;
    cerr << status << endl;
    ots->exit(1);
}
```

Before the server can coordinate transactions with the database, SQL Server must be registered as an XA resource manager with the transaction service. Registering an XA resource manager requires the creation of database-specific open and close strings. These pass information to the database about the TP monitor, and often other details such as the account to use to establish a connection. Finding the format of the open and close strings is not always easy. The TP monitor documentation usually refers to the database documentation, and the database documentation often refers straight back to the TP monitor documentation! The most reliable sources are the examples that accompany the TP monitor product. These will show the format of the open and close strings in the code, and also specify any additional database configuration needed to establish XA communications.

With SQL Server, the open and close strings are the same, and have the format:

`Tm=TPMonitorName, RmRecoveryGuid=uuid`

The interesting part here is the `RMRecoveryGuid`. This requires a unique universal identifier (uuid) string, which can be used to uniquely identify each server process with the database. A uuid can be created using the `uuidgen` utility that is part of Windows NT. If the server process fails unexpectedly during a transaction, when it restarts it presents the uuid to database so that they can coordinate recovery and complete any in-flight transactions.

In this example, a table of uuids is created, called `uuidTable`. The server uses its identifier from the command line (`argv [1]`) to index in to this table for a uuid to use. It then constructs the open string in the correct format using `sprintf`, and uses the `ots` object's member function `register_xa_rm` to correctly establish the XA connection.

```
// Continuation of server main() function..

char openString[256];
char *recoveryGuid = 0;

// A unique RecoveryGuid is needed for each instance of an XA server on
// the system.

recovery_uuid = uuidTable[ atoi(argv[1]) ] ;
sprintf(openString, "Tm=OrbixOTS, RmRecoveryGuid=%s", recovery_uuid)

// Register SQL Server as an XA resource manager with OrbixOTS.
CORBA::Long rm_id = ots->register_xa_rm(&msqlsrvxa1, openString,
                                                    openString, 0);

// Initialise the OrbixOTS server object. Recovery from a failure will
// be performed here

ots->init();

// more code in this function - see below…
```

The variable `msqlsrvxa1` represents the XA switch that defines the function pointer table for XA routines in the SQL Server XA library. It is defined as:

```
extern "C" struct xa_switch_t msqlsrvxa1;
```

This structure is provided by SQL Server in an object file, which must be linked into the application at build time.

Once the XA resources have been registered, initialization of the transaction service can commence by calling the `init()` member function. At this stage, if the server has failed and is recovering, the OTS will communicate with the database to resolve any in-doubt transactions.

Creating the server object

Before the server can accept client requests, it must create a server object that implements the transaction defined in the IDL. This is done simply by creating an object of type `Stock::SubscriberServices_i`. This class will be examined in more detail later in this chapter. Note however the use of the Orbix-generated `Stock::SubscriberServices_var` class to manage the server object. Objects of this type will ensure that the destructor or the server object is called automatically when it goes out of scope, simplifying memory management.

```
// Continuation of server main() function..
// Create an instance of Stock::SubscriberServices_i
Stock::SubscriberServices_var
     subServer = new Stock::SubscriberServices_i;
```

After creating the server object, its object reference must be advertised in OrbixNames so that clients can connect to it. The `nameServerClient` class is again used for this purpose. The server connects to OrbixNames and creates the name object for the object group it will use. It then calls the member function `addObjectReference` to store the object reference to the object group.

```
 // Bind to OrbixNames
nameServerClient ns (argv[2] ) ;

ns.init() ;

// Construct a Name....
CosNaming::Name_var tmpName;
tmpName = new CosNaming::Name(2);
ns.new2LevelName ( tmpName, "StockSubClient", "rgroups" ) ;

bool result;
if ((result = ns.addObjectReference
                  ( subServer,tmpName, argv[1] ) ) != true ) {
    TRACE ("Name Server Error Encountered");
    exit (1);
}
```

`addObjectReference` is shown below. It first resolves the provided name `tmpName` to the object group in the name server. It then attempts to remove any existing object references with the same member identifier as it wishes to register. Member identifiers must be unique in an object group. This ensures that any old references are cleaned up before the new one is added. If there is no matching object reference to remove, the exception is caught, and the new object reference is added anyway.

```cpp
bool nameServerClient::addObjectReference (
            Stock::SubscriberServices_var& subObj,
            CosNaming::Name_var tmpName, char * id )
{
    try {
        CORBA::Object_ptr tmp =
                    rootCtx->resolve_object_group(tmpName);
        LoadBalancing::ObjectGroup_var og =
        LoadBalancing::ObjectGroup::_narrow(tmp);
        LoadBalancing::member mem;
        mem.obj = CORBA::Object::_duplicate(subObj);
        mem.id = CORBA::string_dupl(id);

        try {
            og->removeMember( mem.id ) ;
        } catch (LoadBalancing::no_such_member) {
            cerr << " No member to remove " << endl ;
        } catch (...) {
            cerr <<"Unknown error on remove, add anyway" << endl;
        }
        og->addMember(mem);
        return true ;
    } catch (LoadBalancing::duplicate_member) {
        cerr << "Already a member of " << tmpName << endl;
        cerr << "Ignoring..." << endl;
    } catch (CosNaming::NamingContext::NotFound &ex) {
        cerr << &ex ;
    } catch (CosNaming::NamingContext::CannotProceed &ex) {
        cerr << &ex;
    } catch (CosNaming::NamingContext::InvalidName &ex) {
        cerr << &ex;
    } catch (CosNaming::NamingContext::AlreadyBound &ex) {
        cerr << &ex;
    } catch (CORBA::SystemException &sysEx) {
        cout << &sysEx;
    } catch(...) {
        cerr << "Unknown exception" << endl;
    }
    return false ;
}
```

Completing server initialization

Finally, the server process enters the Orbix message loop by calling the `impl_is_ready()` member of the `ots` object. This function takes one parameter, called the `ConcurrencyMode`. The two most common values for `ConcurrencyMode` are:

concurrent: This allows the server process to handle many concurrent transactions. The `ots` object creates a thread pool,[5] and incoming transactions are passed to the threads to execute in parallel.

SerializeRequestsAndTransactions: This effectively serializes access to the server process, which behaves as if it has only one thread available for client applications. It is the default value.

[5] Default thread pool size is 5, and can be configured by setting the environment variable ENCINA_TPOOL_SIZE.

The decision on which to use depends on two factors. First, if the XA resource managers used by the process have thread-safe implementations of their XA library, then the `concurrent` option can be used safely. If the XA libraries are not thread-safe, then there's no choice. The server must be effectively single-threaded and serialize transactions from clients. If transactions are not serialized, the server will fail.

Most recent versions of resource managers such as Oracle, SQL Server and MQSeries are thread-safe. This means the `concurrent` option is possible. However it does introduce another requirement on the software, namely that the application server objects must also be thread-safe. Any global data or data members that maintain state must be protected against concurrent access using appropriate locking mechanisms. In objects that maintain significant state, this can make the code considerably more complex and expensive to write and maintain. On the other hand, if the objects have no state, and only manipulate parameters and local data, then no code changes are needed for thread-safety.

In general, multi-threaded server processes will perform better than many replicated single-threaded processes. The lightweight nature of threads leads to faster context switching times and more efficient use of system resources. It also means that there are fewer processes to manage.

In this example, the SQL Server XA library is thread-safe, and hence either value for `ConcurrencyMode` is possible. In order to illustrate the differences in implementations, with Orbix the example will use the default `SerializeRequestsAndTransactions` as below, and in the next chapter, multi-threaded servers will be constructed.

```
// Continuation of server main() function..
try {
    cout << "main: waiting for requests" << endl ;

    // Wait for requests. Default serialization mode is
    // serializeRequestsAndTransactions which only allows a single
    // transaction to be active in the server at any one time.

    ots->impl_is_ready();

} catch (const CORBA::SystemException &sysEx) {
    cerr << "Unexpected system exception" << endl;
    cerr << sysEx << endl;
    ots->exit(1);

} catch (...) {
    cerr << "Unknown Exception raised in impl_is_ready" << endl;
    ots->exit(1);
}
```

▶ IMPLEMENTING THE SERVER OBJECT

Client transaction requests are handled by implementations of the server object functions defined in the IDL interface. The Orbix IDL compiler generates the code necessary to accept client requests and marshall parameters at the server process. The IDL compiler also generates a class definition for a class called `SubscriberServicesBOAImpl`.[6] This class has a set of C++ abstract member functions that correspond to the functional interface defined in the IDL interface. In order to implement the desired behavior for server objects, we simply have to inherit from `SubscriberServicesBOAImpl` and add the code to carry out the transactions. When client requests arrive at the server, the ORB transparently passes the requests on to the programmer defined functions to deal with.

In StockOnLine, the server object class is known as `SubscriberServices_i`, and its C++ class definition is as follows:

[6] BOA stands for Basic Object Adapter. See the CORBA specification for more details on this.

```
namespace Stock {

class IT_DECLSPEC_stock SubscriberServices_i
    : public virtual SubscriberServicesBOAImpl {
public:
```

```cpp
SubscriberServices_i();
~SubscriberServices_i();
virtual void CreateAccount ( const TSubscriber& subscriberInfo,
                             CORBA::ULong& subAccNo,
                             CORBA::Environment
                                 &IT_env=CORBA::default_environment)
    throw (DBError);

virtual void UpdateAccount ( CORBA::ULong subAccNo,
                             CORBA::ULong sCredit,
                             CORBA::Environment
                                 &IT_env=CORBA::default_environment)
    throw (DBError);

virtual void QueryStockValueByID ( CORBA::ULong stockID,
                                   CORBA::Float& currentVal,
                                   CORBA::Float& highVal,
                                   CORBA::Float& lowVal,
                                   CORBA::Environment
                                       &IT_env=CORBA::default_environment)
    throw (DBError);

virtual void QueryStockValueByCode (const char * stockCode,
                                    CORBA::Float& currentVal,
                                    CORBA::Float& highVal,
                                    CORBA::Float& lowVal,
                                    CORBA::Environment
                                        &IT_env=CORBA::default_environment)
    throw (DBError);

virtual void BuyStock (    CORBA::ULong subAccNo,
                           CORBA::ULong stockID,
                           CORBA::ULong amount,
                           CORBA::Environment
                               &IT_env=CORBA::default_environment)
    throw (DBError);

virtual void SellStock    (CORBA::ULong subAccNo,
                           CORBA::ULong stockID,
                           CORBA::ULong amount,
                           CORBA::Environment
                               &IT_env=CORBA::default_environment)
```

```
       throw (DBError);

   virtual void GetHoldingStatement (  CORBA::ULong subAccNo,
                                       CORBA::ULong startStID,
                                       TStockHoldingSeq*& stockList,
                                       CORBA::Environment
                           &IT_env=CORBA::default_environment)
       throw (DBError);
};
```

In general, all the server object functions follow the same pattern of behavior, namely:

1. Create the business objects necessary to handle the transaction.

2. Call the appropriate business object member function, which will access the database and carry out the business logic.

3. Get the results of the transaction from the business objects and return them to the client.

As an illustration of this, let's look at the code for the `CreateAccount` transaction.

```
void Stock::SubscriberServices_i::
CreateAccount (   const Stock::TSubscriber& subscriberInfo,
                  CORBA::ULong& subAccNo,
                  CORBA::Environment &IT_env)
{
     SubscriberAccount sub ;

     int result = sub.NewAccount ( subscriberInfo.sName,
                                   subscriberInfo.sAddr,
                                   subscriberInfo.sCredit, subAccNo ) ;
     if (result != SUCCESS ) {
         DBError ex ;
         char msg[ERRMSGLEN];
         switch (result) {
         case GET_CONNECTION_FAILED:
              sprintf ( msg,
              "Create Account Failed to Connect to Database" );
              ex.reason = CORBA::string_dup ( msg ) ;
              cerr << "Create connect failed" << endl ;
```

```
                break;
        default:
            sprintf ( msg,
            "Create Account Failed: SQL error = %d", result );
            ex.reason = CORBA::string_dup ( msg ) ;
        } // end switch
        throw ex ;
    }
}
```

In `CreateAccount()`, the first step is simple. It creates a business object of type `SubscriberAccount`, which encapsulates all the business logic needed to create a new subscriber account. It then calls the `NewAccount` member function, and waits for it to return. If `NewAccount()` returns a value indicating a successful outcome, the function exits, returning the newly created account number to the client. However, if an error value is returned from `NewAccount()`, an exception object is constructed. The exception is thrown, and the ORB ensures that it is correctly returned to the calling client process, which can then abort the transaction. The exception also contains an error message that can be displayed at the client.

Most of the remaining server object functions are all very similar in form, and the interested reader should refer to the code on the website. `GetHoldingStatement()` is however worthy of closer examination, as shown below. At first it follows a similar pattern to `CreateAccount()`. It constructs a business object of type `StockHolding` and calls one of its member functions to perform the transaction. If an error code is returned, it creates and throws an exception that is passed back to the client. If the `GetHoldingList()` function succeeds, it returns an array of objects of type `CStockHolding` that contain the transaction results. These results must be passed back to the client for display.

```
void
Stock::SubscriberServices_i::GetHoldingStatement
                (CORBA::ULong subAccNo,
                 CORBA::ULong startStID,
                 Stock::TStockHoldingSeq*& stockList,
                 CORBA::Environment &IT_env)
{
```

```
        CStockHolding list[20] ;
        short len ;

        StockHolding s ;
        int result = s.GetHoldingList ( subAccNo, startStID, list, len) ;

        if (result != SUCCESS ) {
            DBError ex ;
            char msg[ERRMSGLEN];
            switch (result) {
            case GET_CONNECTION_FAILED:
                sprintf ( msg,
                "Get Stock Holding Failed toConnect to Database" );
                ex.reason = CORBA::string_dup ( msg ) ;
                cerr << "Get connect failed" << endl ;
                break;
            default:
                sprintf ( msg,
                "Get Stock Holding: SQL error code = %d", result );
                ex.reason = CORBA::string_dup ( msg ) ;
            } // end switch

            throw ex ;
        }
        // return results to the client
        stockList = new TStockHoldingSeq ; // ORB frees this...
        stockList->length(len);
        for (int i = 0; i < len ; i++ ) {
                (*stockList)[i].stock_id = list[i].stock_id;
                (*stockList)[i].amount = list[i].amount;
        }
}
```

The server object function returns the results to the client in a `TStockHoldingSeq` object. This is an `out` parameter in the IDL for the function. The server object must therefore create the object on the heap, fill it with the transaction results, and pass it to the ORB. This means the contents of the `CStockHolding` array must be copied in to the `TStockHoldingSeq`. The ORB is then responsible for returning the results to the client, and freeing up the allocated memory on behalf of the server object.

The implementation of `GetHoldingStatement()` illustrates an important design style. In the server IDL, a structure called `TStockHolding` is defined. This is the structure that makes up the individual elements of the `TStockHoldingSeq` structure returned from `GetHoldingStatement`. The Orbix IDL compiler produces the following C++ definition for `TStockHolding` (in `stock.hh`):

```
struct IT_DECLSPEC_stock TStockHolding {
      CORBA::ULong stock_id;
      CORBA::ULong amount;

      void encodeOp (CORBA::Request &IT_r) const;
      void decodeOp (CORBA::Request &IT_r);
      void decodeInOutOp (CORBA::Request &IT_r);
      TStockHolding(const TStockHolding &);
      TStockHolding();
      ~TStockHolding();
      TStockHolding& operator= (const TStockHolding&);
};
```

The structure contains the two data members declared in the IDL, along with specific constructors and member functions to marshall the data members between clients and servers. In the application code, an array of `CStockHolding` objects is used to get the results of the transaction from the business object. `CStockHolding` has the following definition (in `server.h`):

```
class CStockHolding {
public:
      unsigned long stock_id;
      unsigned long amount;
};
```

Note that the two structures contain essentially the same two data members. In fact, it would have been perfectly possible to create an array of `TStockHolding` objects and pass this directly to the business object. The results could then have been used to construct the `TStockHoldingSeq`, making the code shorter, less complex and maybe even more efficient. It seems that `CStockHolding` is just not needed.

There is however, a very good reason for using `CStockHolding`. Its purpose is to isolate, or decouple, the business objects from the middleware layer. If we had passed `TStockHolding` objects to the

`StockHolding` business object, then the `StockHolding` class would have had a compile-time dependency on the IDL compiler-generated code (i.e. it would have to include `server.hh`). In general, this is a bad idea. It means that any changes to the CORBA IDL for the application always impact on the business object code. In a large system, this could cause a considerable amount of unnecessary recompilation. More seriously, it closely couples the business logic to the classes used by the middleware product. This scheme is illustrated in Figure 7.2.

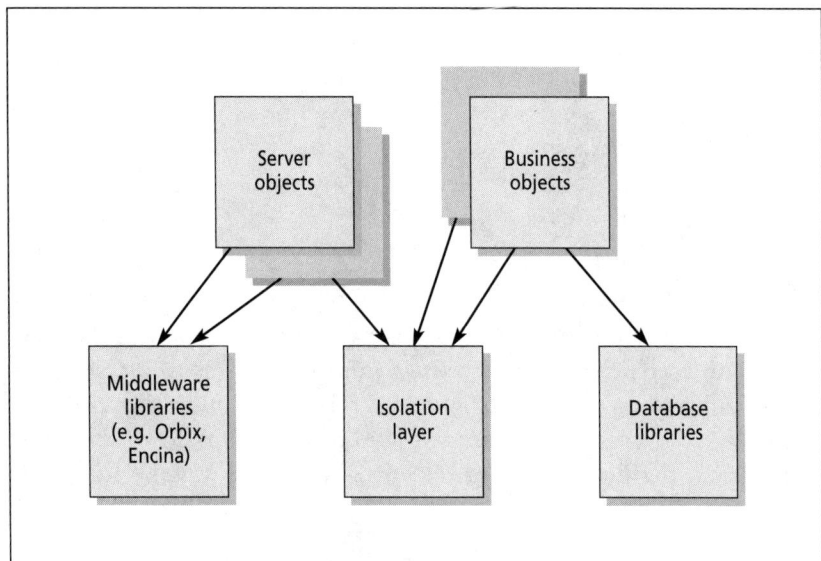

Figure 7.2   **Isolating business objects from middleware dependency**

The isolation layer means that it is possible to completely replace:

- the SQL Server-dependent database access code in the business objects with, say, an Oracle interface, without impacting on the server objects; and
- the Orbix-dependent server object code with, for example, Encina++ objects, without impacting on the business objects.

This simple but highly effective architecture makes great sense in practice, and is used widely.

▶ COMMUNICATING WITH MS SQL SERVER

The StockOnLine example uses SQL Server 6.5 as a resource manager. The application communicates with SQL Server through the ODBC API. Transactions are coordinated using XA. With SQL Server, Microsoft's Distributed Transaction Controller (DTC) participates in the transactions, providing XA mapping for the database calls.

Once SQL Server has been registered as a resource manager with the transaction service the application needs to open a database connection. Before the server can connect to the database, two administrative steps need to be carried out. These are:

1. Create an ODBC data source for the OTS server to use which gives connectivity to the required database.

2. Create an SQL server user for the OTS server to log in to SQL Server with, and make that user the database owner.

Now, the data source name and user and password must be used by the OTS server to open a database connection. This is done as follows:

```
// global ODBC environment handle
static HENV gHenv = SQL_NULL_HENV;
// global ODBC connection handle
static HDBC gCon = SQL_NULL_HDBC;
// global synchronization object
static Sync_i *freeConnectionSync = 0;

int db_init()
{
    int  rc ;
    CHAR *dataSource = 0;
    CHAR *user = 0;
    CHAR *passwd = 0;
    // get ODBC DSN name
    if ( (dataSource = getenv("SQLSERVER_DATASOURCE")) == NULL ) {
        dataSource = DEFAULT_DATA_SOURCE;
    }
    // get database owner
    if ( ( user = getenv("SQLSERVER_USER")) == NULL ) {
        user = "Stock";
```

```
    }
    // get database owner password
    if ( (passwd = getenv("SQLSERVER_PASSWORD")) == NULL ) {
            passwd = "OnLine";
    }
    // Initialize ODBC environment and connection
    rc = SQLAllocEnv(&henv)
    if ( !(rc = SQLAllocEnv(&gHenv)) ) {
            if ( !(rc = SQLAllocConnect(gHenv, &gCon)) ) {
                rc = SQLConnect(gCon, (UCHAR*) dataSource, SQL_NTS,
                        (UCHAR*) user, SQL_NTS, (UCHAR*) passwd, SQL_NTS) ;
            }
    }
    freeConnectionSync = new Sync_i();
    return rc;
}
```

The data source name, user and password are retrieved from the server's environment, and used to call the standard ODBC functions to allocate an environment and database connection handle, and finally to connect to the database. This is standard ODBC code, and will be familiar to ODBC programmers. The interesting part is the use of the CORBA OTS synchronization object, `freeConnectionSync`.

The CORBA OTS defines an interface for the synchronization object in the `CosTransactions` module. It is defined as:

```
interface Synchronization : TransactionalObject {
        void before_completion();
        void after_completion(in Status status);
};
```

The two methods `before_completion` and `after_completion` provide the application with hooks to register callback functions that are used during the two-phase commit process. The application can register a synchronization object with the transaction coordinator. The coordinator will then call the `before_completion` method prior to the prepare phase of the transaction, and will call the `after_completion` method once the transaction has committed or rolled back. The `after_completion` operation is used in this example to release the database connection, as will be illustrated below.

To achieve all this, the synchronization object must be registered with the transaction coordinator. First, a global variable representing the coordinator is declared, and initialized to zero to indicate that there are no active transactions at the server, and hence no database connections in use.

```
CosTransactions::Coordinator_ptr gCoord = 0;
```

The above variable is set during the process of establishing a database connection at the start of a transaction. As the server object is defined as transactional, an OTS transaction must have been started prior to the request arriving at the server. Consequently, when the server object wishes to get a database connection, it is safe to attempt to set the global coordinator, `gCoord`. This is done in the `GetConnection` function. Using the OTS API, a reference to the transaction coordinator is obtained and stored in the `pCoord` local variable. The code then checks to see if `gCoord` is zero, indicating there is no transaction using the database connection. If this is the case, the following will take place:

1. The ODBC API `SQLSetConnectOption` is called to mark this connection as an XA connection.

2. `gCoord` is initialized to indicate a database connection is in use.

3. The synchronization object `freeConnectionSync` is registered with the coordinator.

```
HDBC GetConnection()
{
     CosTransactions::Coordinator_var pCoord;
     CosTransactions::Control_var pControl;
     HDBC hdbc = SQL_NULL_HDBC;
     // Get the Current Transaction Coordinator reference
     try {
          pControl = CosTransactions::Current::get_control();
          pCoord = pControl->get_coordinator();
     }
     catch (CORBA::SystemException &ex) {
          cerr << "get_coordinator() - system exception" << ex << endl;
     } catch (CORBA::UserException &ex) {
          cerr << "get_coordinator() - user exception" << ex << endl;
     }
```

```
catch(...) {
    cerr << "get_coordinator() - unknown exception" << endl;
}

if ( CORBA::is_nil(pCoord) ) {
    return hdbc;
}
if ( CORBA::is_nil(gCoord) ) {
    retcode = SQLSetConnectOption (gCon,
                    SQL_COPT_SS_ENLIST_IN_XA, TRUE);
    if ( retcode == SQL_SUCCESS ) {
        gCoord =
        CosTransactions::Coordinator::_duplicate(pCoord);
        pCoord->register_synchronization(freeConnectionSync);
        hdbc = gCon;
    } else {
        TRACE(("Failed to enlist in transaction %s", rc));
    }
} else {
    // check this transaction is the current transaction
    if ( gCoord->is_same_transaction(pCoord) ) {
        hdbc = gCon;
    } else {
        cerr << "Server must be single-threaded" << endl ;
    }
}
return hdbc;
}
```

Once `GetConnection` returns a valid database connection, the server will access the database and carry out the necessary business logic. Eventually, the transaction will attempt to commit or roll back, and after an outcome is determined, the coordinator will call the synchronization object's `after_completion` operation.

In the Stock-OnLine application, the servers each have only a single connection to the database. In this case the synchronization object is used to release this ODBC connection once the transaction is complete. This is done in the `after_completion` function, as shown in the class definition:

```
class Sync_i : public virtual CosTransactions::SynchronizationBOAImpl {
public:
    void before_completion(CORBA::Environment& IT_env) {};
    void after_completion(CosTransactions::Status status,
                CORBA::Environment& IT_env)
    {
        CORBA::release(gCoord);
        // indicate that there is no transaction
        gCoord = 0;
    }
};
```

The `Sync_i` class provides an implementation of the `Synchronization` interface. When the transaction service calls `after_completion`, the transaction is complete and the database connection must no longer be required. The code indicates this by releasing the global coordinator object and setting its value to zero. This effectively marks the connection as available for a new transaction to utilize.

Typically with distributed transaction processing, care must be taken in establishing and freeing XA connections according to the requirements of the particular resource manager. This example illustrates how XA connections are set up with ODBC and SQL Server. Unfortunately, the code to set up XA connections with Oracle and the Oracle Call Interface (OCI) API is very different. When in doubt, look for examples to show the correct method for handling database connections.

Fortunately, once the XA connections are set up, the database access code is pretty much standard for the selected API. In Stock-OnLine, straightforward ODBC APIs are used to store and retrieve data from SQL Server. As this is really the realm of the database programmer, it isn't covered here, and interested readers are referred to the code on the website.

One thing should be noted, however. As the transaction control is performed by the object transaction service, the database code must not attempt to use the native APIs to commit the updates. The transaction coordinator drives the commit logic, and it will commit the transaction at the database using XA. Any attempt by the application code to commit the transaction itself will result in an error.

▶ **SUMMARY**

This chapter has explained an example OrbixOTM application written in C++. The example has introduced and discussed the following:

- designing CORBA interfaces for transaction servers;
- initializing the client and server applications to use the OTS;
- controlling transactions from the client;
- implementing transactional services using CORBA and OrbixOTM;
- establishing XA database connections with ODBC and SQL Server;
- designing servers to enhance maintainability and portability of the code;
- using the OrbixNames directory service to advertise and access server objects using object groups; and
- enabling objects to operate with OrbixManager.

OrbixOTM has many other features that haven't been covered here. These include implementing security with OrbixSSL and messaging with OrbixEvents. These topics are beyond the scope of this book, as they have their own APIs and complexities. The code presented in this chapter provides a straightforward example that can be used as a basis for adding security and messaging into the application. The OrbixOTM documentation is the best place to look for details on how to do this.

Chapter 8

Building the case study with Encina++

Overview	164
The Stock-OnLine Encina interfaces	164
Initializing the Encina++ client	169
Performing transactions	172
The Encina++ StockDBMSAccess server	176
Security in Encina++	191
Deploying and managing the server	193
Summary	196

▶ OVERVIEW

This chapter demonstrates how the Stock-OnLine case study can be constructed using Encina and the Encina++ API. We'll follow a similar pattern to Chapter 7, starting with the Encina++ IDL for Stock-OnLine, and then focusing on the implementation of the client and server processes. The setup of the XA connection to the database is also explained. The chapter includes code examples for the key parts of the Encina++ system. The complete Encina++ code listing is provided on the website.

▶ THE STOCK-ONLINE ENCINA INTERFACES

Encina defines server interfaces using DCE's interface definition language, with some simple extensions. An interface comprises an interface header and an interface body. The interface header contains interface attributes, such as an interface identifier, version information and exception declarations. The interface body contains data and operation declarations.

An interface header begins by specifying a unique identifier for the interface. The unique identifier is known as a Universal Unique identifier, or *uuid*. A DCE utility known as *uuidgen* produces uuids based on the machine's network address and the time the utility is invoked. The number generated is sufficiently large to guarantee it can be used to uniquely identify this interface definition. The uuid is utilized by the DCE RPC libraries to ensure that the client and server both agree that they are communicating using the same interface definition. This subverts problems with different systems using the same interface name for entirely different applications.

```
[
    /* Interface Header */
    uuid(f2ab66e0-5063-11d3-abb1-00c04f6834ba),
    version(1.0),
    exceptions (DBError)
]
```

The interface header includes a version definition. This allows interface designers to explicitly manage the evolution of interfaces in a system. The version number has major and minor version number components. For example, if the version is 3.2, the major version number is 3 and the minor version number is 2. This is important, as when a client attempts to call an operation in a server interface, the following rules must be satisfied:

1. The uuid of the client and server must match.

2. The major version number at the client and server must be the same.

3. The minor number version at the client must be less than or equal to the minor version number at the server.

This means that interface designers can use the minor version number to indicate that an interface is upwardly compatible with previous versions at the same major version level. For example, the addition of a function to an interface would only necessitate a minor version increment. When a change to an interface is not compatible with previous versions, a new major version level should be used. An example of this would be the addition of a parameter to an existing operation in an interface.

The interface header can also contain exception declarations. The exception statement simply names the exception that an Encina++ server can throw. Encina++ enables exceptions to be thrown and caught across a client–server communications boundary using standard C++ exception handling.

The interface body names the interface, and declares the datatypes and operations supported by the interface. The Stock interface contains a simple collection of constants, strings and structures for use in server operations. This is all straightforward, showing that in many ways all IDLs are somewhat similar. Points worth noting are:

- The [string] attribute is used to indicate that the character data types are NULL-terminated strings.

- A variable size array is used to hold the statement information in the TStockHoldingSeq structure. DCE IDL enables the designer to specify the length of the array in the size attribute of the structure. This essentially provides the same functionality as sequences in CORBA IDL.

- Individual operations in the interface are marked as transactional (the alternative is nontransactional). Transactional operations must be called within the boundary of a transaction. Non-transactional operations may or may not be called within a transaction but, in any case, no transactional context is carried with the call. This means the server does not become a participant in the transaction.

There is no problem in mixing transactional and non-transactional operations in the same interface. In fact this is often a useful facility, allowing interface operations to be tuned to appropriately reflect their needs.

```
/*
**    Encina++ interface body for StockOnline Example
*/

interface Stock
{
    /* Consts/Typedefs for zero terminated strings
    */
    const short SUB_NAME_LEN = 30 + 1;
    typedef [string] char TSubscriberName[SUB_NAME_LEN];

    const short SUB_ADDR_LEN = 60 + 1;
    typedef [string] char TSubscriberAddr[SUB_ADDR_LEN];

    const short STOCK_CODE_LEN = 4 + 1;
    typedef [string] char TStockCode[STOCK_CODE_LEN];

    const short MAX_ENTRIES =20 ;

    /* structures
    */

    typedef struct TSubscriber {
        TSubscriberName    sName      ;
        TSubscriberAddr    sAddr      ;
        unsigned long      sCredit    ;
    } TSubscriber;

    typedef struct TStockHolding {
        unsigned long stock_id   ;
        unsigned long amount  ;
    } TStockHolding;

    /* Struct with conformant array to handle return of
    Stock   Holdings (0-20 possible)
    */

    typedef struct TStockHoldingSeq {
        long                            size ;
        [size_is(size)] TStockHolding   list[*] ;
    } TStockHoldingSeq ;
```

```
/* Interface Methods
********************
*/

[transactional]
void CreateAccount (
     [in] TSubscriber subscriberInfo,
     [out] unsigned long * pSubAccNo
) ;

[transactional]
void UpdateAccount (
     [in] unsigned long subAccNo,
     [in] unsigned long sCredit
) ;

[transactional]
void QueryStockValueByID   (
     [in] unsigned  long stockID,
     [out]float      * pCurrentVal,
     [out]float      * pHighVal,
     [out]float      * pLowVal
) ;

[transactional]
void QueryStockValueByCode (
     [in]   TStockCode stockCode,
     [out]float       * pCurrentVal,
     [out]float       * pHighVal,
     [out]float       * pLowVal
) ;

[transactional]
void BuyStock  (
     [in] unsigned long subAccNo,
     [in] unsigned long stockID,
     [in] unsigned long amount
);

[transactional]
void SellStock (
     [in] unsigned long subAccNo,
     [in] unsigned long stockID,
     [in] unsigned long amount
);
```

```
        [transactional]
        void GetHoldingStatement (
            [in] unsigned long subAccNo,
            [in] unsigned long startStID,
            [out] TStockHoldingSeq **stockList
        );
    }
```

In general, Encina IDL is more C-oriented than CORBA IDL, reflecting its age. The most obvious manifestation of this is the use of pointer types as [out] parameters in operations such as GetHoldingStatement. This shows through even more strongly in the implementation of operations, as we'll see when we examine the server code later in this chapter.

The Encina++ interfaces are run through the Encina TIDL and DCE IDL compilers to produce the client and server stub files for linking with applications. The –*ots* option must be used in the TIDL command to instruct the compiler to produce C++ client and server header and stub files that support the Encina++ API. Figure 8.1 shows the files generated by the TIDL and IDL compilers. These must be compiled and linked with the client and server application code.

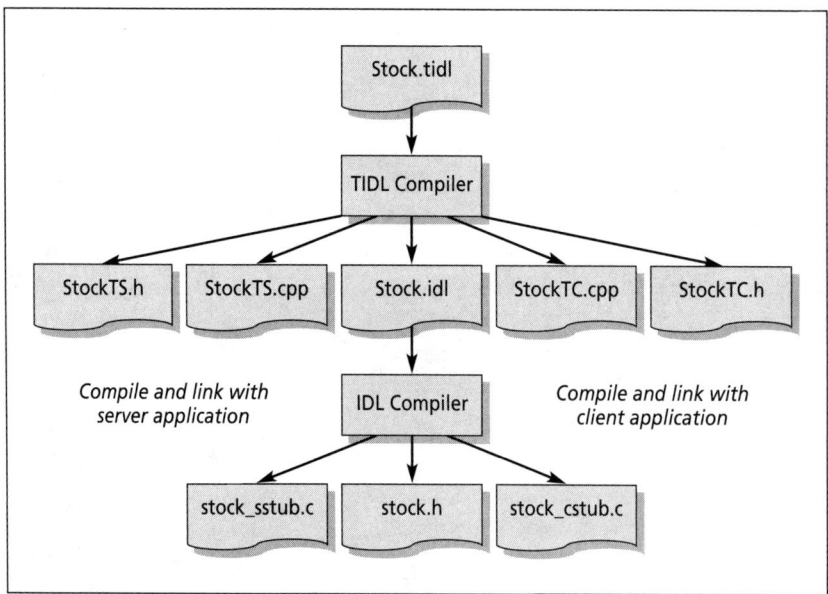

Figure 8.1   **Outputs of the TIDL and IDL compilers**

▶ INITIALIZING THE ENCINA++ CLIENT

Client initialization is trivial in Encina++. A single `OtsClient` object needs to be correctly constructed, and this takes responsibility for correctly initializing all the underlying Encina++ libraries. The single argument passed to the `OtsClient` object is the name of the Encina cell that the client belongs to. In the Stock-OnLine example, the cell name is provided through a command line argument. An alternative is to set the ENCINA_CELL_NAME environment variable in the client's environment.

The format of the Encina cell name provided should be a fully qualified DCE name. Each Encina cell belongs to one (and only one) DCE cell. If the name of the Encina cell is `StockCell`, then the fully qualified Encina cell name is:

`/.:/StockCell`

The `/.:/` notation is shorthand for the name of the DCE cell that the host belongs to. Each DCE cell also has a name, but this notation simply means that we don't have to specify it in the Encina cell name.

```
int main(int argc, char* argv[])
{
    if (argc != 2) {
      cerr << "usage: " << argv[0] << " <Encina Cell Name>" << endl;
      exit(1);
    }
    // Initialise OrbixOTS (client side).
    OtsClient theClient(argv[1]);

    // create the client object
    StocksubObj;

    // pass name server host name in argv[1]
    doSubClient(&subObj) ;

    return 0;
}
```

In order to communicate with the server application, the client must create a client proxy object. The client stub files generated by the TIDL compiler contain a class with the same name as the interface, in this case a `Stock` class, which is used for this purpose. The `Stock` class inherits from a base class known as `OtsBinding`. `OtsBinding` encapsulates the code needed to connect client objects to server objects that implement the required interface, in this case, the `Stock` interface. It utilizes a variable generated by the IDL compiler known as an *interface handle*. This is declared as:

```
extern rpc_if_handle_t Stock_v1_0_c_ifspec;
```

The interface handle contains the following information that is used by the underlying DCE libraries for binding to a server object that supports the required interface:

- the interface name; and
- the major and minor version numbers of the interface.

The use of the `OtsBinding` class and the interface handle is hidden from the application programmer. The application simply constructs the client proxy object, and the C++ inheritance mechanism constructs the `OtsBinding` object. The actual process of binding to a server object entails the client querying the DCE Cell Directory Service (CDS), which server objects use to advertise their location. Again, all this detail is completely hidden from the application, requiring the programmer to write no code in order to exploit the CDS.

The client `Stock` class contains four overloaded constructors, as shown in the extract from the TIDL-generated code below:

```
class Stock: public OtsBinding
{
public:
    Stock():
    OtsBinding(Stock_v1_0_c_ifspec){}

    Stock(char* name):
    OtsBinding(Stock_v1_0_c_ifspec, name){}

    Stock(OtsServerName &name):
    OtsBinding(Stock_v1_0_c_ifspec, name){}

    Stock(ObjectRef* ref):
    OtsBinding(Stock_v1_0_c_ifspec, ref){}
    // REMAINDER OF CLASS NOT SHOWN
```

The selection of a constructor for the client object is important, as it dictates how the client binds to server objects.

Stock(void): This constructor binds the client proxy object to any server object that supports the interface. Selection is random from the pool of objects that are advertised to support the interface in the CDS. In practice, this is the most commonly used option. It is similar to the use of random groups in OrbixNames.

Stock (char * name): This constructor binds the client proxy object to the server object specified by the `objectName` parameter. Server objects can specify a name that identifies them for binding purposes.

Stock (OtsServerName &name): This constructor binds the client proxy object to an Encina Monitor Application Server (MAS) that exports the `Stock` interface. The parameter specifies the name of MAS as specified when the MAS is registered with the Enconsole tool. The main use of this constructor is to access non-Encina++ servers. An example would be an Encina MAS that supports the interface but is written in C.

Stock (ObjectRef *Ref): This binds the client proxy object to a server object via an existing object reference. Encina++ supports factory objects that can be used to dynamically create server objects upon client request. This mechanism is particularly useful for server objects that maintain state about the client that is using their services. Clients use a factory proxy object, which returns the `ObjectRef` that is then used to construct the client proxy. The `ObjectRef` identifies a particular object in a particular application server.

In the Stock-OnLine application, the default constructor is selected. Constructing client proxy objects is rapid, as the objects do not bind to a server object until they are used, therefore the object will bind to the server when one of its member functions is called. It subsequently uses that server object for the remainder of its lifetime, and only rebinds if there is a server failure. This mechanism leads to a static distribution of load across server objects.

In high performance systems, a much more dynamic load distribution is needed so that client load is regularly redistributed across the available server objects. To achieve this with Encina++, the client proxy objects must be forced to rebind relatively frequently. The easiest way to achieve this is to delete the existing proxy and construct a new one. Rebinding on every call would be expensive due to the overheads of accessing the CDS, so application designers need to devise a simple and efficient client rebinding strategy that suits their application performance needs.

▶ PERFORMING TRANSACTIONS

The structure of the Encina++ client application is essentially the same as the structure of the OrbixOTM client discussed in Chapter 7. The function `doSubClient` controls interaction with the user and uses the class `subCommand` to perform the transactions. As this structure is explained in Chapter 7, we won't repeat it here. Instead, let's look at the Encina++ code needed to call the server object transactions, starting with `CreateAccount`.

```
void subCommand::CreateAccount (Stock *   subObject )
{
    TSubscriber subInfo ;

    cout << "Create Accout" << endl ;
    cout << "Enter Account Name (max 30 chars): " ;
    cin.ignore(256, '\n');
    cin.getline(subInfo.sName, SUB_NAME_LEN);
    cout << "Enter Address (max 60 chars): " ;
    cin.getline(subInfo.sAddr, SUB_ADDR_LEN);
    cout << "Enter Requested Credit Limit: " ;
    cin >> subInfo.sCredit ;

    try {
        Current::begin();
        subObject->CreateAccount (subInfo, &subAccNo ) ;
        Current::commit();
        cout << "Create Account OK: Account Number is: " <<
        subAccNo << endl ;
        return;
    } catch (TransactionRolledBack) {
        cerr << " OTS rollback !" << endl;
    } catch (const Stock::DBError ex) {
        cerr << " (Database error occured)" << endl ;
        Current::rollback();
    } catch (OtsExceptions::Any exc) {
        cerr << "Encina exception: " << endl << (const char *) exc
            << endl ;
        Current::rollback();
    } catch (...) {
        cerr << " (unknown exception - transaction failed)" <<
```

```
            endl;
        Current::rollback();
    }

    subAccNo = 0;   // it failed
}
```

As with the OrbixOTM client, `CreateAccount` first gets name, address and credit information from the user.[1] These details are stored in a `TSubscriber` structure. `TSubscriber` is defined in the application TIDL file, and the generated C++ code is:

[1] *User input validation code is deliberately omitted for simplicity and brevity.*

```
#define SUB_NAME_LEN (31)
typedef IDL_char TSubscriberName[31];
#define SUB_ADDR_LEN (61)
typedef IDL_char TSubscriberAddr[61];
#define STOCK_CODE_LEN (5)
typedef IDL_char TStockCode[5];
#define MAX_ENTRIES (20)
typedef struct TSubscriber {
    TSubscriberName sName;
    TSubscriberAddr sAddr;
    IDL_ulong_int sCredit;
} TSubscriber;
```

Once the user input is complete, a transaction is started by calling `Current::begin()` and the client proxy `CreateAccount` method is called. This causes the client proxy to make a remote call to the server object it has bound to, and to pass the operation parameters and transaction context to the server. The MAS to which the server object belongs will take responsibility for the role of transaction coordinator, as it will be a recoverable server. The MAS will log the transaction state, and communicate with the database to carry out the business logic for `CreateAccount`.

If the remote call returns successfully, the client attempts to commit the transaction using `Current::commit`. This will cause the client-side OTS libraries to make a remote call to the transaction coordinator on the server instructing it to attempt to commit the transaction. The coordinator will then communicate with the database to see if it is ready to commit the transaction. Assuming the database can commit, by default the coordinator will immediately return from the client's `commit` call, informing the client that the transaction has succeeded. This means the client application does not have to wait for the second phase of the two-phase commit protocol to complete. Clients can specify that they wish to wait for the full distributed outcome of the transaction, and receive reports on any heuristic hazards that occur. This of course will impact on application performance.

If for some reason the transaction fails, the client needs to catch the appropriate exception that is thrown to indicate the problem. The `TransactionRolledBack` exception is thrown by the OTS if one of the transaction participants votes to rollback. In this case, the client does not need to roll back the transaction itself. When other exceptions are caught, including the application-defined `DBError`, the client must roll back the transaction.

Most of the remaining transactions are all similar in behavior to `CreateAccount`. The code for these is on the website. The one interesting exception is `GetHoldingStatement`. This illustrates the DCE memory management rules for variable length data that is returned from the server objects. Essentially, for each server invocation, the client must:

1. Allocate a pointer to the memory that the server will use to return the results.

2. Pass the address of this pointer to the server object operation.

3. After the server operation returns, use the pointer to access the results from the server.

4. Free the memory returned from the server.

These rules are followed using the `pList` pointer in `GetHoldingStatement`. The important thing to note is that the client application itself does not allocate the memory used to hold the server's results. It simply provides a pointer that the underlying DCE libraries set to inform the client where DCE has placed the results in memory. The DCE runtime allocates the memory that it needs to hold the server results, and leaves the responsibility of freeing this memory to the client application. If the client forgets to deallocate the memory, then there is a memory leak in the application.

```
void subCommand::GetHoldingStatement (Stock *    subObject )
{
    char choice = 'y';
    unsigned long startStID = 0;
    int i;
```

```cpp
    cout << "STATEMENT LISTING" << endl;
    while ( tolower(choice) == 'y' ) {
        TStockHoldingSeq * pList = NULL;
        try {
            Current::begin();
            subObject->GetHoldingStatement
                        (subAccNo, startStID, &pList ) ;
            Current::commit();
            cout << "Stock ID \t " << "Amount" << endl ;
            cout << "---------------------------" << endl ;
            for (i = 0 ; i < pList->size ; i++ ) {
                cout << pList->list[i].stock_id << "\t\t" <<
                        pList->list[i].amount << endl ;
            }
            if (pList->size == MAX_ENTRIES ) {
                startStID = pList->list[i].stock_id ;
                // remember last one returned
                cout << "Next Page? ((y/n)" << endl ;
                cin >> choice ;
            } else {
                choice = 'n';
            }
            if ( pList != NULL ) free( pList) ;
    } catch (TransactionRolledBack) {
        // exception handling not shown - as in CreateAccount
```

The memory management rules illustrated in this example are in reality very much the norm for remote procedure call or remote method invocation implementations. For variable length out parameters, and new data returned from the server to the client, the underlying client and server middleware libraries coordinate to pass the results from the server to the client. Generally, the client application cannot predict the size of the returned data before the remote call is made. This means the client cannot allocate the memory for the results, as it doesn't know how big they will be. This is why the client middleware libraries allocate the memory when the results are received, tell the client application where the data is stored, and leave it to the client to free the data when it is complete. As long as you understand the rules, it's then just a matter of implementing them using the syntax of the middleware that is in use.

The server side of the `GetHoldingStatement` transaction will be explained in the following sections which cover the server implementation.

▶ THE ENCINA++ STOCKDBMSACCESS SERVER

The StockDBMSAccess server supports the IDL interface defined in the `Stock` interface. During its initialization, it establishes the connection with the stock database and creates server objects to respond to client requests. First, we'll examine the initialization code and then look into the processing of client transactions and database access.

Server initialization

Initializing the Encina++ server is relatively straightforward, and typically takes place in the `main()` function. Encina++ provides the `Encina::Server` class to encapsulate much of the detail of initializing the Encina and DCE run-time environments. The server object is used to initialize and terminate a server application, register resource managers with a server, and make the server start listening for client calls.

The application server object is of type `TStock_i`, and this is constructed after the Encina server object is constructed. Encina++ generates a constructor for server objects that takes a string representing the object's name. In this example a name is supplied. This would enable client objects to bind to server objects by name, as described in the previous section.

Next the resource manager is registered with Encina. As the server will access SQL Server using XA, the application must supply the correct open and close strings to set-up communications. As SQL Server requires a recovery uuid, this example creates a uuid dynamically using the API `uuid_create`. This is then transformed into a string using the API `uuid_to_string` and used to construct the identical open and close strings required by SQL Server.

Registering the XA resource manager is carried out by calling the `Encina::Server::RegisterResource` function. The address of the SQL Server-supplied XA switch is passed, along with the open and close strings, and a flag to indicate if the XA library is thread-aware. In this example, the Encina++ server will be multi-threaded, as SQL Server has a thread-safe XA implementation. For this reason, a TRUE value is passed to indicate that the XA library can accommodate multi-threaded applications.

```c
int main(int argc, char **argv)
{
   try{
     // Declare the server object
     Encina::Server theServer;
     //
     // Declare an instance of the server object
     TStock_i theStockMgr("StockServerObject");

     //
     // Recoverability initialization section

     /* generate recoveryGuid for the open/close string */
     char mssql_openstring[256];
     char mssql_closestring[256];
     char *recoveryGuid;
     uuid_t uuid;
     unsigned32 st;

     uuid_create(&uuid, &st);
  if (st == uuid_s_ok) {
       uuid_to_string(&uuid,
           (unsigned char **)&recoveryGuid, &st);
       if (st == uuid_s_ok) {
       sprintf(mssql_openstring,
           "Tm=Encina\\, RmRecoveryGuid=%s", recoveryGuid);
       sprintf(mssql_closestring,
           "Tm=Encina\\, RmRecoveryGuid=%s", recoveryGuid);
       }
  }
  theServer.RegisterResource(&msqlsrvxa1, mssql_openstring,
                             mssql_closestring, TRUE);
  //this function exits if it fails...
  mssql_dbConnect() ;
  //
  theServer.Initialize();
  //
  // Call Listen. Server is ready to accept calls now.
  // This thread will be blocked until shutdown.
  theServer.Listen(Encina::Server::SERIALIZE_NOTHING);
  mssql_dbDisconnect() ;
```

```
    } catch(OtsExceptions::Any &exc) {
      cerr << "Exception in server main: " << (const char *) exc
      << endl;
    } catch(...) {
      cerr << "Caught Unknown Exception" << endl;
    }
    return 0;
}
```

After the resource manager has been registered successfully, the server calls the `mssql_dbConnect` function to set up connections to SQL Server. The details of `mssql_dbConnect` will be examined later in this chapter, so at this stage we'll just assume that it successfully opens a connection to SQL Server, or fails if it encounters problems.

Finally `main` completes server initialization by calling the `Encina::Server Initialize` and `Listen` member functions. The `Initialize` function initializes the underlying Encina run-time components and registered XA resource managers, and registers exported objects and interfaces with the DCE services. `Initialize` is optional. If it is not called separately, the subsequent call to `Listen` will perform the necessary set-up work. Calling `Initialize` gives the server application the opportunity to perform application-specific initialization before the server itself starts to receive client requests. After `Initialize` is called, the server can create transactions, communicate with registered resource managers, and make outgoing calls to other application servers.

The `Listen` function makes the server available to receive incoming client requests. Its single parameter specifies the concurrency mode that the server supports. Three options are possible, namely:

```
enum ConcurrencyMode {
      SERIALIZE_TRPCS_AND_TRANSACTIONS,
      SERIALIZE_TRPCS,
      SERIALIZE_NOTHING
};
```

The default is `SERIALIZE_NOTHING`, which creates a multi-threaded server capable of handling multiple transactions concurrently in multiple threads. This is appropriate for thread-safe XA implementations and thread-safe server objects. Otherwise, the usual option is `SERIALIZE_TRPCS_AND_TRANSACTIONS`, which effectively gives a single-threaded server.

`Listen` creates a thread pool to service client requests. The application can specify the size of the thread pool by setting the ENCINA_TPOOL_SIZE environment variable for the server. Encina++ takes care of creating the threads and passing incoming client requests to the threads for servicing.

In Encina++, `Listen` will not return until the server is closed down using Encina's administrative tools. Once it returns, the server can carry out any application-specific clean-up tasks. In this example, the server calls the `mssql_dbDisconnect` function which closes down the database connections that the server has utilized. Again, `mssql_dbDisconnect` is examined in detail later in this chapter.

Implementing the server object

Encina's TIDL compiler generates a skeleton class that can be used to implement the server object for the `Stock` interface. The generated class definition for the server object is as follows:

```
class TStock_i : public StockMgrAbstract
{
public:
    virtual ~TStock_i();

    TStock_i(Uuid &obj,
        char *localObjectName = (char *) 0,
        char *defaultAcl = TPM_DEFAULT_ACL,
        int numThreads = 0) ;

    TStock_i(char *localObjectName = (char *) 0,
        char *defaultAcl = TPM_DEFAULT_ACL,
        int numThreads = 0) ;

    virtual void ENCINA_STUB_CALLING CreateAccount(
        TSubscriber subscriberInfo,
        IDL_ulong_int *pSubAccNo
        );

    virtual void ENCINA_STUB_CALLING UpdateAccount(
        IDL_ulong_int subAccNo,
        IDL_ulong_int sCredit
        );
```

```
virtual void ENCINA_STUB_CALLING QueryStockValueByID(
    IDL_ulong_int stockID,
    IDL_short_float *pCurrentVal,
    IDL_short_float *pHighVal,
    IDL_short_float *pLowVal
    );
virtual void ENCINA_STUB_CALLING QueryStockValueByCode(
    TStockCode stockCode,
    IDL_short_float *pCurrentVal,
    IDL_short_float *pHighVal,
    IDL_short_float *pLowVal
    );
virtual void ENCINA_STUB_CALLING BuyStock(
    IDL_ulong_int subAccNo,
    IDL_ulong_int stockID,
    IDL_ulong_int amount
    );
virtual void ENCINA_STUB_CALLING SellStock(
    IDL_ulong_int subAccNo,
    IDL_ulong_int stockID,
    IDL_ulong_int amount
    );
virtual void ENCINA_STUB_CALLING GetHoldingStatement(
    IDL_ulong_int subAccNo,
    IDL_ulong_int startStID,
    TStockHoldingSeq **stockList
    );
};
```

The server class, in this case `TStock_i`, must inherit from the TIDL-generated `StockMgrAbstract` class. `StockMgrAbstract` has a pure virtual member function for each of the operations that the server object must support. `StockMgrAbstract` in turn inherits from `OtsInterfaceMgr`, which is the base class for all Encina++ server objects. When constructed correctly, `OtsInterfaceMgr` exports the server object's details into the DCE name space so that clients can bind to it and submit requests. This is all performed automatically during the construction of the server object, and hence requires no application code.

The constructors and destructor of `TStock_i` present the application with the opportunity to initialize any state that the object must maintain. As Stock-OnLine uses stateless objects, there are no specific application requirements. The only obligation of the server object is to correctly call the constructor for `StockMgrAbstract` in its member initialization list, as shown in the following TIDL-generated code.

```
TStock_i::TStock_i(    Uuid &obj,
                       char *localObjectName,
                       char *defaultAcl,
                       int numThreads )
    :
    OtsObjectMgr(&obj, localObjectName),
    StockMgrAbstract(obj, localObjectName, defaultAcl, numThreads)
{ // initialize things here }
```

To illustrate the implementation of the server operations, let's look at the `CreateAccount` member function. Like the OrbixOTM example in Chapter 7, a `SubscriberAccount` object is created and its `NewAccount` method is called to communicate with the database and execute the business logic. The detailed implementation of this business logic can be seen on the website.

If `NewAccount` returns successfully, the newly allocated subscriber account number is returned to the client. Otherwise, an exception is thrown to indicate to the client that the transaction has failed and should be rolled back. And that's really all there is to it.

```
void TStock_i::CreateAccount( TSubscriber subscriberInfo,
             IDL_ulong_int *pSubAccNo )
{
    SubscriberAccount sub ;

    int result = sub.NewAccount (
                    (const char *) subscriberInfo.sName,
                    (const char *) subscriberInfo.sAddr,
                    subscriberInfo.sCredit,
                    *pSubAccNo ) ;

    if (result != SUCCESS ) {
        DBError ex ;
        switch (result) {
```

```
            case GET_CONNECTION_FAILED:
                cerr << "Create Account connect failed" << endl ;
                break;
        default:
            cerr << "Create Account Failed: SQL error code =" <<
                result << endl ;
        } // end switch
        throw ex ;
    }
}
```

Apart from the `GetHoldingStatement` member function, the remaining `TStock_i` member functions follow a similar pattern to `CreateAccount`, and therefore are not discussed in detail here. `GetHoldingStatement` is more interesting though. It clearly illustrates some of the differences between the C++-based style of programming that Orbix employs for passing results from servers to clients, and Encina++'s C-based style due to its use of DCE's RPC service.

The major issue with `GetHoldingStatement` is the allocation of the memory required to return the statement information from the server to the client. A `StockHolding` object is used to execute the business logic to read the statement entries from the database, and up to 20 entries are returned in an array of `CStockHolding` objects. Next, the statement entries must somehow be made available to the DCE run-time to return to the client using the `out` parameter `stockList`. Note `stockList` is defined as a pointer to a pointer in `GetHoldingStatement`'s parameter list. This is DCE's C language mapping for handling variable length parameters. In DCE, these are known as *conformant arrays*. A conformant array has its length set at run-time. The IDL definition for a conformant array uses a size variable that is used to control the amount of memory transmitted. Conformant arrays are declared in the IDL using an asterisk in place of the array dimension value. An example of this is shown in the `list` member of `TStockHoldingSeq` in the `stock.tidl` file shown earlier in this chapter.

```
void TStock_i::GetHoldingStatement( IDL_ulong_int subAccNo,
                                    IDL_ulong_int startStID,
                                    TStockHoldingSeq **stockList )
{
```

```cpp
    CStockHolding list[20] ;
    short len ;
    StockHolding s ;

    int result = s.GetHoldingList ( subAccNo, startStID, list, len) ;

    if (result != SUCCESS ) {
        DBError ex ;
        switch (result) {
        case GET_CONNECTION_FAILED:
            cerr << "Get Statement: Couldn't Connect to Database"
                 << endl ;
            break;
        default:
            cerr << "Get Statement Failed: SQL error code = " <<
                    result << endl ;
        } // end switch
        throw ex ;
    }
    // now put results in memory for DCE to pass back to the client.
    // allocate the memory. which is big enough for:
    // a TStockHoldingSeq, which includes 1 TStockHolding structure

    int size ;
    // calculate the size
    if (len != 0 )
        size =      sizeof (TStockHoldingSeq) +
                    ( ( sizeof(TStockHolding) * (len - 1) ) ) ;
    else
        // just return an empty
        size = sizeof (TStockHoldingSeq) ;

    // Allocate the memory - DCE will free this
    *stockList = (TStockHoldingSeq *)
            rpc_ss_allocate ( (unsigned) size ) ;
    (*stockList)->size = len ;
    // copy the data to the new memory
    for (int i = 0; i < len ; i++ ) {
        (*stockList)->list[i].stock_id    = list[i].stock_id ;
        (*stockList)->list[i].amount= list[i].amount ;
    }
}
```

To understand the conformant array mechanism, it's important to first examine the C structures generated from the application IDL. The `TStockHoldingSeq` structure has two members, an array of `TStockHolding` structures of length 1, and a long integer that is used to specify the size of the accompanying `TStockHolding` array.

```
typedef struct TStockHolding {
    IDL_ulong_int stock_id;
    IDL_ulong_int amount;
} TStockHolding;
typedef struct TStockHoldingSeq {
    IDL_long_int size;
    TStockHolding list[1];
} TStockHoldingSeq;
```

As a statically allocated `TStockHoldingSeq` only has enough space for a single `TStockHolding` structure, the server code must carry out the following steps:

1. Dynamically allocate a `TStockHoldingSeq` with sufficient memory to hold all the statement entries to be returned to the client, and make the output parameter `*stockList` point to the memory.

2. Copy the results into this dynamically allocated structure.

3. Set the size member to inform DCE how many entries there are in the conformant array.

The implementation of these three steps can be seen in `GetHoldingStatement`. The size of the memory block to allocate is calculated based on the number of entries needed by the array. The size calculation subtracts one from the number of entries in the array, as the declared structure's size already accommodates one array element. The memory is then allocated using the DCE memory management routine `rpc_ss_allocate`. This behaves similarly to `malloc`. It must be used, however, because the DCE run-time is responsible for freeing this memory, not the application code. DCE frees the memory after `GetHoldingStatement` returns and the RPC code has transmitted its contents back to the client.

Communicating with SQL Server

SQL Server communications first require a database connection to be opened. The Encina++ server exploits the thread-safe XA library for SQL

Server and can consequently open more than one simultaneous connection. The constant `NUM_CONNECTIONS` in the code fragment below is used to configure the number of connections to use. `NUM_CONNECTIONS` is used to set the size of the `connections` table of ODBC connection/transaction identifier (tid) pairs. The Encina-defined data type `tran_tid_t` is used to represent the tid for the transaction that is currently using the associated database connection.

Two variables are also defined to ensure that access to the `connections` table is thread-safe. The DCE pthreads library data types `pthread_mutex_t` and `pthread_cond_t` represent mutual exclusion locks and condition variables respectively. These are used to serialize access to the `connections` table and signal to any waiting threads that there are now ODBC connections free for use.

```
// This array holds available ODBC connection/transaction pairs
// These variables are used to synchronize access to the "connections"
// array by application server threads, spawned by each client/server
// call .

char* dataSourceName = "STOCK";
const int NUM_CONNECTIONS = 5 ;

typedef struct {
    HDBC hdbc;
    tran_tid_t tid;
} tran_connection_t;

static tran_connection_t connections[NUM_CONNECTIONS];

static HENV henv;

static pthread_mutex_t lock;
static pthread_cond_t freeCon;
```

The ODBC connection table and synchronization variables are first set in the `mssql_dbConnect` function. The pthread's API is used to correctly initialize the `lock` and `freeCon` variables, and the ODBC API is used to allocate the ODBC environment. The user name, password and ODBC data source name are then set so that ODBC connections can be established. Finally, each ODBC connection handle in the `connections` table is allocated and an attempt to connect to the database is made. If everything works successfully, the function returns, otherwise any error condition causes the function to exit the process. Also, each transaction identifier in the `connections` table is set to the Encina-defined `TRAN_TID_NULL` value. `TRAN_TID_NULL` is never generated by a TRAN function as a valid tid value, and indicates that there is not an active transaction using its associated ODBC connection.

```cpp
void mssql_dbConnect(void)
{
    int i, retcode;

    // Initialize global mutex variable
    retcode = pthread_mutex_init(&lock, pthread_mutexattr_default);
    if (retcode != 0) {
        cerr << "pthread_mutex_init() failed." << endl ;
        exit(1);
    }

    // Initialize global condition variable
    retcode = pthread_cond_init(&freeCon, pthread_condattr_default);
    // error handling code omitted

    retcode = SQLAllocEnv(&henv);
    // error handling code omitted

    // Set datasource, user and password
    CHAR *user = 0;
    CHAR *passwd = 0;
    CHAR *dataSource = 0 ;
    if ( (dataSource = getenv("DB_DATASOURCE")) == NULL )
        dataSource = dataSourceName;
    if ( (user = getenv("DB_USER")) == NULL )
        user = "encina";
    if ( (passwd = getenv("DB_PASSWORD")) == NULL )
        passwd = "encina";

    for (i = 0; i < NUM_CONNECTIONS; i++) {
        connections[i].tid = TRAN_TID_NULL;

        // Allocate an ODBC connection
        retcode = SQLAllocConnect(henv, &connections[i].hdbc) ;
        // error handling code omitted

        //Connect to ODBC data source
        retcode = SQLConnect(connections[i].hdbc, (UCHAR*)
```

```
                    dataSource, SQL_NTS, (UCHAR*) user, SQL_NTS,
                (UCHAR*) passwd, SQL_NTS) ;
        // error handling code omitted
    } // end for
}
```

Once the connections are established, the server application will drop into the Encina message loop and subsequently receive client transactions. When a new transaction arrives at the server object, the allocated thread from the server application thread pool calls `GetConnection`. This function must select a database connection from the table and return it for use in the transaction.

`GetConnection`'s first task is to obtain the transaction identifier for the current transaction associated with the executing thread. The Encina API `threadTid_Lookup` is used for this purpose. The object must then check to see if this is a new transaction or if the transaction has already touched this server, most likely in another transactional server object function. If the transaction is not new, it will already be associated with an ODBC connection in the `connections` table. It is the role of the `FindConnection` function to establish this.

```
HDBC GetConnection(void)
{
    tran_tid_t tid;
    HDBC hdbc;

    tid = threadTid_Lookup();
    // see if the transaction is already associated with a connection
    hdbc = FindConnection(tid);
    if (hdbc != SQL_NULL_HDBC)
        return hdbc;
    // it's a new transaction so get a free ODBC connection
    hdbc = FindFreeConnection(tid);
    return hdbc;
}
```

The transaction identifier is passed as a parameter to `FindConnection`. The function searches through the table looking for the tid and, if it is found, it simply returns the associated ODBC handle. If the tid is not found in the table, a value of `SQL_NULL_HDBC` is returned, indicating that this is a new transaction at this server. Note the use of the Encina `tran_TidEqual` API to compare the two transaction identifiers. Encina's TRAN service provides a number of functions for reliably comparing transaction identifiers and for obtaining the identifiers for related transactions.

```
HDBC FindConnection(tran_tid_t tid)
{
    HDBC hdbc;
    int i;

    for (i = 0; i < NUM_CONNECTIONS; i++) {
        if (tran_TidEqual(connections[i].tid, tid)) {
            hdbc = connections[i].hdbc;
            return hdbc;
        }
    } // end for

    // no existing connection, return a NULL connection handle
    return SQL_NULL_HDBC;
}
```

Assuming the thread is dealing with a new transaction, it must obtain a free database connection. This is performed in the `FindFreeConnection` function. As `FindFreeConnection` modifies the global `connections` table, its code must be bracketed with a pair of lock/unlock operations on the mutual exclusion variable `lock`. This ensures that only one thread at any time can execute the table searching and modification code, thus minimizing potential data corruption.

Once the thread finds a free entry in the `connections` table, it assigns its transaction identifier to the table element's tid member to indicate that it has selected the associated database connection. It then calls the ODBC API `SQLSetConnectOption` to mark this connection for use with XA. Next, so that the server object can release the connection, it registers the `FreeConnection` function to be called back by the transaction service when the transaction completes. The Encina API `tran_CallAfterResolution` is used for this purpose.

It is interesting to note `FindFreeConnection`'s behavior when all the allocated ODBC connections are in use. If this state occurs, the thread drops out of the `for` loop and blocks on the `pthread_cond_wait` operation. This routine automatically releases the `lock` mutual exclusion variable and causes the calling thread to wait on the `freeCon` condition. The thread then blocks until another thread in the server calls `pthread_cond_signal` on `freeCon`. This will happen when another transaction completes. When this occurs, the `lock` mutual exclusion variable is automatically reacquired and the routine returns. It then searches the table again for a free ODBC connection handle.

```
HDBC FindFreeConnection(tran_tid_t tid)
{
    HDBC hdbc;
    RETCODE retcode;
    int i;

  //Lock the mutex.
  if (pthread_mutex_lock(&lock) != 0)
      exit(1);

  while (TRUE) {
      for (i = 0; i < NUM_CONNECTIONS; i++) {
          if(tran_TidEqual(connections[i].tid, TRAN_TID_NULL)){
              connections[i].tid = tid;
              hdbc = connections[i].hdbc;

              // Enlist the connection in an XA transaction.
              retcode =
              SQLSetConnectOption(hdbc,
                  SQL_COPT_SS_ENLIST_IN_XA,
                  TRUE);
              // error handling code omitted

              // Set the transaction resolution handler.
              tran_CallAfterResolution(tid,
                              FreeConnection, NULL);

              // Unlock the mutex.
              if (pthread_mutex_unlock(&lock) != 0)
                  exit(1);
              return hdbc; // all ok
          } // end if

      } // end for

      // No free ODBC connection was found.
```

```
        // So wait until woken up by some terminated transaction.
        if (pthread_cond_wait(&freeCon, &lock) != 0)
            exit(1);
        // and try again....
    } // end while

    //
    // Weird stuff happening if we get here
    // A connection should have been found ..... eventually .
    cerr << "Failed to find ODBC connection " << endl ;

    // Unlock the mutex lock.
    if (pthread_mutex_unlock(&lock) != 0)
            exit(1);
    return SQL_NULL_HDBC;
}
```

The `FreeConnection` function's execution must also be protected using matching lock/unlock operations on the `lock` variable. After acquiring the lock, it searches the table to find its transaction identifier, and sets the tid member of the appropriate table element to `TRAN_TID_NULL`. This indicates that the connection is free to use in another transaction. It then performs a `pthread_cond_signal` operation on the `freeCon` variable to wake up any threads that may be blocked trying to get a free connection, and finally releases the lock. At the end of `FreeConnection`, the thread's get/release cycle for the database connection is complete.

```
void ENCINA_CALLING FreeConnection(tran_tid_t tid, void* arg)
{
    int i;

    / Lock the mutex.
    if (pthread_mutex_lock(&lock) != 0)
        exit(1);
    for (i = 0; i < NUM_CONNECTIONS; i++) {
        if (tran_TidEqual(connections[i].tid, tid)) {
            connections[i].tid = TRAN_TID_NULL;

            // wake up blocked transactions
            if (pthread_cond_signal(&freeCon) != 0)
                exit(1)
```

```
            // Unlock the mutex. */
            if (pthread_mutex_unlock(&lock) != 0)
                exit(1);
            return;
        } endif
    } // end for

    // if we get here, something's horribly wrong!
    cerr << "Failed to find ODBC connection used in transaction" << endl
;
    if (pthread_mutex_unlock(&lock) != 0)
```

Finally, when the server is closed down, it calls `mssql_dbDisconnect` to free the ODBC connections and environment, and releases the resources associated with the synchronization variables.

```
void mssql_dbDisconnect(void)
{
    int i, retcode;
    for (i = 0; i < NUM_CONNECTIONS; i++) {
        SQLDisconnect(connections[i].hdbc);
        // error handling code omitted
        retcode = SQLFreeConnect(connections[i].hdbc);
        // error handling code omitted
    } // end for

    pthread_mutex_destroy(&lock);
    pthread_cond_destroy(&freeCon);

    SQLFreeEnv(henv);
    // error handling code omitted
}
```

▶ SECURITY IN ENCINA++

Encina++ MASs exploit the underlying DCE services to implement security. With security enforced, client applications must log into DCE to obtain valid DCE credentials. These credentials are then used when the client calls the application server to carry out authentication and access control.

The authentication level required by a MAS is set administratively using Enconsole. When a client is authenticated with the DCE security service, the client receives an encrypted ticket. When authentication is required, the client must pass this ticket to the MAS as proof of their identity. In addition, the MAS can require clients to use at least a specified level of RPC protection. Protection levels determine the level of security needed on RPCs between clients and servers. Seven protection levels are provided, as follows:

`rpc_c_protect_level_default`	Use the DCE default protection level defined in the DCE configuration.
`rpc_c_protect_level_none`	No authentication required.
`rpc_c_protect_level_connect`	Perform authentication only when the client establishes a connection to the server.
`rpc_c_protect_level_call`	Perform authentication at the start of each RPC.
`rpc_c_protect_level_pkt`	Perform authentication at the start of each RPC and check that packet headers have not been modified.
`rpc_c_protect_level_pkt_integrity`	Perform authentication at the start of each RPC and check that none of the data has been modified.
`rpc_c_protect_level_pkt_privacy`	Perform authentication at the start of each RPC and check that none of the data transferred has been modified, and encrypt each RPC.

If a client makes an RPC with a lower protection level than a server requires, the monitor rejects the RPC and the client sees a security exception. No application code is required in the MAS to handle security.

In addition, when a MAS is configured in Enconsole, DCE Access Control Lists (ACLs) are created for the interface supported by the server and potentially each function defined in the interface. The administrator can then grant DCE users permission to call any of the operations in the interface. This provides effective access control for Encina++ servers.

It's important to note that security in Encina++ is fully integrated with the Encina monitor. Security is configured administratively and exploits DCE's Kerberos-based security service to implement authentication, protection and access control.

▶ DEPLOYING AND MANAGING THE SERVER

Encina provides a system deployment and management architecture for applications to exploit. Each Encina application must belong to an Encina cell. A cell is a management domain that includes configuration and application information. The three major components are:

Cell Manager (ecm): Each cell has a single ecm that manages the cell persistent cell repository.

Node Manager (enm): Each machine that hosts an Encina server runs a single enm process. This starts and stops application servers under administrator control, automatically restarts failed servers and provides transaction logging services for local recoverable servers.

Monitor Application Server (MAS): Encina application servers are typically built as MASs. This means they rely upon the Encina monitor environment to provide them with various services.

Figure 8.2 depicts the relationship between these components. The arrows between components indicate management responsibilities of a component. This means the ecm must be started before an enm can start, and the enm for a node must be started before any MASs can run on that node. In turn, all MASs on a node must be stopped before the enm can stop. It is possible to stop the ecm without stopping any enms. This means the cell's applications can continue to process transactions, and merely disallows administrative operations that would alter the cell's configuration in the repository.

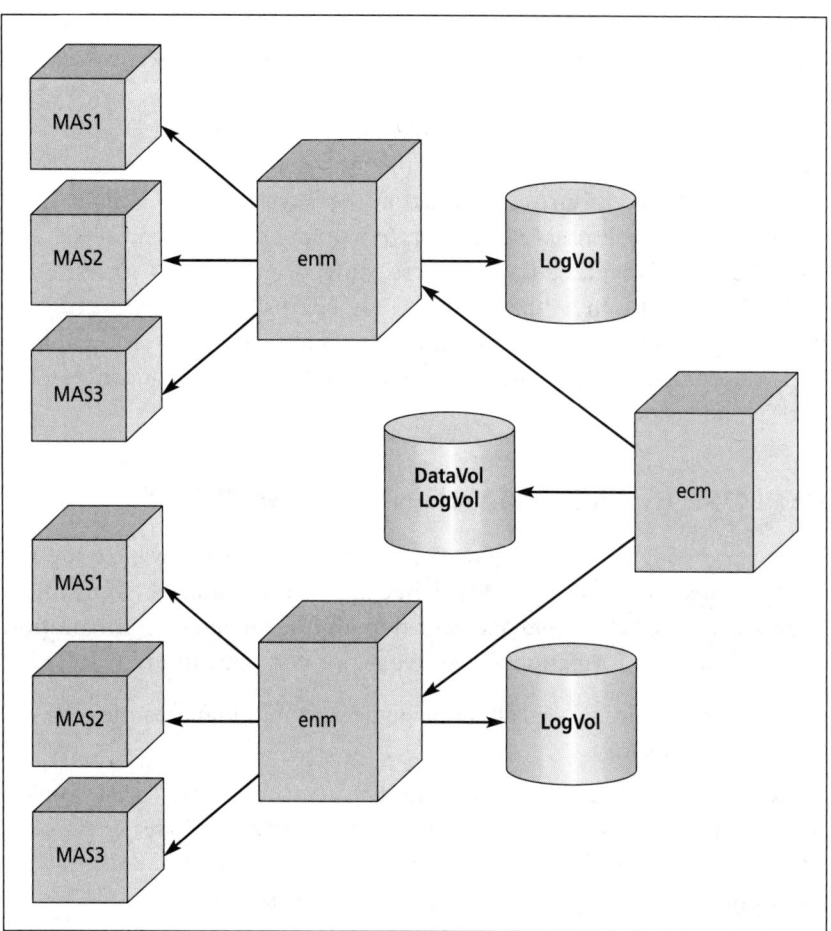

Figure 8.2 Encina monitor basic cell architecture

Each MAS can be replicated across nodes to improve scalability and fault tolerance. In addition, a MAS on a single node can be run in a multiple processing agent (PA) configuration. Each PA is essentially a replicated version of the server process. Configuring a MAS in an Encina cell is a simple task, and is supported by scriptable command line tools and an graphical administration tool known as *Enconsole*. A screendump of the main enconsole window is shown in Figure 8.3.

Enconsole provides a graphical user interface for configuring Encina cells, node managers and MASs, as well as registering resource managers and servers that are not so tightly integrated with the monitor environ-

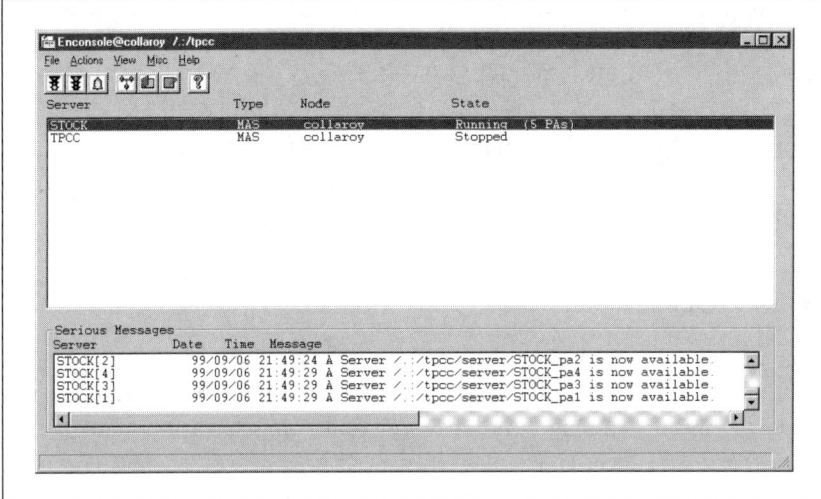

Enconsole main screen   Figure 8.3

Setting the number of PAs for an Encina MAS   Figure 8.4

ment (e.g. DCE or Encina Toolkit servers). For MASs, an example configuration window is shown in Figure 8.4. The number of PAs for a MAS is set using this window. Importantly, once a MAS is up and running, Enconsole can be used to change the number of PAs, and the change will take effect immediately. The node manager will start new PAs or stop existing PAs so that the number executing matches the amount set by the administrator.

▶ SUMMARY

This chapter has presented the design and program code for the Encina++ version of Stock-OnLine. The Encina transactional IDL for the server has been explained, and a server object has been implemented to support the interface. It has also illustrated how a pool of database connections can be shared safely amongst multiple application threads in a multi-threaded application server.

Some of the benefits of Encina's tightly integrated design should have become apparent. No or little code is needed to exploit a directory service in both the client and server. Security is set up administratively, with a single client API allowing each client to decide what level of security it requires. Access control can be enforced administratively at both the interface and operation level, and application servers do not even have to process client calls that violate the security levels enforced. Application server management requires no program code, and Enconsole provides a basic but highly practical management tool for Encina systems.

Chapter 9

Performance issues

Introduction	198
Understanding application performance	198
Test environment and results	200
Base timings	200
Performance under load	203
Improving performance	206
General performance tips	208
Summary	212
Further reading	213

▶ INTRODUCTION

Performance is often a make or break issue for enterprise transaction processing systems. It's therefore important to have a good understanding of where distributed transaction processing systems spend their execution time, and how some of the overheads can be reduced. In this chapter, the behavior and performance profile of the Stock-OnLine application is described, and the results of some experiments are shown to put some real performance figures to these profiles. Next, the OrbixOTM and Encina++ Stock-OnLine programs are run with varying numbers of clients and servers to see how their performance scales as client load increases. Finally, some general areas and techniques for improving application performance are discussed.

▶ UNDERSTANDING APPLICATION PERFORMANCE

Transaction processing introduces some additional performance overheads on top of those normally experienced in a distributed object system. Obvious rules like minimizing remote calls and the data transported between clients and servers apply, just like in any distributed system. However, passing transaction contexts around, logging transaction state and two-phase commit messages all have performance implications.

Figure 9.1 depicts the interactions that occur during the `CreateAccount` transaction in Stock-OnLine. All the lines between components represent inter-process calls, which will be remote calls if the components are distributed across different machines. Subscriber clients are ephemeral and therefore cannot act as transaction coordinators, as they do not have the ability to log transaction state. In Encina++ and OrbixOTM, the first recoverable server that a transaction touches becomes transaction coordinators. This means an instance of the StockDBMSAccess server process will act as the transaction coordinator. As the Stock-OnLine examples start and end the transaction on the client, the commit call thus represents a remote method invocation to the transaction coordinator on the server.

Note also that the `commit` call returns to the client as soon as the coordinator has made a decision. This is a standard optimization used in OTMs to increase the speed of the commit operation. The CORBA OTS makes this behavior configurable through the `report_heuristics` parameter for the `commit()` operation. By setting `report_heuristics`

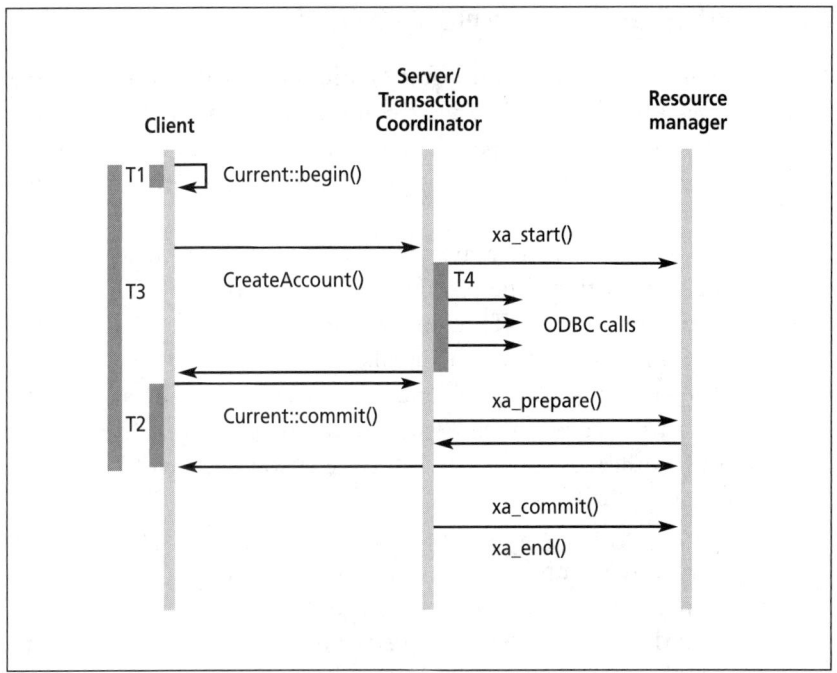

Figure 9.1 Component interactions during a CreateAccount transaction

to `true`, clients will be informed of any heuristic decisions made by transaction participants.

Figure 9.1 shows four time periods, marked by solid grey boxes, which we are interested in measuring in the application code. These are:

T1: the time it takes to begin a transaction.

T2: the time it takes to commit a transaction from the client.

T3: the total time taken at the client to complete the transaction, as measured from start to finish.

T4: the time taken at the server to execute the ODBC/SQL calls and business logic associated with the transaction.

T3 is usually known as the client response time, and is one of the most important measures of a system's performance. If an application's response time is poor, it's unlikely to be seen as a successful system. The other time intervals are components of the overall response time. By understanding their values, we can see which parts of the response time are fast or slow, and look at optimizing those.

▶ TEST ENVIRONMENT AND RESULTS

The test environment used is three fast Pentium PC workstations running Windows NT 4.0. The machines were connected over a 10 Mb local area Ethernet network. Whenever possible, tests were run at times when there was low network activity, and the results are averages of at least two test runs.

The software versions used are OrbixOTM 1.0c and Encina++ from TxSeries 4.2 GA Edition. The resource manager used is SQL Server 6.5 communicating with the OTS using XA and Microsoft's Distributed Transaction Controller (DTC). The database is initialized before each test run with 100 subscriber accounts and 200 stock items. The application servers run on the same machine as the database server. Clients run across the two other test machines. All code is compiled with Microsoft Visual C++ 5.0.

When digesting the results that follow, it's worth noting that the available hardware set-up is very much a low-end configuration in terms of expected performance. In fact, the cost of the three workstations is a combined total of around $10K. This is not a configuration likely to produce a high-performance, scalable application! Also, the set of test run and results presented is not comprehensive. Running tests, tuning components for performance and capturing results takes a lot of time and effort. See the Further Reading section for more comprehensive sources of information.

The value of these results is in showing the relative performance of OrbixOTM and Encina++ in the test environment, and illustrating how the constituent parts of a transaction vary in value as load increases and designs are improved. So, like any set of benchmarks, be aware of the limitations of the figures presented.

▶ BASE TIMINGS

In order to measure the time intervals in Figure 9.1, the code in the examples was instrumented to time operations and log the intervals to an application-defined, thread-safe performance logging object. Timestamps were taken before and after events occurred and the time differences were recorded. When a client or server ends, the performance log object's destructor is fired to dump the results to a file. All times in the following are in milliseconds unless stated otherwise.

It's important to understand initially what is the best performance level that the application will yield. To measure this, a single application server is run with a single client. After running a transaction mix for a few minutes, a set of transactions is measured and averaged. The initial system ramp-up time attempts to ensure that start-up costs such as filing database caches do not adversely influence the results.

The base response times are shown in Figure 9.2. This represents time interval T3 in Figure 9.1. Not surprisingly, the read-only transactions are considerably faster than transactions that update the database. Also in general Encina++ is marginally faster than OrbixOTM, but this is a minor difference at this client load level.

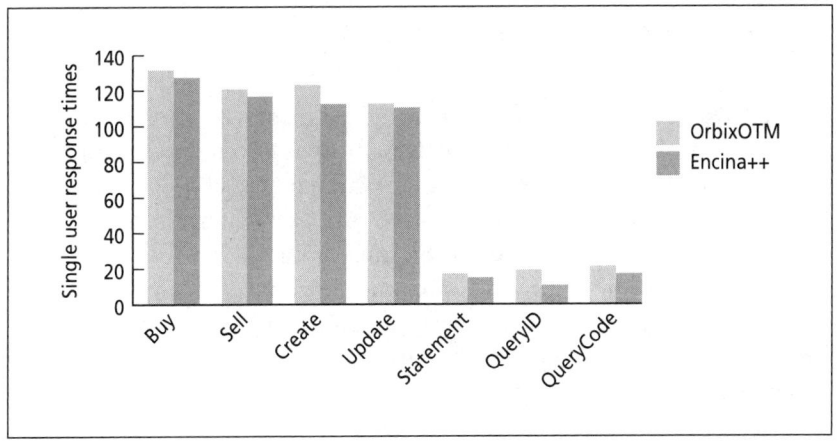

Base Stock-OnLine response times   **Figure 9.2**

To understand why the read-only transactions are faster, the different transactions `begin()` (interval T1) and `commit()` times (interval T3) were measured in the Encina++ code.[1] The duration for the `begin()` operation was always under a millisecond, because this simply initializes a transaction context structure locally within the client, and hence is not a very interesting figure to measure. Figure 9.3 shows the results obtained for the `commit()` operation.

Figure 9.3 shows the overheads introduced by the OTS commit operation. This includes a remote call to the transaction coordinator from the client, and the time for the coordinator to prepare the transaction with SQL Server and log the outcome. Read-only transactions are faster

[1] Similar times were observed for OrbixOTM.

202 Performance issues

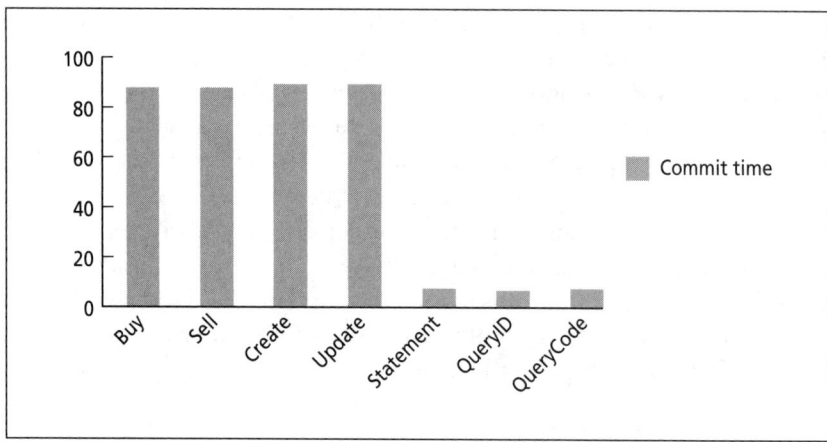

Figure 9.3   Encina++ commit operation times

because resource managers can respond with `votereadonly`, making the coordinator aware that no modifications have been made to the database. This means the transaction cannot fail, and the coordinator doesn't have to send a `commit` message to the resource manager. Transactions that modify data must wait until the transaction is prepared. This takes longer as the coordinator must communicate with the resource manager.

Time interval T4 adds the final piece to the picture by showing how long each transaction takes to do database-related work and associated business logic. Figure 9.4 depicts this and, as common code is used for

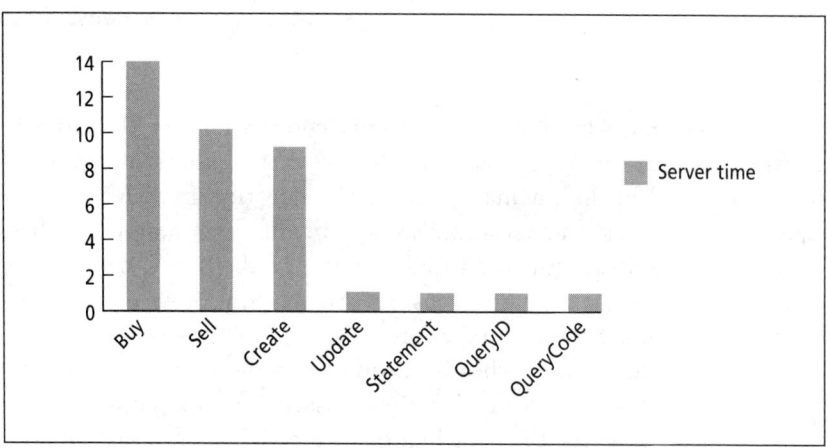

Figure 9.4   OrbixOTM and Encina++ server times

the business logic in both applications, the times for OrbixOTM and Encina++ are combined. In general, these times are relatively quick when compared to the overall transaction duration, which for transactions that update the database is dominated by the commit time.

▶ PERFORMANCE UNDER LOAD

In order to see how the two implementations perform under heavier client load, a client test driver was put together. Each client was modified to execute the following loop, in which transaction demarcation, input value generation and performance monitoring code has been omitted for clarity:

```
for (i = 1; i <= ITERATIONS ; i++ ) { // ITERATIONS = 100 by default
    cout << "Starting Iteration " << i << endl ;
    subObject->BuyStock( subAccNo, randVal, randVal) ;
    Sleep (3000) ;

    subObject->CreateAccount (subInfo, &subAccNo ) ;
    Sleep (3000) ;

    subObject->QueryStockValueByID(stID,&currVal,&highVal,&lowVal ) ;
    Sleep (3000) ;

    subObject->BuyStock( subAccNo, stID, i + 10) ;
    Sleep (3000) ;

    subObject->BuyStock( subAccNo, stID, i + 10) ;
    Sleep (3000) ;

    subObject->SellStock( subAccNo, stID, i + 10) ;
    Sleep (3000) ;

    SubObject->GetHoldingStatement (subAccNo, 0, &pList ) ;
    Sleep (3000) ;
}
```

Each iteration performs seven transactions, made up of:

- Three BuyStock transactions.
- One SellStock transaction.
- One CreateAccount transaction.
- One QueryStockValueByID transaction.
- One GetHoldingStatement transaction.

After each transaction, the client sleeps for a minimum of three seconds. Each iteration therefore takes at least 21 seconds, plus the time to execute each transaction.

Each of the test runs that followed employed five single-threaded application servers for both OrbixOTM and Encina++. All application servers ran on the same workstation as the database, meaning that all database accesses went through a local ODBC driver to a local database.

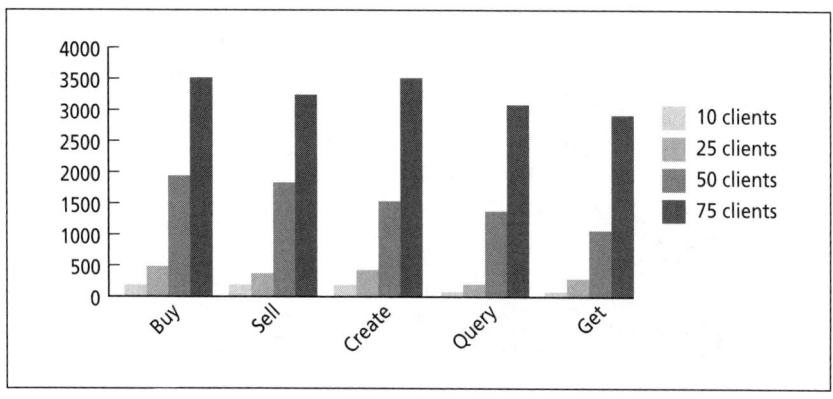

Figure 9.5 OrbixOTM client response time with five application servers

In Figure 9.5, the client response times for the OrbixOTM application are shown. As the client load increases past 25 concurrent subscribers, the response time starts to grow rapidly. This indicates clearly that the server capacity to process client requests has been exceeded. Each client is attempting to issue a transaction every three seconds. This means that to deal with the increased client load, the server transaction processing rates must scale to roughly 8, 16 and 25 transactions per second (tps) for 25, 50 and 75 clients respectively. The tests showed that the server configuration was capable of sustaining around 11 tps. Consequently, once the required transaction servicing rate rises above 11 tps – somewhere around 35 clients – outstanding client requests start to be delayed for progressively longer periods.

Part of the reason for this becomes clear when the server execution times for the same test runs are examined (*see* Figure 9.6). As the client load increases, contention for database resources increases, especially for the transactions that modify the database. The `BuyStock`, `SellStock` and `CreateAccount` transactions all access the databases's `KeyTable` to get a new key value. As the client load increases, and because five out of every seven transactions are updates, the database becomes the bottleneck. This forces client requests to be queued longer at the application servers, and this blows out the overall response times.

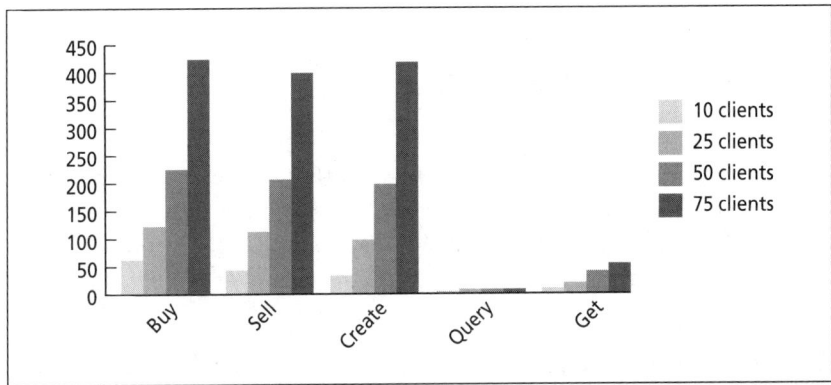

OrbixOTM client response times with five application servers Figure 9.6

A similar effect is seen with Encina++, as shown in Figure 9.7. Client response times for Encina++ are slightly better than OrbixOTM for lower client loads, but when there are 75 clients, the results are pretty much on a par with OrbixOTM. As the same server code is used in both applications, not surprisingly the server execution times observed were similar with Encina++, and therefore we won't show them separately.

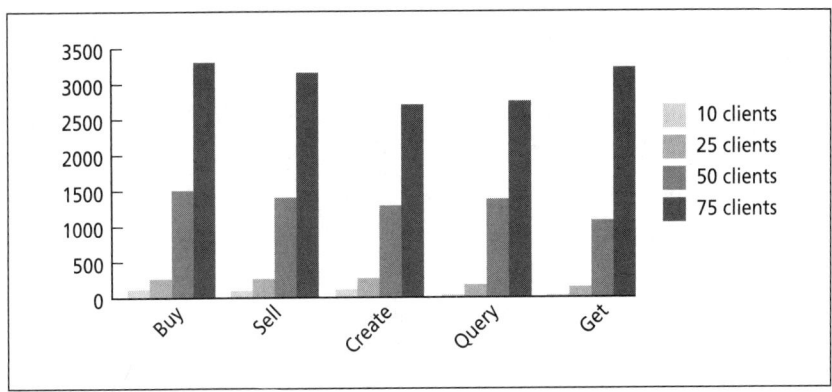

Encina++ client response time with five application servers Figure 9.7

Interestingly, the commit times that were measured with Encina++ stayed remarkably stable. With 75 clients, the commit times only increased about 10% over the times observed with 10 clients. So while the commit time was the major component of the update transactions when client loads were low, it became a minor part of the response time as client loads rose.

▶ IMPROVING PERFORMANCE

One way to improve the application's performance is to reduce the contention in the database for the `KeyTable`. If the number of updates to the `KeyTable` was reduced, this would in turn reduce the locks placed on the table in database, and improve concurrency in the application.

In this application, it's possible to build a simple caching scheme for the entries in the `KeyTable`. The basic design is:

1. Initialize a thread-safe cache object for each key (i.e. account and transaction keys) to an empty value, and pass it an update *interval* value such as 100.

2. When a transaction needs a new key, it asks the correct cache object for a value. If the cache is empty, the cache object locks the `KeyTable`, reads the current key value, and writes back the current key value plus the value of its update interval. This means it has effectively gained ownership of a number of key values to distribute on demand. It then returns a key value to the calling transaction, increments the key value, and decrements the update interval value.

3. Each time a transaction asks for a key value, if the cache object has not run out of values, it simply returns the next key value. It does not have to read the value from the database, so this is fast.

4. When the cache has distributed all the values it owns, it must read again and update the `KeyTable` and take ownership of another set of key values.

Figure 9.8 illustrates this scheme.

The aim of this scheme is to reduce the number of times the `KeyTable` is updated from once every update transaction, to 1/*interval* times, where interval is an application selected value such as 100. This will reduce transaction times at the database by lowering the number of reads and writes and improving concurrency of queries by reducing locking.

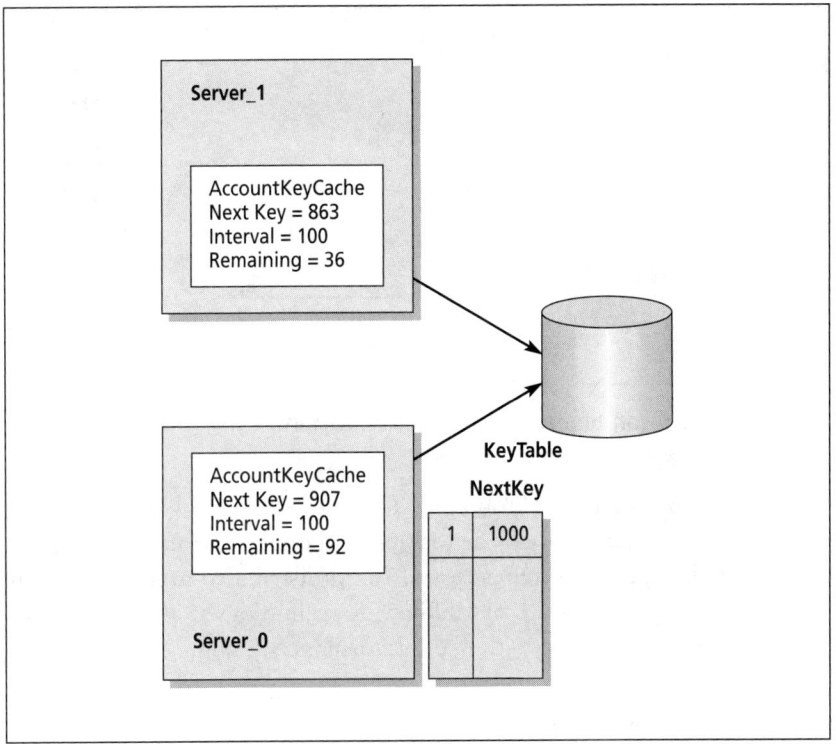

Caching account keys **Figure 9.8**

For this scheme to work, the application must be able to live with some constraints, such as:

- Key values do not reflect the order in which records are created. This is because different application servers will process transactions at different rates, and refresh their keys at different rates.
- If a transaction rolls back, the key value is lost and will never be used.
- If an application server fails and recovers, the remaining keys it owns are lost and will never be used, unless the server implements its own state management and recovery.

In order to investigate the effectiveness of this scheme, it was implemented and tested with the Encina++ application. An update interval of 100 was selected to initialize the key caches. The client response times and server execution times for 50 clients and five single-threaded application servers are shown in Figure 9.9.

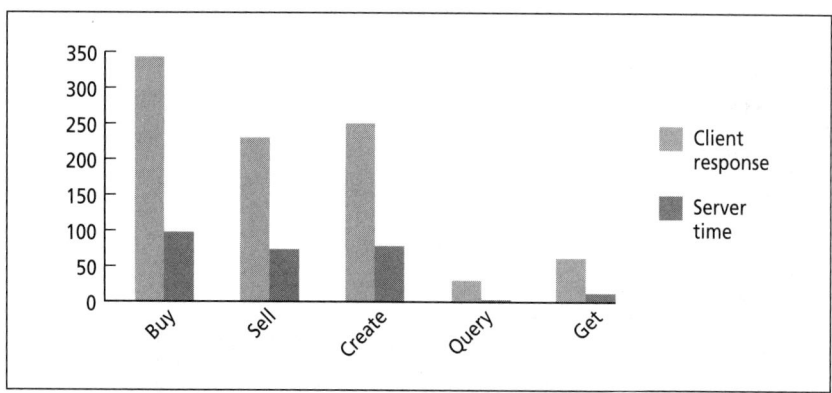

Figure 9.9 Encina++ execution times with application caching

The improvements are dramatic. They emphasize how no OTM can perform to its full capacity if the locking in the resource manager is effectively serializing most of the accesses. Good distributed architectures can only exploit the capabilities of middleware technology if all the key components are well designed with high performance in mind.

▶ GENERAL PERFORMANCE TIPS

Transaction processing introduces specific performance overheads in the areas of:

- the overheads of XA and the two-phase commit protocol;
- the overheads of logging transactions state; and
- load-balancing.

Let's briefly examine each of these in turn. As OrbixOTM and Encina++ share the same underlying transaction service, both have similar features and hence similar potential for optimizing performance

Two-phase commit

When a server application connects to resource managers using XA, the two-phase commit protocol is used to ensure that all transaction participants agree on the transaction outcome. Specifically, when a transaction arrives at a recoverable server, the transaction service will send an `xa_start` message to every XA resource manager registered with the server. This also means that each resource manager will participate in the two-phase commit protocol. Of course, a given transaction may not access all the resource managers at a server. Unfortunately, the transaction service has no way of knowing this application-specific information, and hence must take a worst-case view of a transaction's behavior.

This scheme is known as *static registration* of XA resource managers. The alternative, *dynamic registration*, is potentially a much more efficient solution for applications with multiple resource managers. With dynamic registration, a resource manager informs the transaction coordinator when it becomes involved in a transaction. If it does not dynamically register in a transaction, it does not participate in the commit protocol, therefore improving application performance. Dynamic registration is usually a resource manager-dependent feature, so it's necessary to consult the resource manager's documentation to see how this can be carried out.

Transaction logs

Depending on the operating system that the application server is run on, it may be possible to use raw disk partitions for the OTS transaction logs. Encina and OrbixOTM both support raw disk partitions, which basically means transaction log writes are considerably quicker as they do not incur the overheads of the operating system's file system operations. Raw disk partitions are even more useful when mirrored logs are utilized: a log mirror gives protection against a disk media failure, as long as the mirror exists on a different physical partition or disk. The transaction service will write log messages serially to each log, thus ensuring that the message is successfully written to at least one log. Hence mirrored logs increase log write times. In a fault-tolerant system, mirrors are a necessary evil, so the use of a single mirror gives the optimal trade-off between performance and fault tolerance.

In Encina, all servers on a particular node utilize their local node manager to log transaction state to a single, shared log. This means each log access incurs a remote call to the local node manager process. OrbixOTM gives the option of setting up a similar scheme to Encina, or dedicating a single log to each OTS server. The latter will undoubtedly give better performance but, in terms of disk usage and system management, it may be preferable to use a logging server. An OTS server can nominate another server to carry out its log accesses. This is done using the following API:

```
OrbixOTS::Server_var ots = OrbixOTS::Server::IT_create();
ots->logServer(``OrbixOTS_LOGGER'');
```

If this scheme is used, it's recommended that the log server is an OTS server that does not service application clients. Its purpose is simply to centralize transaction logging for a group of servers. In this way, the extra costs of the remote call for each log access should be minimized.

Load-balancing

An OrbixOTM or Encina++ application has a finite application server capacity in terms of the overall application throughput. Achieving maximum throughput requires all processing resources to be used to their maximum capacity. This should ensure relatively consistent transaction loads on each application server.

Simple-load balancing with OrbixOTM and Encina++ is provided through the use of selection policies for server objects in the name server. To measure the effectiveness of these mechanisms, during test runs the number of transactions each server process received was measured. The OrbixOTM client test driver was designed to get a new server object reference from OrbixNames approximately every ten transactions[2]. This attempts to frequently redistribute client load, which is necessary in a dynamic system.

[2] This strategy is probably not ideal in practice, as a client could potentially end up with open connections to every OTS server, which could be a large number in a major application. It is simply used in this example to show how how load-balancing can be improved. It would be more sensible to initialize a fixed-size cache of object references at client start-up, and cycle through these as the client executes transactions to disperse load.

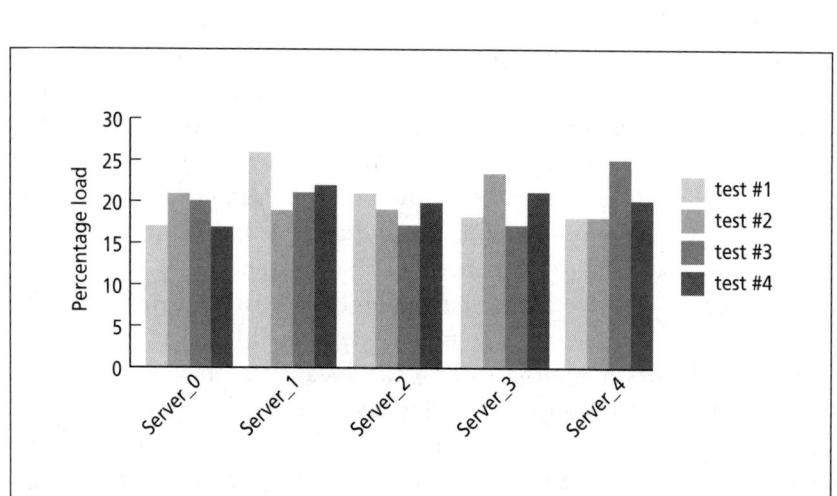

Figure 9.10   Example load distribution across OrbixOTM servers

Ideally each of the five application servers would receive 20% of the overall client load. As Figure 9.10 indicates, the tests get close to achieving this, but the results could be better. In test #1 for example, Server_1 process 26% of the overall client load, whereas Server_0 gets just 17% of the transaction. Clients who bind to Server_1 are therefore likely to experience longer response times than those who bind to Server_0.

The execution time for getting a new object reference from OrbixNames was also measured. In these tests, OrbixNames was running on its own workstation remote from the clients. The results are shown in Figure 9.11. Access is fast when lightly loaded but, as the client load grows, it takes on average 33 milliseconds for the `resolve()` operation to return successfully[3].

[3] *OrbixOTM version 3.0 now has multithreaded implementation of OrbixNames, which should provide faster access times.*

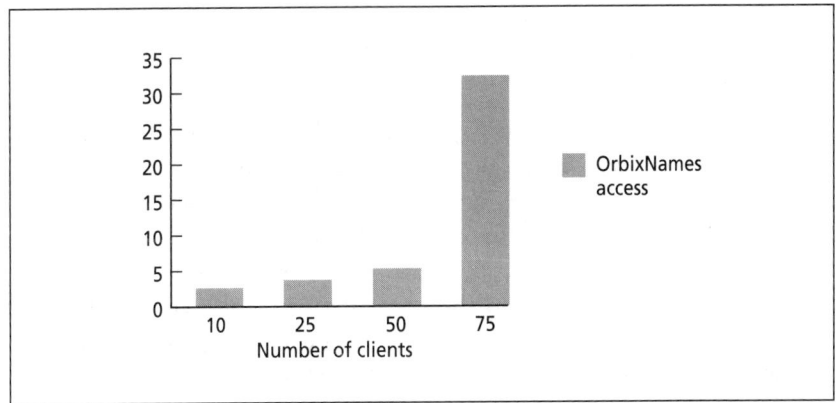

OrbixNames `resolve()` operation execution times   **Figure 9.11**

With Encina++, two sets of tests were run, namely:

Set #1: Each client binds at start-up to a server object, and uses this for the whole test duration. This is the 'out of the box' Encina++ behavior.

Set #2: Each client binds at start-up to a server object, and after ten transactions deletes the client proxy and creates a new one in order to get a new server object binding.

The average results of these tests for a MAS with five PAs are shown in Figure 9.12. This shows clearly that load is much more evenly dispersed around 20% when clients take active steps to distribute their load across the available server objects.

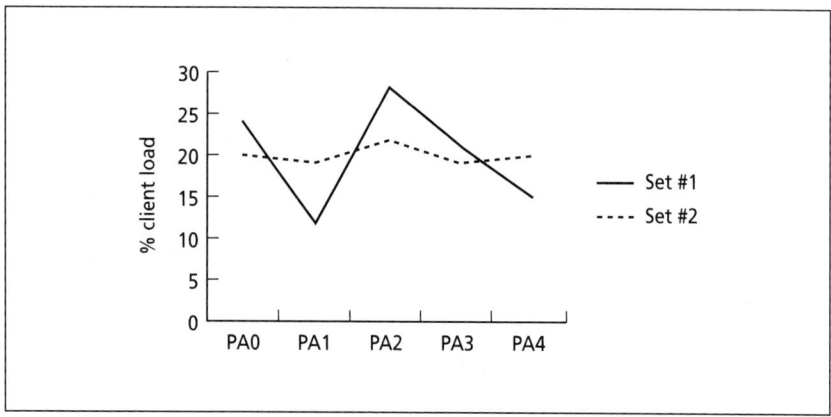

Figure 9.12 Comparing the results of Encina++ load distribution strategies

▶ SUMMARY

It's a fact of life and software engineering that performance is a major issue in most enterprise transaction processing systems. For this reason, performance should be a key design driver throughout the development of a system, from initial technology evaluation and exploring architectural options to final coding, deployment and system configuration.

This chapter has explored the performance of the OrbixOTM and Encina++ Stock-OnLine applications. The constituent phases of a transaction have been shown and timings measured for these by instrumenting the code in the examples. The results show that, as client load increased, the database became a bottleneck due to the serialization of requests. By introducing a simple cache, the performance results for 50 clients improved considerably.

Many other aspects of a system impinge on performance, and the chapter concluded by mentioning three of these:

- dynamic XA registration has the potential to reduce the overheads of two-phase commit;
- suitably configured transaction logs can improve the performance of logging transaction state; and
- effective load balancing makes excellent use of system resources. Under- and over-used resources can impact adversely on system performance, making load-balancing a critical success factor in many high performance systems.

▶ FURTHER READING

Detailed performance studies of OTMs are few and far between. Most vendors have White Papers that tell you how to get the best out of your middleware by adjusting tuning parameters and turning on various optimizations. Independent consulting agencies often compare products but few, if any, actually write code and report the results. The following are worth checking out:

www.ovum.com

www.cutter.com

www.MiddleTier.com

For links to new sources of information in this area, check out **www.cmis.csiro.au/adsat**. The ADSaT group produces detailed and rigorously founded product evaluations based on actual use of the different technologies.

Index

access control 193
Access Control Lists (ACLs) 90
access times, distributed systems 112–13
account creation
    Encina 181–2, 172–4
    OrbixOTM 135–8, 152–3
ACID properties
    subtransactions 32
    transactions 8, 20–1
ACLs *see* Access Control Lists
administration services, TP monitors 9, 40
application server architectures 48–65
    caching 62–4
    load balancing 49–54
    multithreaded servers 56–9
    publish-subscribe 64–5
    service partitioning 54–6
    stateless/stateful servers 59–62
applications
    development 9
    see also transactions
architecture
    application servers 49–65
    business objects/middleware isolation 155–6
    CORBA ORB 68–9
    CORBA OTS 71–2
    distributed transaction processing systems 44–66
    Encina 85
    Encina monitor cell 194
    issues 44–6
    OrbixOTM 97
    overview 46–8
    publish–subscribe 64–5

Stock OnLine system 110
    see also CORBA
arrays 165, 182–4
atomicity, transactions 8, 20
authentication 99–100
availability, enterprise applications 3–4

`_bind` function 77–8
binding
    DCE 88–9
    Encina++ 169–71
    server objects 125–31
`BindObject` 128–30
business logic layer 5, 6
business objects
    middleware isolation 155–6
    Stock OnLine system 111–12

C++ class interfaces 96
CA *see* Certification Authority
caches
    key values 206–8
    scrolling transactions 139
    stateful servers 61, 62–4
case study 108–17
    binding 169–71
    CORBA interfaces 120–3
    database design 115–16
    design 110–14
    Encina++ 164–96
    interactions 198–9
    interfaces 120–3, 164–8
    OrbixOTM 120–62
    requirements 108–10
    security 191–3

case study *contd*
   Services package 113–14
   StockDBMSAccess 111–13, 142–50, 176–91
   subscriber client 123–41
   transactions 172–6
CDS *see* Cell Directory Service
Cell Directory Service (CDS) 86, 88–90
Cell Manager (ecm) 193–4
cells
   DCE 86, 90
   Encina 92–4, 169, 193–4
Certification Authority (CA) 100
class interfaces, Encina 96
client access layer 5, 6
client object, constructor 170–1
client stubs 69–70, 87
client-server systems 11–14
clients
   case study 110, 123–41
   initialization 169–71
   response times 199, 204–5
   TP system architecture 47
coarse-grain locking 38
COBOL 2
COM+ 15
commit times 201–3, 206
Common Object Request Broker Architecture *see* CORBA
communications, Encina/mainframe 95
communications resource manager (CRM) 22
`ConcurrencyMode` 149
conformant arrays, DCE 182–4
consistency, transactions 8, 20
constructor, client object 170–1
`Control` interface 73
`Coordinator` interface 73, 74
CORBA (Common Object Request Broker Architecture) 3, 82
   background 68–71

   interfaces 25, 120–3
   pseudo-objects 75
CORBAServices 69, 71
   Event Service 102
   Naming Service 98
   OTS 71–82
`CosTransactions` 73, 76–80
`CreateAccount`
   Encina 172–4, 181–2
   interactions 198–9
   OrbixOTM 135–8, 152–3
creation, server object 146–8
CRM *see* communications resource manager
`Current` pseudo-object 73–5, 76

data access layer 5, 6
data type definitions 120–1
databases
   access 112, 204–5
   connection 157–61, 184–91
   design 115–16
   non XA-compliant 80–1
   open and close strings 145
   transaction control 161
DCE *see* Distributed Computing Environment
deadlocks
   RM locking 38–9
   XA libraries 28–9
decoupling, business objects/middleware 155–6
DII *see* Dynamic Invocation Interface
directory services 5
   object reference allocation 50–4
   publish-subscribe architectures 65
   system architecture 48
   see also Cell Directory Service; Naming Service
Distributed Computing Environment (DCE) 85–91

Cell Directory Service 88–90
cells 86
components 86
Remote Procedure Call 87–8
Security Service 90–1
Threads library 91
Distributed Time Service (DTS) 86
distributed transaction processing 2
    advantages 11–14
    monitor 8–9
Distributed Transaction Service (TRAN), Encina 91
downtime 4, 14
DSI *see* Dynamic Skeleton Interface
DTS *see* Distributed Time Service
durability, transactions 8, 20
Dynamic Invocation Interface (DII) 69–70
dynamic registration, XA resource managers 208–9
Dynamic Skeleton Interface (DSI) 69–70

ecm *see* Cell Manager
EJB *see* Enterprise Java Beans
Encina++ 14, 96
    client initialization 169–71
    security 191–3
Encina
    architecture 85
    cells 194
    monitor 92–4
    overview 84–96
    Peer-to-Peer Communications (PPC) Services 95
    Recoverable Queuing Service (RQS) 94–5
    server initialization 176–9
    server interfaces 164–8
    server object implementation 179–84
    Structured File System (SFS) 95
    subtransactions 34–5
    toolkit 91–2

TX API functions 24–5
Enconsole 194–5
encryption 99–100
endpoint information 89
enm *see* Node Manager
enterprise applications 2–8
Enterprise Java Beans (EJB) 15
Event Service 102
    see also publish–subscribe architectures
exceptions
    CORBA interfaces 120–1
    Encina++ interfaces 165
    remote function call 137–8
execution time 199, 207–8
explicit transaction propagation 76, 78

factory objects 60–2
failure
    stateful servers 61
    stateless servers 59
    transaction managers 30–1
    transaction processing 20–1
fault tolerance
    architectural considerations 45
    replica application servers 49
file system, Encina SFS 95
fine-grain locking 38
Forte 15

heuristic outcomes 30–2

IBM, Transarc 84
IDL *see* Interface Definition Language
IIOP *see* Internet Inter-ORB Protocol
implementation, server object 179–84
implicit transaction propagation 76, 78–9
initialization
    clients 124–5, 169–71
    pseudo-objects 131
    servers 142–6, 149–50, 176–9

integration, departmental systems 11, 13
integrity, enterprise applications 4
Interface Definition Language (IDL) 87
    compiler outputs 168
    modules 120
    sequences 121
interface handle 170
Interface Repository (IR) 70
interfaces
    DCE 87
    department systems 11
    Encina++ 164–8
    OTS 73–7, 80–1
    Stock-OnLine system 120–3
Internet Inter-ORB Protocol (IIOP) 71
interoperability
    DCE 86
    OTM products 15
Iona Technologies 84, 105
IR see Interface Repository
isolation, transactions 8, 20, 37

Java 15

key value cache 206–8

libraries, Encina 91–2
Listen 178–9
load balancing
    application servers 49–54
    case study 126, 134
    Encina++ 171
    OrbixNames 99
    performance 210–12
    stateful servers 61–2
Lock Service, Encina 91
locks 37–9, 59
Log Service (LOG), Encina 92
logs 23, 209–10

M3 14
MAC see message authentication code
mainframes 2, 95
management
    architectural considerations 45
    enterprise applications 5, 6
    OrbixManager 100–1
    system architecture 48
    TP monitor 32, 40
marshalling 87
MASs see Monitor Application Servers
memory management 175, 184
message authentication code (MAC) 100
message broker system 7
middleware 4, 5
    business object isolation 155–6
    function 12–13
    memory management 175
Monitor Application Servers (MASs) 93–4, 193–6
    Encina++ security 191–3
multi-threaded servers 56–9
mutex lock 59

name server, system architecture 48
Naming Service 98
nesting, transactions 32–5
Node Manager (enm) 193–4
node managers 93

Object Concurrency Control Service (OCCS) 81, 97–8
Object Management Architecture (OMA) 68
Object Management Group (OMG) 3, 68
object reference allocation, directory services 50
Object Request Broker (ORB) 68–71
Object Transaction Monitors (OTM) 3
    products 14–15
    see also Encina++, OrbixOTM

Object Transaction Service (OTS) 3, 4, 6, 71–82
   Encina++ 96
   features 71–2
   interfaces 73–7, 80–1
   non-XA-compliant objects 80–1
   Orbix 97–8
OCCS *see* Object Concurrency Control Service
OMA *see* Object Management Architecture
OMG *see* Object Management Group
Open Group 105, 86
Open Software Foundation (OSF) 86
ORB *see* Object Request Broker
OrbixOTM 14–15
   architecture 97
   case study 120–62
   interfaces 103–4
   OrbixEvents 97, 102
   OrbixManager 97, 100–1, 144
   OrbixNames 97, 98–9, 125
   OrbixOTS 97–8
   OrbixSSL 97, 99–101, 104
   Overview 97–104
OSF *see* Open Software Foundation
OTM *see* Object Transaction Monitors
OTS *see* Object Transaction Service
`OtsBinding` 169–70
`OtsInterfaceMgr` 180
overheads, performance 208–10

PA *see* processing agent
Peer-to-Peer Communications (PPC) Services 95
performance 198–213
   architectural considerations 45
   client-server systems 10
   distributed system design 112–14
   improving 206–8
   load balancing 210–12
   overheads 208–10

system testing 200–6
unbounded sequences 121
see also load balancing; service partitioning
`-persistent` 143
physical constraints, architectural considerations 46
POSIX Pthreads library 91
PPC *see* Peer-to-Peer Communications
prepare phase, two-phase commit protocol 23
procedural interfaces, Encina 95–6
processing agent (PA) 93–4, 194–6
processing time
   load balancing 53–4
   service partitioning 55–6
programming, Encina applications 95–6
protection levels
   Encina++ 192
   RPCs 90–1
prototypes 46
pseudo-objects
   CORBA 75
   initialization 131
pthreads library 91, 185
public key cryptography 99–100
publish–subscribe architectures 64–5
   see also Event Service

queuing
   Encina RQS 94–5
   slow transactions 35–6

read locks 37
read-only transactions, performance 201–2
Recoverable Queuing Service (RQS) 94–5
recovery 39–40
   database transactions 145–6
Recovery Service (REC), Encina 92
registration, XA resource managers 145–6, 176, 208–9

reliability, three-tier systems 13
remote function calls 112–13
remote procedure call (RPC) 86, 87–8,
        90–1
    protection 192–3
    transactional 29–30, 91
replication
    application servers 49
    Cell Directory Service 90
resolution phase, two-phase commit
        protocol 23
`Resource` interface 73, 75, 80–1
resource manager (RM) 22
    locks 37–9
    recovery 39–40
    TP monitors 9
    TP system architecture 48
    XA protocol 26–9
resource usage, load balancing 49–54
response times 199, 204–5
RM see resource manager
round robin approach, object reference
        allocation 50–2
RPC see Remote Procedure Call
RQS see Recoverable Queuing Service
runtime environment, TP monitors 9

scalability 4
    architectural considerations 45
    replica application servers 49
scrolling transaction 138–9
Secure Socket Layer (SSL) 97, 99–101
    website 105
security
    architecture 45, 48
    Encina++ 191–3
    enterprise applications 4–5
    stateful servers 60
Security Service, DCE 86, 90–1
server stubs 87

servers
    binding 125–31
    creation 146–8
    implementation 150–6, 179–84
    initialization 142–6, 149–50, 176–9
    interfaces, Encina 164–8
    load balancing 49–54, 61–2
    log access 209–10
    recovery 39–40
    stateful 60–4, 139
    stateless 59, 114
    TP system architecture 47–8
    transactions 172–6
    see also application server; SQL server;
        Monitor Application Servers
service layer, distributed system design
        113–14
service partitioning, application server
        architectures 54–6
SFS see Structured File System
SII see Static Invocation Interface
single-threaded server 57
software system architecture, definition 44
SQL Server 157–61, 184–91
SQL statements, table creation 115–16
SSL see Secure Socket Layer
stateful servers 60–4, 139
stateless servers 59, 114
Static Invocation Interface (SII) 70
static registration, XA resource managers
        208–9
Stock-OnLine system see case study
`[string]` attribute 165–6
Structured File System (SFS) 95
subscriber client 123–41
    binding 125–31
    initializing 124–5
    transactions 131–41
subtransactions 32–5
synchronization object 158–9
system services, TP system architecture 48

table creation, SQL statements 115–16
technological change 2, 9
`Terminator` interface 73, 74
testing
   architectural considerations 45
   performance 200–6
thread pools 58, 179
thread-safety
   resource managers 149
   XA libraries 27–9
threads
   database connections 184–91
   library 86, 91
ThreadTid, Encina 92
three-tier client-server systems 11–14
tid *see* transaction identifier
TIDL *see* Transactional IDL
timings, performance tests 200–6
TM *see* transaction manager
toolkit, Encina 92
TP *see* transaction processing
Tran-C *see* Transactional-C
transaction identifier (tid) 23
transaction manager (TM) 22
   failure 30–1
   resource manager interactions 26–9
Transaction Manager-XA Service (TM-XA), Encina 92
transaction processing (TP) monitors 9
   management tools 32, 40
transaction processing (TP) systems 2–8
Transactional-C (Tran-C) 96, 33
Transactional IDL (TIDL) 91
   compiler outputs 168
transactional objects 76–80
transactional operations, Encina interfaces 165–6
transactional queuing technology 35–6
Transactional Remote Procedure Call (TRPC) 29–30, 91
`TransactionFactory` interface 73

transactions
   ACID properties 8, 20–1
   architectural considerations 44
   control 161
   definition 18–21
   demarcation 24–6
   Encina++ 172–6
   logs 23, 39–40, 209–10
   nested 32–5
   propagation 76–9
Transarc 84, 105
Transarc/Encina DCE utilities library 91
two-phase commit protocol 21–4, 208–9
two-phase locking rule 37
two-tier client-server systems 10–11
TX API 22, 24, 96

unique universal identifier (uuid) 145, 164
use-case diagram, case study 109
utilities library, Encina 91
uuid *see* unique universal identifier

Visibroker ITS 14–15
Volume Service (VOL), Encina 91

websites
   CORBA 82
   middleware technology 66
   performance issues 213
   product documentation 105
   publish-subscribe 66
write locks 37
WWW clients and servers 47–8

X.509 certificate, public keys 99–100
X/Open distributed TP model 21–2, 34
XA+ 23
XA 22
   resource manager access 26–9
   resource manager registration 145–6, 176, 208–9